T0323452

Organization Theories in the Making

Organization Theories in the Making

Exploring the leading-edge perspectives

Linda Rouleau
HEC Montréal

OXFORD
UNIVERSITY PRESS

Great Clarendon Street, Oxford, OX2 6DP,
United Kingdom

Oxford University Press is a department of the University of Oxford
It furthers the University's objective of excellence in research, scholarship,
and education by publishing worldwide Oxford is a registered trade mark of
Oxford University Press in the UK and in certain other countries

Impression: 2

Published in the United States of America by Oxford University Press
198 Madison Avenue, New York, NY 10016, United States of America

British Library Cataloguing in Publication Data

Data available

Library of Congress Control Number: 2022936088

ISBN 978–0–19–879202–4

DOI: 10.1093/oso/9780198792024.001.0001

Printed and bound by
CPI Group (UK) Ltd, Croydon, CR0 4YY

This book is dedicated to all of the PhD students who have attended my doctoral seminar on organization theories over the years, as well to all those who will do so in the future!

A special thanks to Marie-Claude Rabeau and Meaghan Girard, from HEC Montréal, for helping me make sure that the words on these pages were faithful to those in my mind!

Contents

List of Figures

List of Tables

Introduction
The Past 25 Years of Theorizing Organizations

We live and work in a world that is in constant flux, where our organizations compete in complex institutional and globalized environments and amidst the emergence of new markets. The development of information technology as well as the rise of the knowledge economy have transformed the way individuals and groups work together to achieve organizational goals. To foster economic and social innovations, organizations are opening their boundaries and decentralizing their governance structures. As a result, managers have to engage multiple stakeholders around legitimate discourses and be ready to roll up their sleeves as they set out to transform and develop new organizational processes and practices. All these changes have challenged organizational scholars to generate new ways of seeing the empirical complexity of contemporary organizations.

Over the past 25 years, organizational researchers have developed leading-edge perspectives that explore new research questions: How do organizations build and maintain legitimacy in their institutional context? How do organizations achieve compromises between stakeholders that have divergent interests? How do they manage the multiple networks that they belong to and that they are composed of? How is organizational knowledge produced and transferred? How are organizational discourses produced, disseminated, and appropriated at different organizational levels? What do managers and people in other roles do in their everyday tasks? This book aims to demonstrate how, over the past 25 years, the field of organization theories (OTs) has been providing stimulating, thoughtful, and innovative perspectives to answer these questions. More pointedly, it provides a synthesis of the latest theoretical advances and developments in the field.

In this book, I use the plural form, organizational theories (OTs), when referring to the field traditionally known as organization theory (OT). Indeed, in order to present an integrated or unified front, the field is generally referred to in the singular form. However, this no longer reflects the rise in perspectives, empirical studies, and paradigms that have made the

Organization Theories in the Making. Linda Rouleau, Oxford University Press.
© Linda Rouleau (2022). DOI: 10.1093/oso/9780198792024.003.0001

field so highly diverse and dynamic over the past 25 years. This shift from the singular to the plural is meant to emphasize the plurality of ways of seeing organizational life as well as a call to include these perspectives under the broad umbrella provided by the field of OTs.

0.1 Why another organization theories book?

Why a new OTs book when there are already so many out there? OTs are essential if we want to understand the world of organizations, whether we are interested in management, consulting, or research. However, I have always been uncomfortable with the material aiming to portray this field of study. Until now, most books on OTs propose the same story, with minor variations. Many are devoted to 'classical readings' or present an overview of their evolution from the beginning of the 1900s to the end of the 1990s. This story has been told countless times. This book adopts a different approach to OTs and zooms in on the relationship between the latest developments in OTs (from 1995s to the present) and the research communities that gave rise to them. OTs develop both in competition against (or even in reaction to) one another, and, on the contrary, in alliance with each other. As you will see, these stories all intersect with each other to form a mosaic of ideas that define today's organizations. Hence the title of this book: *Organization Theories in the Making*.

The book you are about to read is a 'hybrid' between generalist and specialist approaches. While it is reasonably accessible for beginners, it goes beyond the mainstream and applied view of OTs to highlight the main debates and challenges at the cutting edge of the field. In addition to introducing the key academic conversations central to the field today, this book also invites graduate students and early career researchers to learn how recent theories view and portray the organization and, more specifically, to understand current research questions, conceptual resources, and methods. In the OTs field, there are rich debates between the diverse epistemic communities, and junior researchers and graduate students need to be well versed in them in order to write a relevant thesis, report, or academic paper. A deep knowledge of recent OTs is key when building a compelling literature review and making meaningful theoretical contributions. Scholars translating a research topic into theoretical terms need to be aware of the conceptual resources offered by the field of OTs. Faced with the realities of 'publish or perish', junior researchers and graduate students are urged to develop their theory-building skills. This book offers readers the opportunity to do this and more by taking a deep dive in the complexities and controversies of OTs. By familiarizing yourself with the 'new metaphors' of organizations, you will be able to make your own contribution to the field of OTs.

0.2 Organization of the book

Throughout this book, I mainly refer to 'perspectives', and avoid as much as possible using the term 'theories'. A theory is a specific set of integrated conceptual relationships or claims to explain an organizational phenomenon. On the other hand, 'perspective', from the Latin *perspiecere*, has the connotation to 'look through' something. Thus, a perspective refers both to the position from which the researcher is looking at an organizational phenomenon and the way the scholar attributes meaning to organizational reality based on their own values. Once produced, perspectives direct attention to what there is to see or what is missing in the organizational world. Since the end of the 1990s, OTs have been providing new views of reality or perspectives rather than developing theories per se. In this book, referring to perspectives allows me, nonetheless, to review the diverse streams of research that comprise them. Behind the notion of perspectives is also that of research communities, whose members share common interests and a common understanding of organizations. These scholarly or epistemic communities in OTs play an important role in setting research agendas and conferring a reputation on emerging perspectives.

Each of the perspectives introduced in this book represents a recent and cutting-edge advancement in the institutional, economic, political, and cultural analysis of organizations. The book comprises eight chapters, each devoted to a perspective, namely organizational institutionalism, convention analysis, network analysis, knowledge studies, discourse studies, and practice studies.

Chapter 1 introduces the *central debates in OTs*. It will help you to better understand the paradigm debate in OTs and why it is so important for those who intend to advance knowledge in this field. This chapter also addresses the long-standing issue of the quest for novelty in OTs—considered by some scholars as a sign of crisis in the field.

Chapter 2 is about *organizational institutionalism*. Even though it originated in the late 1970s, organizational institutionalism has been and still is the most influential perspective in OTs all over the world. Since the beginning of the 2000s, there have been many significant turns in the very nature of the institutional project. The book's second chapter explores the greatness and miseries of organizational institutionalism.

Chapter 3 presents *convention analysis* or the heterodox model of the economy of worth, developed primarily in France. This research programme puts forth an original way of seeing how coordination is achieved within and between organizations and proposes an innovative approach to combining social and economic dimensions. Convention analysis is currently being disseminated all around the world, and this chapter reflects on the future of this perspective.

Chapter 4 looks at *network analysis*, another important perspective that has been advanced since the beginning of the 2000s. Various approaches have articulated themselves around the idea of 'network' and have helped the field of OTs take a relational turn. On one end of the spectrum, mainstream network analysis aims to explain the centrality or power positions of individuals or organizational actors in networks. On the other end, particular attention is devoted to actor–network theory, which is considered one of the most leading-edge perspectives developed over the past few decades. The chapter ends by discussing why these research streams are grouped together, despite their apparent differences, and what makes network analysis so popular in OTs.

Chapter 5 is devoted to *knowledge studies*. In a knowledge economy where the words technology, innovation, and creativity are on everybody's lips, knowledge studies represent one of the major research areas within OTs that has been developed over the past 25 years. This perspective, also called the 'knowledge movement', consists of several interconnected research topics, such as competence, capabilities, learning, and more recently, communities of practice. The chapter is organized around an intriguing question: are knowledge managers the 'Taylors' of the new century?

Chapter 6 explores *discourse studies*. Since the end of the 1990s, OTs took the linguistic turn under the growing influence of post-modernism. Organizational discourse has been one of the 'new metaphors' that has provided relevant and exciting sets of notions aimed at renewing our understanding of the contextual and pluralistic nature of organizing. After exploring the pros and cons of discourse studies, the chapter will introduce the post-linguistic turn in OTs, in which discourse and materiality are considered as inseparable.

Chapter 7 is about *practice studies*, which are a cornerstone within OTs. Affiliated with social constructionism, practice studies emerged and became widespread during the 2000s in almost every subfield of management. This chapter addresses how practice studies in OTs offer a perspective aimed at achieving a better understanding of how organizational members—managers and non-managers alike—accomplish their work through multiple micro- and macro-level activities. Finally, the chapter questions the practice turn in OTs as a potential way to engage scholars in a more reflexive and inclusive dialogue with practitioners.

Chapter 8 encourages you to imagine 'OTs in the making' for the next 25 years! To do so, I first explore the complex relationships between organization and organizing. I then argue that OTs constitute a survival toolkit for new academics. The chapter ends by introducing the latest trends not discussed elsewhere within the book, such as open theorizing, multimodality research, and new forms of organizational agency.

For each chapter, the context and influences in which the perspectives emerged and evolved serve as an introduction. The core of each chapter is a selective immersion into the different research streams associated with the chapter's featured perspective. In order to illustrate the main arguments, I draw on specific exemplars from academic journals that also demonstrate how they can be used to study contemporary organizational issues. Each chapter ends by highlighting the pros and cons of the perspective introduced and provides some thought-provoking questions in order to open the dialogue with the reader. It is also worth noting that each chapter contains a synoptic table summarizing the main scholarly components within each perspective and its research substreams (e.g. definition, research question, level of analysis, influences, disciplines, view of the organization, conceptual resources, methods, and current examplars). Moreover, each chapter ends with a list of bibliographic references that constitutes a set of recommended core readings for those who wish to dig deeper into the debates, arguments, and examples provided throughout each chapter. In addition to providing an introduction to the world of OTs as it now stands, I hope that this comprehensive overview will help early career researchers and graduate students to make sense of the recent developments in the field of OTs and to find their own way in this field.

1
Central Debates in the Field of Organization Theories

Though the often-used label of 'organization theory' (OT) may project a certain sense of stability and uniformity, the field of OTs is in fact a much-contested domain (Westwood and Clegg, 2003; Reed, 2006) that features a diversity of positions—a diversity which is itself hotly debated as to whether this is a positive or negative quality of the field. Two central debates continue to structure the field of OTs: the paradigm debate and the debate surrounding theoretical novelty (i.e. what is the role of knowledge and how does one advance it?). What does this imply, tangibly, for junior scholars and PhD students?

The way you position yourself in these debates has immense implications for how you conduct your research. As a researcher, you need a deep knowledge of the paradigmatic debates to conceive and constitute your object of study. Additionally, to make theoretical contributions that advance the state of knowledge on organizations, you need to think about the origins of theoretical novelty. Though you may have been tempted to take these things for granted, this chapter explains why these debates should be taken seriously, and in so doing lays the groundwork for what follows. Indeed, by presenting a global portrait of the latest advancements in OTs, this book aspires to help you advance your own thinking about your onto-epistemological position, which will help you pursue your own quest for novelty.

1.1 'Paradigms are dead' vs 'Long live paradigms!'

A book on OTs must begin by reviewing the never-ending paradigm debate that has been central to this field since the late 1970s. Even though there is little agreement on the exact definition of paradigm, this notion has been generally associated with a tool or disciplinary matrix that maps the intellectual journey characterizing knowledge production in the field of OTs.

Organization Theories in the Making. Linda Rouleau, Oxford University Press.
© Linda Rouleau (2022). DOI: 10.1093/oso/9780198792024.003.0002

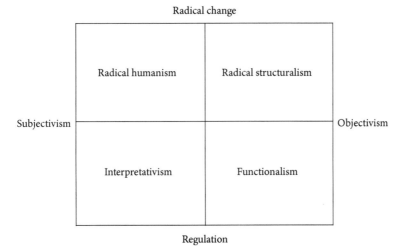

Figure 1.1 Paradigms in OTs*
*Adapted from Burrell and Morgan, 1979, p. 23.

In their book *Sociological Paradigms and Organizational Analysis*, Burrell and Morgan (1979) suggest the presence of four distinct paradigms in organization analysis: radical humanist, radical structuralist, interpretive, and functionalist. Represented by a 2×2 matrix (see Figure 1.1), each paradigm is based on explicit or implicit meta-theoretical assumptions on the nature of science and society as conveyed by knowledge producers. The 'subjective–objective' dimension located on the horizontal axis of the matrix is built on four sets of explicit or implicit assumptions about the nature of science; namely, ontology, epistemology, human nature, and method. The vertical axis refers to the 'regulation versus radical change' dimension unique to the assumptions about the nature of society. Burrell and Morgan (1979) suggest that these paradigms are 'incommensurable' or 'exclusive'; in other words, it is almost unthinkable that researchers producing knowledge based on opposing assumptions could engage in the same conversation. By arguing that paradigms 'offer different ways of seeing "the world" that are inherently incompatible', Burrell and Morgan (1979, p. 25) set the stage for what has since been coined the 'paradigm war'. Proponents of paradigm incommensurability are generally mainstream scholars who are fighting to achieve the unity of the field. Opposing them are critical scholars who argue for paradigm plurality by assuming the existence of transition zones between the paradigms and promoting different ways of using diverse paradigmatic orientations.

The merits of Burrell and Morgan's paradigmatic classification are undisputable. First, writing in the context of the 1970s, when contingencies and systems theories were hegemonic, this classification highlighted the existence of alternative approaches in OTs (Deetz, 1996). As a result, the field has been recognized as a 'contested terrain' (Reed, 2006), meaning that multiple perspectives coexist among researchers. Second, OTs scholars responding to the 'paradigm war' debate that was triggered by this classification have, over the years, proposed diverse integrative solutions and demonstrated that drawing on different standpoints can in fact enhance scientific conversations (Schultz and Hatch, 1996; Hassard and Kelemen, 2002; Morgan, 2006). Finally, the notion of paradigm developed through this framework has also been used as a tool to map the territory in diverse management literatures, such as marketing, entrepreneurship, and so on. If you are interested in the paradigm war debate, Shepherd and Challenger (2013) provide an excellent rhetorical analysis of the strategies used by academics who have chosen to engage in this intellectual debate in the past decades.

In the past decade, OTs scholars have mapped the paradigms' underlying philosophical assumptions in keeping with recent research developments. So how did this play out within the different positions? For instance, in the case of the constructionist worldview, its rise and subsequent dissemination questioned the dualistic object–subject dimension at the heart of Burrell and Morgan's view of the nature of science. And in fact, OTs researchers today are more interested in capturing the fluid, shifting, and even contested nature of organizing than in considering the organization as an entity delineated by more or fewer boundaries. In other words, in a 'post-paradigmatic time', as Hassard et al. (2013) put it, it may appear to some that it is less relevant to pay attention to the paradigm informing our theoretical and methodological choices. However, this is an illusion. Indeed, as these choices have expanded and become more complex, such paradigmatic issues seem more important than ever. The problem is to find the map or tool to guide such a reflection that will recognize both the permeability of frontiers between multiple theoretical frames and the constructed and processual character of organizing.

Let us now turn to two recent propositions that aim to inject new momentum for reinvigorating the paradigmatic debate in OTs. Revisiting the Morgan and Smircich (1980) typology, Cunliffe (2011) substitutes the notion of paradigm for one of 'knowledge problematic'. A knowledge problematic refers to a set of related ideas on theoretical issues (e.g. relationality, durability, historicity, mediation, and forms of knowledge) and methodological assumptions (e.g. the nature of reality, knowledge, human action, and research approaches and methods) and linguistic features specific to certain research approaches. Cunliffe (2011) suggests three knowledge problematics: intersubjectivism, subjectivism, and objectivism (Figure 1.2).

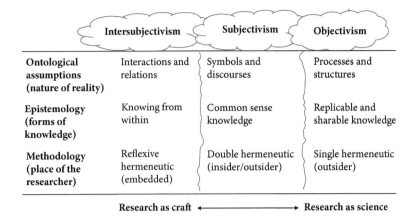

Figure 1.2 Knowledge problematics*
*Adapted from Cunliffe, 2011, pp. 654–655.

Intersubjectivism is based on the idea of 'intersubjective agreement' where reality is seen as constructed with others through mutual relationships. Essentially concerned about 'human experience', researchers belonging to the subjectivism realm are interested in the multiple ways human beings shape, maintain, and interpret the world around them. The objectivism problematic considers reality to exist independent of human beings and focuses on dynamics and relationships between structures, events, entities, and even discourses.

By adding intersubjectivism into the continuum and introducing theoretical and methodological issues other than those put forth by Burrell and Morgan (1979), this renewed typology offers additional avenues for debating the forms and nature of knowledge. For instance, nowadays, it is common for researchers to claim to belong to the subjectivist form while their research design and interpretation are largely 'objectified'. This typology also recognizes the existence of tensions and competing discourses characterizing diverse fields of knowledge. Each problematic takes the shape of clouds overlapping one another (see Figure 1.2) to indicate the fluidity that exists between knowledge problematics. Conceptualized in this way, each knowledge problematic can embrace practice, process, and even a critical ontology. As Cunliffe (2011, p. 666) states, beyond our differences, it is rather 'the interplay and tensions within and between different problematics and methodologies [that] inform, differentiate, and make our work significant'.

Allard-Poesi and Perret (2014) offer an 'epistemological orientations and tensions' model to encapsulate the issues relevant to the ongoing paradigmatic debate. This model is based on four questions that junior researchers

Orientations	Realism		Constructivism
Ontological question: what is reality?	Essentialism	←———————→	Non-essentialism
Epistemological question: what is knowledge?	Objectivism	←———————→	Relativism
Methodological question: what validity criteria apply?	Consistency	←———————→	Commensurateness
Axiological question: does knowledge make a tangible impact on reality?	Autonomy	←———————→	Performativity

←———————————————————————————————————→

| Positivism | Post-positivism | Critical realism | Interpretativism | Engineered constructivism | Post-modernism |

Figure 1.3 Orientations and epistemological tensions*
*Adapted from Allard-Poesi and Perret, 2014, p. 21.

and graduate students should ask themselves when designing a research project (see Figure 1.3): What is the nature of social reality? What is the nature of knowledge? What are the criteria for valid knowledge? How does the knowledge produced impact reality? The answers to these questions are positioned on a continuum between 'realism' and 'constructionism', which are, according to these authors, the two main paradigmatic orientations of the OTs in the 2000s.

A realist orientation is inspired by a view of reality as being embedded in objective and structural constraints—though it does recognize that the organizational and scientific worlds are influenced by culture. Inspired by Bhaskar's *A Realist Theory of Science* (1978), such an orientation is grounded on a 'stratified ontology' and is alternatively labelled 'post-positivism' or 'critical realism'. While positivists are concerned with empirical facts and actual events, according to Reed (2005), realists argue that there are underlying structures, mechanisms, and conventions that produce organizational and objective constraints in organizational life. What's more, these underlying and 'deep' structures must be theoretically modelled and explained and are subject to adjustments over time. A realist orientation thus recognizes the discursive and cultural dimensions of reality and science. However, its focus remains on causal relationships between the structures, mechanisms, and conventions underlying observable empirical facts and events that can be generalized to other organizations.

A constructionist orientation is based on a set of philosophical arguments around the nature of organization and science that are quite different from realism. According to constructionists, organizations are first and foremost social constructions that are negotiated, contested, and subject to organizational rules and social beliefs. Inspired by Berger and Luckmann's *The Social Construction of Reality* (1966), a constructionist orientation suggests that the properties of organizations are socially built on agreements between multiple actors' interpretations, including those of researchers. A constructionist orientation considers that knowledge is relative in a world that is socially constructed in time and space; hence, what is true or useful knowledge in one setting is not necessarily true or useful in another setting, regardless of the cognitive structures of the observer. Put differently, knowledge needs to be adapted to the social reality that it explains. Of course, a constructionist orientation acknowledges that the social is embedded in the material world. However, the focus of such an orientation is on the ongoing intersubjective processes and practices created, negotiated, resisted, and of interest for the understanding of the nature of organizing.

Within these orientations, there are a number of significant differences that give rise to a set of tensions and generative debates. According to Allard-Poesi and Perret (2014), these tensions revolve around the view of the nature of reality and knowledge as well as the way of assessing knowledge validity and effects on the reality observed (see the fourth question raised in Figure 1.3). For example, a realist orientation seeks stable and singular patterns and mechanisms that structure organizational reality and generally addresses the 'what' research questions, while a constructivist orientation considers organizational reality as a web of ongoing processes and practices and privileges the 'how' research questions. Realists assess value to knowledge as long as this knowledge appears to satisfy the dominant validity criteria in a given research discipline, whereas constructionists principally consider the transferability of the knowledge produced to other situations and settings. While realists consider that their research exists separately from reality (i.e. it does not impact the reality), constructionists recognize the intrinsic performative effects of knowledge on the reality studied. The literature proposes different spectrums to characterize these two positions: realism is 'strict or mild' while constructivism is 'weak or strong' or 'conventional versus relational' (Newton, Deetz, and Reed, 2011). Both can be described as 'radical', which means that they push their central assumptions within the limits of their boundaries. Simply put, radicality implies that critical realism supports assumptions closer to post-positivism and that critical constructionism bears a family resemblance to post-modernism.

Cunliffe (2011) and Allard-Poesi and Perret (2014) recently revisited the paradigm debate to offer a more complex view of how organizational knowledge is produced today. Try mapping the work of your favourite scholars, and even that of your colleagues and professors, on one these continuums; it will give you greater insight into the state of knowledge in your own field. More importantly, positioning yourself on these continuums allows you to question your own assumptions about the nature of reality, science, method, and so on. This is an essential exercise for improving your abilities to write coherent research proposals, conference and review papers, as well as theses and reports.

1.2 The desperate search for theoretical novelty

This quest for theoretical novelty, or neophilia (a term used by hackers and Internet fans referring to being excited and pleased by novelty) in the OTs is a long-standing debate. The *Academy of Management Review*, a scholarly journal devoted to publishing papers that advance our theoretical understanding of managerial and organizational life, has set up a tradition of organizing a special topic forum (STF) on theory development every 10 years. These STFs, held in 1989, 1999, 2011, and 2021, have been strong catalytic moments in this quest for novelty. In each STF, the debate around the diversity of theories arises, which inevitably raises the question of whether or not such diversity should be promoted. For example, the main goal of the first STF was to help scholars strengthen their theory-building skills to make relevant theoretical contributions in a field that was at the time largely practitioner oriented. Ten years later, Elsbach, Sutton, and Whetten (1999) argued for more integrative solutions, such as metatheories, in order to advance the field. A decade later, Suddaby, Hardy, and Nyugen (2011) posited that organization scholars were drawing on the same set of theories, and they called on scholars to develop new theories of organization. The last STF forum (which was in preparation at the time of writing and guest edited by Haveman, Mahoney, and Mannix) was poised to look at how we can enlarge our ways of theorizing from empirical data.

And indeed, the field of OTs has been driven by what I consider to be a 'desperate' scholarly search for improving and developing new and exciting theories. From the beginning of the twentieth century to the 1970s, new ways of approaching organizations were regularly introduced in response to the critics of previously dominant theories (e.g. Human Relations School, decision-making, system and contingency theory). In the 1970s, the OTs expanded tremendously, bringing to the forefront new disciplinary dimensions to organizational analysis (e.g. institutional, ecological, economic, political, cultural, and symbolic). However, since the 1990s, the OTs have been extended through the exploration of new territories or perspectives, as featured in this book (e.g. networks, knowledge, discourse, practice, and materiality). These latest developments have accentuated the theoretical pluralism of the field, which has allowed scholars to craft new insightful contributions to a huge diversity of topics. As a result of this effervescence, theoretical novelty has become the nexus of obsession and controversy.

For some scholars, the OTs have never been so active, theoretically speaking (Barry and Hanses, 2008; Hassard, Wolfram Cox, and Rowlinson, 2013; Cornelissen and Durand, 2014). There may not be any 'new theories' per se emerging at the moment, but there is a multitude of new topics (e.g. organization aesthetics, organizational silence, socio-materiality, emotions, the body), as well as innovative methods (e.g. data mining, video-ethnography, visual research methods) being developed. Moreover, each passing decade bears witness to original research programmes or novel perspectives that push the field forward (e.g. process and practice studies). According to these scholars, the field is constantly moving, providing a wealth of possibilities for promoting and combining various perspectives in order to produce new knowledge that is adapted to the increasing diversity of organizational forms and realities.

Other scholars, such as Suddaby et al. (2011), Davis (2010), and Daft and Lewin (1993), have a completely different understanding of the field. Following Davis (2010), they claim that the field of OTs is presently jammed in a 'living museum of the 1970s' (Davis, 2010, p. 691 in Suddaby et al., 2011). According to them, the theoretical pluralism characterizing current OTs is less important than we think. Below the surface of the OTs mosaic is a stock of established and legitimated theories that were formulated years ago and remain in use to advance the field (e.g. contingency, system, institutional, and sensemaking theories). These scholars not only claim that organizational theorists fail to propose new theories, but that the field of OTs appears to be detached from organizational reality more than ever, as it is not keeping pace with the actual challenges faced by the organizational world, such as globalization, outsourcing, open collaboration, and so on.

Concomitant to this debate, scholars in the OTs field also spend a great deal of effort reflecting on how theoretical advancement is currently produced in the field. Scholars generally recognize that organizational theories are built upon the foundational building blocks of theoretical concepts, metaphors, and empirical material (Boxenbaum and Rouleau, 2011). Together, these building blocks provide a wide range of propositions and models explaining how organizations function and relate to their environment. Theory building is the process by which these building blocks are put together to produce specific arrangements of plausible and/or transferable explanations about organizational life. Of course, these arrangements are not 'fixed' and immutable; their interpretation and appropriation provide us with different ways of thinking and producing knowledge on organizations.

At the risk of oversimplifying, theoretical advancement in the field of OTs seems to be generally achieved in three different ways.

1.2.1 Borrowing from other disciplines

Since the founding of OTs, it has been quite common for organizational scholars to borrow concepts and theories from neighbouring disciplines, most notably sociology (e.g. organizational structure and actor–network theory), psychology (e.g. organizational commitment and attribution theory), economics (e.g. organizational decision-making and evolutionary theory of change), and anthropology (e.g. organizational culture and myth). Over the past decades, the OTs have also been importing from more distant or foreign disciplines, such as technology (e.g. organizational artefacts and socio-materiality), literary studies (e.g. narratives and translation), and geography (e.g. organizational space and place). Reading classics in social sciences and humanities, as well as demonstrating some interest for other related expertise and domains, can be theoretically refreshing and helpful to the advancement of knowledge on organizing.

Unquestionably, borrowing from other disciplines has been and remains very helpful. Nevertheless, it also has some drawbacks. Importing ideas, whether they are theories or concepts, from other disciplines has unintended effects, including impeding the development of 'indigenous theory' and constraining the development of new theory. OTs theorists spend a lot of time recontextualizing, translating, or domesticating foreign ideas, which often has the result of reducing the inherent potential of these ideas instead of generating new insights. Additionally, what is significant in social sciences at any given time may only become important in OTs five or ten years later.

1.2.2 Hybridizing theories and/or metaphors

Novelty lies in the unique combination of ideas rather than in the introduction of new ideas. Tension, inconsistency, and contradiction between theories and metaphors generate opportunities to extend knowledge and add complexity to the ways organizational life is perceived and described. Oswick,

Fleming, and Hanlon (2011) refers to 'conceptual blending' to characterize this approach to advancing theory. Before the 1970s, papers in the field of OTs were strongly aligned with a single specific theoretical influence, but this is significantly less true today. Indeed, it is fairly common to see the influences of multiple theoretical sources when reading OTs texts produced after the 1970s. More than ever, the majority of OTs papers are anchored in multiple theoretical foundations. This embedded multiplicity makes it difficult for novice theorists to understand the underlying theoretical and epistemological influences of the theories they use.

Indeed, in the past 25 years, scholars have focused on hybridizing to develop new knowledge in the OTs field. There are several ways to do this. In previous works, I demonstrated how institutional theory and the strategy-as-practice perspective are based on a specific set of pre-existing but recombined metaphors (Boxenbaum and Rouleau, 2011; Rouleau, 2013). Working with bridging concepts (e.g. sensemaking can take multiple forms, and related constructs, such as sense-breaking or sensegiving, can be developed) or finding ways of collapsing false binary oppositions (e.g. unifying agencies and structural explanations) are also popular ways of hybridizing theory for new knowledge. Hybridizing can also be achieved through conceptual blending, or by unifying notions from two or more lenses. For instance, Zaheer and Bell (2005) link social network research to the resource-based view of the firm in their studies of firms' innovation by proposing the notion of 'network-enabled capabilities' (capabilities held by innovative firms that bridge structural holes).

1.2.3 Building theory from empirical facts

Another common way of building theory in the OTs is by drawing on inductive or, more realistically, abductive theorizing (Shepherd and Sutcliffe, 2011; Stæner & Van de Ven, 2021). The growing popularity of the 'Gioia method' (Gioia, Corley, and Hamilton, 2012) has created widespread recognition for the fact that theory building often starts with a rigorous analysis of empirical observations. From the multiple iterations between empirical observations and relevant literature, novel conceptual categories emerge.

Another approach to creative theorizing from empirical data is the notion of constructing an empirical mystery focusing on the differences and inconsistencies between empirical material and prevailing ideas, as proposed by Alvesson and Kärreman (2007). For example, traditional literature on strategy and identity often investigates, from a top-down perspective, how newly appointed top managers breathe life into organizational identity when outlining strategic changes for organizations. Rather than adopting this top-down orientation, scholars can construct an empirical mystery by reversing the perspective and investigating how new top managers are subject to, and constituted by, the discursive practices of their subordinate managers and organizational members in a context of strategic change.

Co-constructing knowledge 'with' practitioners instead of 'on' practitioners could also be another way to rejuvenate or build new theory from empirical facts. More specifically, extending what was previously called 'Mode 2 of knowledge production' might introduce new knowledge, and in so doing help fill some of the gaps between theory and practice. Knowledge developed through transdisciplinary and/or partnership-based approaches tends to generate and lead to a reconfiguration of knowledge, particularly around 'grand challenges' such as globalization, artificial intelligence, climate change, and inequality. This approach to producing knowledge might help organizational theorists create new insights about organizational life.

The popularity of this debate on theoretical novelty in the field of OTs is a consequence of the 'publish or perish' context. The system of publishing is built on the need to generate strong and relevant theoretical contributions. In principle, such a requirement should renew our theoretical practices and resources. However, the publication system creates a desperate quest for novelty in the OTs while simultaneously hindering the generation of novelty. In order to be seen as relevant, contributions need to be made in continuity with prior literature and theorizing claims. At the same time, the paper format is not always well suited to the generation of new knowledge and theory. For instance, it would probably not have been possible for Giddens to develop the theory of structuration or for Latour to elaborate the actor–network theory by writing papers in journals with today's standards. As a PhD student or a junior researcher, it is difficult, if not impossible, to escape this tension.

These central debates constitute the bedrock of OTs and reverberate to the longstanding complementarity between the European and the American traditions of research in this field—a theme that is frequently revisited throughout this book. While the paradigm debate has given rise to a lively set of conversations in European journals (e.g. *Organization Studies, Organization*), the theoretical novelty debate continues to be disputed largely in North American forums (e.g. *Academy of Management Review*), where it originated. Given that these traditions have different roots, this is understandable. The European tradition is more concerned with discussing philosophical issues, whereas its American counterpart is more pragmatically oriented. This is why this book introduces the latest developments in both traditions. The embeddedness of the field in these two grand traditions of research is strongly inscribed in the institutional structure of the field. Take, for example, its two main international associations: EGOS (European Group of Organization Studies) and the OMT division of AOM (Organization and Management Theory Division of the Academy of Management). Over the years, both European and American scholars have benefited from each other's influence—something that remains true to this day.

References

Allard-Poesi, F. & Perret, V. 2014. Fondements épistémologiques de la recherche. *In*: Thietart, R. A. (ed.) *Méthodes de recherche en management*. Paris, Dunod.

Alvesson, M. & Kärreman, D. 2007. Constructing Mystery: Empirical Matters in Theory Development. *The Academy of Management Review*, 32, 1265–1281.

Barry, D. & Hanses, H. 2008. *The Sage Handbook of New Approaches in Management and Organizations*. London, Sage Publications.

Berger, P. L. & Luckmann, T. 1966. *The Social Construction of Reality*. New York, Anchor Books.

Bhaskar, R. 1978. *A Realist Theory of Science*. London, Routledge.

Boxenbaum, E. & Rouleau, L. 2011. New Knowledge Products as Bricolage: Metaphors and Scripts in Organizational Theory. *The Academy of Management Review*, 36, 272–296.

Burrell, G. & Morgan, G. 1979. *Sociological Paradigms and Organizational Analysis*. London, Tavistock.

Cornelissen, J. P. & Durand, R. 2014. Moving Forward: Developing Theoretical Contributions in Management Studies. *Journal of Management Studies*, 51, 995–1022.

Cunliffe, A. L. 2011. Crafting Qualitative Research: Morgan and Smircich 30 Years On. *Organizational Research Methods*, 14, 647–673.

Daft, R. L. & Lewin, A. Y. 1993. Where are the Theories for the 'New' Organizational Forms? An Editorial Essay. *Organization Science*, 4, i–vi.

Davis, G. F. 2010. Do Theories of Organizations Progress? *Organizational Research Methods*, 13, 690–709.

Deetz, S. 1996. Describing Differences in Approaches to Organization Science: Rethinking Burrell and Morgan and their Legacy. *Organization Science*, 7, 191.

Elsbach, K., Sutton, R. I., & Whetten, D. 1999. Introduction: Perspectives on Developing Management Theory, Circa 1999: Moving from Shrill Monologues to (Relatively) Tame Dialogues. *The Academy of Management Review*, 24, 627–633.

Gioia, D. A., Corley, K. G., & Hamilton, A. L. 2012. Seeking Qualitative Rigor in Inductive Research: Notes on the Gioia Methodology. *Organizational Research Methods*, 16, 15–31.

Hassard, J. & Kelemen 2002. Production and Consumption in Organizational Knowledge: The Case of the 'Paradigms Debate'. *Organization*, 9, 331–355.

Hassard, J., Wolfram Cox, J., & Rowlinson, M. 2013. Where Are the Old Theories of Organization? Prospects for Retrospection in Organization Theory. *The Academy of Management Journal*, 38, 309–313.

Morgan, G. 2006. *Images of Organizations*. Thousand Oaks, CA, Sage Publications.

Morgan, G. & Smircich, L. 1980. The Case for Qualitative Research. *Academy of Management Review*, 5, 491–500.

Newton, T., Deetz, S., & Reed, M. 2011. Responses to Social Constructionism and Critical Realism in Organization Studies. *Organization Studies*, 32, 7–26.

Oswick, C., Fleming, P., & Hanlon, G. 2011. From Borrowing to Blending: Rethinking the Process of Organizational Theory Building. *The Academy of Management Review*, 36, 318–337.

Reed, M. 2005. Reflections on the 'Realist Turn' in Organization and Management Studies. *Journal of Management Studies*, 42, 1621–1644.

Reed, M. 2006. Organizational Theorizing: A Contested Terrain. *In*: Clegg, S. R., Hardy, C., Nord, W. R., & Lawrence, T. (eds.) *The Sage Handbook of Organization Studies*. 2nd edition. London, Sage Publications, pp. 20–54.

Rouleau, L. 2013. Strategy-as-Practice Research at a Crossroads. *M@n@gement*, 16, 547–565.

Schultz, M. & Hatch, M. J. 1996. Living with Multiple Paradigms: The Case of Paradigm Interplay in Organizational Culture Studies. *The Academy of Management Review*, 21, 529–557.

Shepherd, C. & Challenger, R. 2013. Revisiting Paradigm(s) in Management Research: A Rhetorical Analysis of the Paradigm Wars. *International Journal of Management Reviews*, 15, 225–244.

Shepherd, D. A. & Sutcliffe, K. M. 2011. Inductive Top-Down Theorizing: A Source of New Theories of Organization. *The Academy of Management Review*, 36, 361–380.

Stæner, A.S., Van de Ven, A. 2021. Generating Theory by Abduction. *The Academy of Management Review*, 46, 684–701.

Suddaby, R., Hardy, C., & Nguyen, H. 2011. Introduction to Special Topic Forum: Where Are the New Theories of Organization? *The Academy of Management Review*, 36, 236–246.

Westwood, R. & Clegg, S. 2003. *Debating Organization: Point-Counterpoint in Organization Studies*. Oxford, Blackwell Publishing.

Zaheer, A. & Bell, G. G. 2005. Benefiting From Network Position: Firm Capabilities, Structural Holes, and Performance. *Strategic Management Journal*, 26, 809–825.

2
Organizational Institutionalism

Since the mid-1990s, organizational institutionalism has emerged as a vibrant and leading approach in organization theories (OTs), in both the United States and Europe. We could almost say that organizational institutionalism is actually 'the' research paradigm in OTs. The adoption or the 'institutionalization' of this stream of research in OTs can first be explained by the fact that it provides researchers with a precise language that allows them to explain how organizations respond to environmental challenges in order to appear legitimate to their stakeholders, which in turn informs the broader relationship between 'business and society'. Second, the growing importance of social responsibility and sustainability issues and the corresponding rise of accreditation programmes in many industries partly explain the noteworthy trajectory of institutional theory in the past decades. In addition to exploring this contextual element, this chapter questions the phenomenal diffusion of the institutional framework in OTs.

Organizational institutionalism emerged in reaction to the objectivist and rational view of contingency and decision-making theories. In this context, scholars were urged to take into account the role that symbolic and broader structures of meanings play in the constitution of organizational structures. Renewing the strong hypothesis of environmental adaptation in the late 1970s, organizational institutionalism develops a new framework to explain 'why organizations adopt behaviours that conform to normative demands' (Suddaby, 2010, p. 15)—sometimes to the detriment of their economic goals. While this research programme has been initially criticized for fostering a rather constraining approach to organizations that suggested they were passively shaped by their institutional environment, organizational institutionalism has taken a new path at the turn of the millennium. Instead of focusing solely on explaining why organizations adopt similar forms and management practices, organizational institutionalism is now aimed at understanding the multiple agentic and innovative ways in which organizations change over time in spite of the constant presence of mimetic, coercive, and normative institutional pressures. In order to shed new light on the past 25 years of significant changes in organizational institutionalism, one needs

Organization Theories in the Making. Linda Rouleau, Oxford University Press.
© Linda Rouleau (2022). DOI: 10.1093/oso/9780198792024.003.0003

to figure out if those changes allow institutionalists to expand and renew their core assumptions and objectives or if they instead push them further away from the crux of their initial research programme; that is, the study of institutions and the embeddedness of social action and values.

The present chapter starts by describing the three fundamental waves of evolution in organizational institutionalism. Then, it explores the main substreams of organizational institutionalism: institutional change; institutional logics; institutional entrepreneurs; and institutional work. Finally, this chapter ends on a discussion of the strengths and weaknesses of organizational institutionalism.

2.1 Three waves of institutional theory

Before introducing the latest developments in organizational institutionalism, one needs to contextualize them in the historical development of the institutionalist school of thought in OTs. This evolution took place in three waves: (i) the old institutionalism; (ii) the new institutionalism; and (iii) the 'renewed' institutionalism, which for the purposes of simplification is currently called 'organizational institutionalism' or institutional theories. Drawing on institutionalist vocabulary, these three waves can be seen as periods of emergence, growth, and maturity for institutional theories. Table 2.1 provides an overview of the main distinctive characters of those three stages of evolution.

The first institutionalist ideas emerged in OTs during the 1940s and 1950s as a counterpoint to rationalist and voluntary explanations, mirroring trends in sociology, economics, and political sciences (for more information, see Scott, 2014). Selznick, who is now considered the 'father' of institutional theories in OTs, was one of their main proponents (Clark (1956) and Zald and Denton (1963) being other well-known institutionalists of this period). In 1949, Selznick studied the *Tennessee Valley Authority* project and demonstrated that organizational goals were diverted in favour of the dominant groups of stakeholders targeted by the federal agency programme. Selznick's monograph demonstrated that intentional projects such as top-down strategic planning always give rise to unexpected consequences owing to the vested and divergent interests of stakeholders. More than ten years later, Selznick (1957) wrote another classical book titled *Leadership in Administration* where he looks at what he calls 'institutional leaders'; that is, company leaders who are capable of instilling values promoted in the community or in greater society within their own organization. As a matter of fact, according to Selznick,

Table 2.1 Old, new, and 'renewed institutionalism'

	Old institutionalism	New institutionalism	Renewed institutionalism
Conflicts of interest	Central	Peripheral	Distributed
Source of inertia	Vested interests	Environmental legitimacy	Legitimacy building and reparation
Level of analysis	Organization	Field, sector, or society	Individuals, organization, field, and society
Institutional locus	Organizational values, culture	Abstracted, societal	Logics, field, and organizations
Behavioural emphasis	Commitment	Habits and rules	Processes and practices
Organizational dynamics	Change	Persistence	Continuous change
Key forms of cognition	Values, norms, and attitudes	Classification, scripts, and schemas	Sensemaking
Social psychology	Socialization	Attribution	Construction
Goals	Negotiable	Symbolic	Shared
Structural emphasis	Informal networks	Formal administration	Organized collective action

* The two first columns have been adapted from Hirsch and Lounsbury (1997).

this is what allows organizations to persist over time. Those studies eventually led Selznick to reflect on the idea of the organization as an institution.

Selznick' work is representative of what has been further called the 'old' institutional school in two ways. First, Selznick's work recognizes the importance of taking into account the existence of the multiple stakeholders around the organization who impact organizational goals. Second, it emphasized how values, socializations, norms, and commitments are embedded in the way leaders shape organizations. According to Selznick (1957, p. 17), to institutionalize is 'to infuse with value beyond the technical requirements of the task at hand'. Therefore, the first wave of institutional theories has been generally described as conveying an 'action' or a 'micro'-based view of organizations as institutions.

The second wave of organizational institutionalism emerged at the end of the 1970s with the seminal works of Meyer and Rowan (1977) and DiMaggio and Powell (1983), pertaining to rationalized myths, and structural isomorphism and decoupling, respectively. These works invigorated the way the relationship between the environment and the organization was conceptualized at the same time as the contingency perspective was losing its momentum. In the 1970s and 1980s, institutionalists sought to understand the process by which management structures are institutionalized; that is, why and how organizations adopt managerial fashions and patterns from their institutional field. Put differently, they suggest that institutional environments have a strong impact on the structural conformity and maintenance of organizations. Typical works of this second wave examine the adoption or the institutional trajectories of a great diversity of management structures and patterns: adoption by cities of civil service employment reforms (Tolbert and Zucker, 1983), adoption of similar structures by schools from around the world (Meyer et al., 1987), adoption by large corporations of incentives plans for executive compensation (Westphal and Zajac, 1994), and adoption of performance appraisal programmes in universities (Townley, 1997). The research agenda of organizational institutionalism thus became dominated by a 'structural' and 'macro' approach dedicated to explaining why organizations share more similarities than differences and how they persist over time. By reorienting the approach towards the institutionalization process of formal structures, new institutionalism (or 'neo-institutionalism') set aside concerns of meaning construction, which had been so dear to the old institutionalism or the first generation of institutionalists and their focus on values, organizational dynamics, and social norms.

Although the institutional scholars injected invigorating new ideas into the OTs field, they soon became the target of extensive criticisms. Broadly speaking, they were criticized for focusing on stability while providing a constraining and homogeneous vision of the institutional features shaping the organizational environment (Hirsch and Lounsbury, 1997). They were also blamed for excluding individuals and leaders from their framework (Oliver, 1991) as well as for failing to take into account the subjective dimension in institutionalization processes. Moreover, they were criticized for not considering the divergent interests of actors or the differentiated power of stakeholders (Scott, 1987). Hence, as a rejoinder, many institutional voices of the 1990s suggested either revisiting the core assumptions of the institutionalist project or unifying the 'old' and the 'new' institutionalism in order to integrate change and agency in the institutional conversation (e.g. Greenwood and Hinings, 1996; Selznick, 1996; Hirsch and Lounsbury, 1997). These authors argued that neo-institutionalism committed the grave sin of abandoning action in favour of structures, and change in favour of stability, and that it was time to reconcile the 'action–structure' or 'micro–macro' debate underlying the development of institutional theories over time. Thus, in the early 2000s, the OTs field saw the emergence of a third wave of works that renewed organizational institutionalism and brought it to maturity.

The third wave of organizational institutionalism aims to bring together the old and the new institutionalism by acknowledging that organizations react differently to similar institutional pressures. Instead of examining how organizations end up looking so alike, institutionalists became concerned about understanding why organizations preserve, adopt, and even abandon structures and patterns that would make them appear legitimate in the eyes of their institutional stakeholders. Despite the pressures they face in their environment, organizations were hence considered as actors having some discretionary power in the way they respond to institutional demands. Therefore, the third wave of organizational institutionalism seeks to explain the range of organizational responses to institutional pressures. Institutional heteromorphism—or, put simply, variations in organizational structures and practices—has now replaced the assumption of structural or ceremonial conformity that was central to the neo-institutionalist research programme. As a consequence of the constructive debate around variation and conformity in organizational institutionalism, change thus became the new focus of the renewed institutional approaches of the 2000s. Since then, new substreams of institutional research have emerged and developed in parallel to the study of institutional change: institutional logics; institutional entrepreneurs; and institutional work (see Table 2.2).

2.2 Institutional change

In a then-provocative paper, Greenwood and Hinings (1996) argue that neo-institutional theory is an adequate lens for understanding organizational change. According to them, the isomorphic argument only makes sense in highly institutionalized contexts and sectors. In other contexts, the variety of institutional pressures (normative, coercive, and mimetic) opened up possibilities for differentiated organizational interpretations. Even more so, the diversity of dissemination mechanisms (governmental, regulative, or professional agencies) could reinforce differentiation in organizational responses to institutional pressures and even alter them. Seo and Creed (2002) further support this perspective by suggesting that the contradictory nature of institutional arrangements enables and fosters the agents' capacities to enter into processes of institutional change. For example, Lounsbury (2001), a central figure in organizational institutionalism, has studied the adoption

Table 2.2 Synoptic overview of organizational institutionalism

	Institutional change	Institutional logics	Institutional entrepreneurship	Institutional work
Definition	The diffusion and adoption of heterogeneous ideas and organizational responses to institutional pressures	The sociocultural forces or cognitive orders that structure a given institutional field	Initiators of a change—involved in mobilizing the resources required to implement it—that breaks with the dominant logics structuring a field	The local and purposive acts of resistance and maintenance of institutions carried out by individuals and groups to shape their institutional environment
Research question	How do organizational structures, patterns or ideas emerge, get maintained, and become disrupted?	How do organizations deal with tensions in the institutional logics they are subjected to, or how do they respond to this institutional complexity?	How can actors, whether individual or collective, adapt, maintain, and change their institutional environment in spite of the strong pressures constraining them?	How does institutional work occur? What activities/practices steer the purposive efforts of creating, maintaining, and disrupting institutions?
Organization	A set of heterogeneous organizational responses to change	The results of conflicting logics	A setting in which embedded actors are promoting new institutional structures, patterns, and ideas	A setting in which actors are working to maintain institutional structures, patterns, and ideas

Influences	Greenwood and Hinings (1996); Selznick (1996); Seo and Creed (2002)	Jackall (1988); Friedland and Alford (1991); Thornton (2004); Thornton et al. (2012)	DiMaggio (1988); Beckert (1999); Battilana et al. (2009)	Lawrence and Suddaby (2006); Lawrence et al. (2009); Lawrence et al. (2011)
Conceptual resources	Translation, institutional trajectories (emergence, maintenance, and disruption)	Institutional complexity; change and shifts over time; compromises between logics; logics hybridity	Dominant and peripheral subject positions; power resources; legitimacy	Types of institutional work (e.g. technical, political, cultural, temporal); theorization; legitimation
Methods	Longitudinal qualitative/quantitative analysis	Longitudinal (often comparative) qualitative/quantitative analysis	Ethnographic case studies	Institutional biographies
Exemplars	Lounsbury (2001); De Holan and Phillips (2002); Harmon, Green, and Goodnight (2015); Glynn (2017)	Lounsbury (2007); Greenwood et al. (2011); Perkmann and Schildt (2015); Durand and Jourdan (2012); Vermeulen et al. (2016)	Rao et al. (2003); Maguire et al. (2004); Lockett et al. (2012); Olsen (2017)	Perkmann and Spicer (2008); Martí and Fernández (2013); Daudigeos (2013); Granqvist and Gustafsson (2016); Wright and Nyberg (2017)

of recycling programmes in American colleges and universities. He showed that the majority of them do adopt recycling programmes, yet they do so in different ways. For instance, some educational institutions have extensive recycling programmes, while others have more restricted ones. The characteristic of the recycling programme depends on the leaders promoting them. When leaders are student groups, they benefit from the support of the ecological movement; therefore, the programmes they put forth have more impact. Conversely, programmes run by local administrators—who are less committed to the environment and whose actions are not supported externally—are of more limited scope.

The emergence and consolidation of organizational institutionalism in Europe presents an interesting case of variations in practices, leading to a distinct stream of research. While organizational institutionalism was largely developed in North America, this research programme took on a different flavour in Europe. For instance, what became known as Scandinavian Institutionalism (Czarniawska and Sevón, 1996; Sahlin and Wedlin, 2008) constitutes an illustrative case of such variation. Throughout the 1970s, Scandinavian professors and PhD students visited the Scandinavian Consortium for Organizational Research (SCANCOR) in Stanford University, the home of prominent institutionalist scholars (e.g., Scott, Meyer, and Powell). As a result, the work of Scandinavian researchers on public reforms and bureaucratic change took on an institutionalist lens. In 1996, Czarniaswka and Sevón published a book called *Translating Organizational Change*, coining the label 'Scandinavian Institutionalism'. Rather than speaking in terms of 'adoption' of structures and patterns, Czarniawska and Sevón (1996) came up with the notion of 'translation', borrowed from Latour (1986), to explain the change in ideas that results from them 'travelling' and hence being 'translated' from one context to another. From there, Scandinavian Institutionalist researchers conducted extensive qualitative research aiming to better understand how intra-organizational dynamics are both affected by and subsequently impact the institutional field. Revisiting the Scandinavian Institutionalist story, Boxenbaum and Pedersen (2009) concluded that the Institutionalist Scandinavian School has largely endorsed a heteromorphic view of organizational responses to institutional pressures. In so doing, this School produced organizational knowledge dedicated to action and comprehension, contrary to North American researchers, whose efforts were generally geared towards standardizing and promoting the normativity of their findings during the first two waves of organizational institutionalism development.

Researchers interested in institutional change examine the multiple ways that structures, patterns, and even institutions are created, maintained, and disrupted. In what I consider an exemplary case study of institutional change, De Holan and Phillips (2002) explore the complex relationships between institutional emergence, stability, and dissipation. These authors study how the management team of MagoTaplan, a medium-sized Cuban manufacturing enterprise, underwent a radical organizational change in a transitional economy dominated by strong ideological pressures. The case study concludes that by taking into account pressures 'for and against' change, institutional research can show how managers are able to adapt their organizational structures to their transitional economic environment while being able to respond to the socialist regime pressures. By analysing the interorganizational, organizational, and managerial levels of MagoTaplan, these authors demonstrated the interactions between capitalist and socialist pressures and how managers adapted their organizational structure in order to respond to their economic environment while maintaining a socialist façade.

Institutional change researchers also investigate the drivers and processes through which change is accomplished (Dacin, Goodstein, and Scott, 2002). For example, the role of legitimacy standards and judgements is a central research theme around institutional change (Greenwood et al., 2017). Harnon, Green, and Goodnight (2015) explore how rhetorical and communication processes play a role in institutional change. Glynn (2017) suggests that identity is a central driver and mechanism by which institutions are changing. Until now, most studies on institutional change were based on longitudinal research design and were conducted in disruptive environments. Despite the efforts to understand change in organizational institutionalism, many questions remain. According to Greenwood et al. (2017, p. 8), 'few studies analyse failed efforts to change institution'. They also make a call for further research on institutional change in mature fields.

2.3 Institutional complexity and logics

It is now widely accepted that institutional theory provides a rich view of the organizational environment. The Old Carnegie School and contingencies theories generally portray the organizational environment as composed of several external stakeholders having divergent interests and resources. By introducing society, culture, and even values in the way they define the environment, organizational institutionalists suggest that the environment—also termed 'institutional field'—is the site of multiple and conflicting cultural norms and practices that both limit and enable organizational responses and goals (Greenwood et al., 2010). Moreover, the sheer variety of characteristics that can make up an institutional field is fundamental to the notion of institutional complexity (Thornton, Ocasio, and Lounsbury, 2012). Not only do institutions shape organizational goals and structures, but they also operate at multiple levels (e.g. the organizational, field, and even society levels). Hence, to address the issue of institutional fragmentation and complexity, the notion of 'institutional logics' has emerged in the early 2000s and has become extremely popular over the years.

Broadly put, institutional logics concern the sociocultural forces or cognitive orders that structure a given institutional field. For example, universities are the site of the twin logics of ambitious research projects and relevant teaching. They contribute to shaping how universities and professors behave with respect to the conflicting goals of pursuing versus transferring knowledge. Similarly, artistic and cultural organizations are subject to the logic of creation, and, at the same time, to that of commerce. Additionally, in these types of organizations, the logic of public education may be factored in as well. Together, these institutional logics influence the way such organizations behave, design their programmes and activities, and make artistic choices. Professional organizations such as financial, law, or medical organizations also experience various tensions resulting from contradictory logics anchored in diverse sets of professional rules and values. Institutional researchers are interested in explaining how such organizations deal with tensions between the different logics they are subject to, or how they respond to this institutional complexity.

Friedland and Alford (1991) were amongst the first scholars to raise the issue of institutional complexity. In their seminal chapter 'Bringing Society Back In', they said:

> The central institutions of the contemporary capitalist West—capitalist market, bureaucratic state, democracy, nuclear family, and Christian religion—shape individual preferences and organizational interests as well as the repertoires of behaviors by which they may attain them. These institutions are potentially contradictory and hence make multiple logics available to individuals and organizations. Individuals and organizations transform the institutional relations with society by exploiting these contradictions. (Friedland and Alford, 1991, p. 232)

Their original claim prompted interest amongst institutional scholars to investigate the links between institutions and organizational responses or decision-making processes. More than a decade later, Thornton (2004) proposed an analysis of the transformation of the American higher education publishing industry from the late 1950s to the early 1990s. In her book *Market from Culture*, she demonstrated how the industry moved from what she called 'editorial logics', based on reputation and networks, to 'market logics' emphasizing growth and profitability. Building on Friedland and Alford (1991), Thornton (2004, p. 69) proposed the following definition of institutional logics: 'The socially constructed, historical pattern of material practices, assumptions, values, beliefs, and rules by which individuals produce and reproduce their material subsistence, organize time and space, and provide meaning to their social reality'.

Thornton, Ocasio, and Lounsbury published a book in 2012 titled *The Institutional Logics Perspective. A New Approach to Culture, Structure and Process* in which they chart the territory of institutional logics and propose a new research programme aimed at pushing this perspective further. The symbolic and material aspects of institutions and their multiple levels of analysis are amongst the new elements that are emphasized to structure the foundations of the institutional logic's perspective. By considering both the symbolic (meaning) and material (structures and practices) aspects of institutions, they provide the means to better theorize about heterogeneity and change. In so doing, their research programme integrates and/or reconciles the old and the new institutionalism. Moreover, Thornton et al. (2012) advance the idea that institutions operate at multiple levels of analysis. First, they suggest a cross-level framework of institutional logics that combines the recursive relationships between the macro and micro level of analysis. In so doing, they affirm the interest of looking at the micro-foundations of institutional logics. Second, they revisit Friedland and Alford (1991)'s model of social institutions in order to come up with a theoretical framework for empirical research. According to Thornton et al. (2012), family, religion, state, market, profession, and corporation constitute the main institutional orders of western societies. Each order is driven by its specific institutional logics and they are therefore in conflict or in tension with each other. This research programme opens up a vast array of possibilities to explore the relationships between the logics at play in a given field and the dynamics and practices by which collective and individual actors contribute to maintain, transform, and change institutions.

Since then, research on institutional logics has expanded very rapidly (Lounsbury, 2008; Greenwood et al., 2011). Most of the research targeted changes and shifts in institutional logics over time. Typically, those changes were depicted as anchored around two logics: a traditional and dominant logic and a new, yet ascending, logic. For instance, Lounsbury (2007) investigated how trustee and performance logics led to different forms of contracts within independent mutual fund firms in the United States. His study shows that over time, the entire mutual fund industry moved from a conservative investment approach held by a trusteeship logic to a speculative one motivated by a performance logic. Also, after being rapidly criticized for emphasizing the study of two logics, institutional researchers now tend to highlight the coexistence of multiple logics. Perkmann and Schildt (2015) argue that organizations durably and even routinely incorporate multiple logics. Hence, institutional researchers aim to 'order' or better understand 'the relative incoherence of enduring institutional logics' (Greenwood et al., 2011, p. 323). Even though institutional logics are typically portrayed as incompatible and contradictory, institutional scholars are studying the mechanisms and practices by which organizations are accommodating and making compromises between institutional logics (Durand and Jourdan, 2012; Smets et al., 2015). The burgeoning literature on hybrid organizations is also contributing immensely to advancing our understanding of institutional logics dynamics and strategic organizational responses to institutional complexity (Vermeulen et al., 2016).

2.4 Institutional entrepreneurship

The 'institutional entrepreneurship' notion was introduced by, or credited to, DiMaggio (1988), and pertains to the activities through which new institutions are created. The notion constitutes an answer to the famous 'embedded agency' paradox; that is, 'how agents can modify or even abolish institutions if their interests and cognitive schemes have been created by these same institutions' (Weik, 2012, p. 568). Thus, institutional entrepreneurship aims to understand how actors, whether individual or collective, can adapt, maintain, and change their institutional environment in spite of the strong pressures that constrain them.

When evoking the notion of institutional entrepreneurship, questions of clarification immediately arise: What, exactly, is an institutional entrepreneur? What is the distinction between an entrepreneur and an institutional entrepreneur? According to Battilana, Leca, and Boxenbaum (2009), two conditions must be met for one to be identified as an institutional entrepreneur. First, an institutional entrepreneur must initiate a change that 'breaks' with the commonly shared understandings and beliefs in a given organizational field—put differently, they must initiate a change that breaks with the dominant logics structuring the field. Second, an institutional entrepreneur should be directly involved in mobilizing the resources needed to implement the change. For instance, in the case of MagoTaplan described earlier, the director of this Cuban enterprise can be considered as an institutional entrepreneur (de Holan and Phillips, 2002). By introducing marketing and purchasing departments as well as an empowering rewards system for employees, he promoted values that contradicted the standards of an enterprise operating in a socialist economy. On the other hand, a director implementing the same organizational reforms in a capitalist enterprise would not be considered an institutional entrepreneur. In the taxi industry, a businessperson who starts a company on the grounds of a corporatist business model would be considered as an entrepreneur, whereas they would be regarded as an institutional entrepreneur should they introduce a new business model entailing a significant breach from the dominant logic shaping the industry.

Institutional entrepreneurs play a key role in the processes of creating and transforming institutions as well as institutional fields. The social or 'subject positions' in which actors are institutionally embedded provide them with opportunities and resources for initiating change. Yet not all actors have the same interests and motivations to initiate institutional change. Institutional research generally establishes a difference between 'dominant' and 'peripheral' or 'fringe' actors in a given institutional field. While dominant actors generally don't have any interests in initiating change, they are the ones who possess the resources needed to mobilize other stakeholders and transform the rules of an institutional field. Therefore, an important part of the literature on institutional entrepreneurs often emphasizes the role of powerful actors such as political agents, technocrats, and professionals in effecting institutional change. Rao, Monin, and Durand, (2003) explain how the *nouvelle cuisine* movement was implemented in France by the most renowned and honoured chefs who abandoned classic cuisine. In this case, the *nouvelle cuisine* movement reinforced the incumbent chef's autonomy and diminished the power of restaurateurs whose operations were anchored in classic cuisine.

Contrary to dominant actors, peripheral actors generally benefit the most from improving their position within a given institutional field, though they generally do not have the resources to initiate substantial change. For instance, Maguire, Hardy, and Lawrence (2004) studied the process of institutionalizing HIV/AIDS treatment advocacy in Canada. They found that institutional entrepreneurs in this emerging field needed to carry a high level of legitimacy in both the gay community and the pharmaceutical industry in order to be able to overcome divergent interests as well as mobilize and rally other stakeholders to their cause. In this case, the institutional entrepreneurs were two individuals, Robert and Turner, who were both HIV positive and had gone through the system to receive the necessary treatments. Maguire et al. (2004) further demonstrate that those key actors were able to bridge the variety of stakeholders involved by developing a vast array of arguments that translated their interests.

In a research project about the healthcare system, Lockett et al. (2012) take into account both the role of dominant and peripheral actors around a given change playing out in different settings. The authors, studying the implementation of new pathways for cancer genetic services within the English National Health Service, zoom in on three different settings and demonstrate that the intermediate actors—rather than the dominant or peripheral ones—were acting as institutional entrepreneurs. Lockett et al. (2012) explain that dominant actors had the resources to implement change but did not have any vested interests to that end as they were privileged and deeply rooted in the field, while peripheral actors were likely to desire some changes but could not easily carry them out since they were used to operating with limited resources. Also, as they combined a mix of both power (structural legitimacy) and resources (normative legitimacy), only intermediate actors had sufficient interests and resources to break the existing rules in this highly institutionalized field and implement new ones.

Research on institutional entrepreneurship has focused on the efforts needed to sustain new organizational practices, philosophies, and roles (Rao et al., 2003; Maguire et al., 2004; Lockett et al., 2012) as well as on the emergence of novel organizational forms (Tracey, Phillips, and Jarvis, 2011; David, Sine, and Haveman, 2013). The notion of institutional entrepreneurs has also been largely used in the contexts of emerging or transitioning economies. For instance, Olsen (2017) examines the role of institutional entrepreneurs in the transformation of the relationship between state and market in emerging economies. Comparing the micro-finance fields in Brazil and Mexico, she showed how institutional entrepreneurs' ability to access the state was key in the co-evolution process of implementing micro-finance as a way to reduce poverty and enhance economic activity in emerging economies.

In order to understand how institutional entrepreneurs transform existing institutions and create new ones, research has focused on different aspects of institutional entrepreneurship. Some researchers have investigated the set of arguments or rationales put forth to build a strong foundation of meaning and coherent identities as a way to instil institutional change. For example, Tracey, Phillips, and Jarvis (2011) studied the creation of Aspire, a hybrid organization combining not-for-profit homeless support and for-profit retail activities. According to the authors, problem framing and counterfactual thinking were essential in order to theorize the need for a new organizational form and create the opportunity to provide a new solution (i.e. a household catalogue business that employed homeless people) to tackle homelessness. Others were rather interested by the wide range of resources—whether financial, political, cultural, or technological—that institutional entrepreneurs mobilize to shape the field in which they operate. Sharma, Lawrence, and Lowe (2014) show how accountants play the role of institutional entrepreneur by implementing an accounting system that contributed to replacing state-bureaucratic routines from newly privatized organizations. Finally, several other authors focused their analysis on the relations and interactions (e.g. collaborations, coalitions, or alliances) that institutional entrepreneurs develop with other allies to build legitimate institutional change. David et al. (2013) studied the founders of early professional management consulting firms in the United States and described how these consulting pioneers (e.g. Booz, Allen & Hamilton, Arthur D. Little, Inc., and McKinsey & Company) developed strong ties outside their emerging field with local and national elites such as individuals and organizations that had high legitimacy and authority in larger society.

By the end of the 2010s, institutional scholars started to criticize institutional entrepreneur research. Some of them lay blame on the fact that institutional entrepreneurship has been and still is typically portrayed in a positive light in institutional literature. Stories of institutional entrepreneurship are usually success stories built around purposive and self-interested entrepreneurial actors often depicted as heroes fighting against highly constraining institutional forces. Other scholars question the fact that institutional entrepreneur research mostly focuses on examining the emergence of new institutions or institutional change in mature fields, largely ignoring what is happening during times of institutional stability and maintenance. Here the notion of institutional work appears to be an alternative and complementary focus to institutional entrepreneurship, bringing a more nuanced view of agency back into organizational institutionalism.

2.5 Institutional work

Rather than focusing on the entrepreneurial figure of institutional change, institutional work is broadly concerned with the local and everyday work of resistance and maintenance of institutions carried out by individuals and groups who produce and reproduce meanings, beliefs, values, and material practices, thereby shaping their institutional environment. Lawrence and Suddaby (2006, p. 215) are the ones who established milestones of institutional work. They define this notion as 'the purposive action of individuals and organizations aimed at creating, maintaining and disrupting institutions'. Lawrence, Suddaby, and Leca (2009, p. 215) then edited a book that established the conceptual core of this notion and proposed a set of related essays and case studies to better understand the recursive relationships between action and institutions. In 2011, the same authors published a paper in which they discuss the 'distinctiveness of institutional work as a field of study'. In this paper, they expand the notion of institutional work to include 'practices of individual and collective actors' aimed at creating, maintaining, and disrupting institutions (Lawrence, Suddaby, and Leca, 2011, p. 52). Interestingly, they come up with the idea of further exploring 'institutional biographies', that is, the 'exploration of specific individuals in relation to the institutions that structured their lives' (Lawrence et al., 2011, p. 55), in order to examine institutional work as a distributed phenomenon and to take into account the institutional work of powerless actors in building alternative institutions.

Generally speaking, research on institutional work looks at '*how* institutional work occurs, *who* does institutional work, and *what* constitutes institutional work' (Lawrence, Leca, and Zilber, 2013, p.1024). For example, to uncover the variety of institutional work efforts and practices, researchers conducted empirical research related to the creation, maintenance, and disruption of institutions. Perkmann and Spicer (2008) looked at the institutional work of multiple actors with different skills working side by side, by which, for instance, management fads (e.g. total quality management, teamworking, sustainability) become institutions. They have identified three types of such institutional work: political; technical; and cultural. Whereas institutional entrepreneurs were essentially concerned about creating institutions, most institutional work research looks at how institutional work contributes to the maintenance of institutions. Rereading the Holocaust, Martí and Fernández (2013) provide an original study of the complex institutional work of oppression accomplished by the Nazis and of resistance from the prisoners. Institutional work in disruptive time was also studied. Maguire and Hardy (2009) proposed the notion of 'defensive institutional work' to illustrate how actors who are 'producing, distributing and consuming texts' can disrupt the institutionalized usage of DDT (dichlorodiphenyltrich) pesticide and trigger a radical change in their institutional field.

Other institutional work researchers centred their work on the types of actors who engage with institutional work, focusing mainly on professionals, elites, and experts at the field level. Arguing that professional projects are the source of institutional change, Suddaby and Viale (2011) explain how professionals play a central role in reconfiguring institutions and organizational fields. The institutional work done by professionals and experts is also closely associated with their efforts to preserve their status. This is the case of professionals in the medical field. Little has been said, however, about the institutional work of peripheral organizational actors who have less collective power and fewer resources than organized professionals, elites, or experts. In order to fill this gap, Daudigeos (2013), for example, studied occupational health and safety managers in a multinational construction company and showed how these peripheral actors draw on their professional and craft-like knowledge in order to overcome their marginal position and the institutional constraints they face. In doing so, these managers simultaneously contribute to promoting and institutionalizing their roles at the field level. However, there remains a need to investigate the work of actors who are resisting and promoting social changes to address the grand challenges of our societies.

Finally, institutional researchers developed new conceptualizations or models extending our comprehension about the nature of institutional work and the relationships between agency and institution. Drawing on a case study of English and German banking lawyers in a global law firm, Smets and Jarzabkowski (2013) develop a relational model of institutional work and institutional complexity. Their model shows how actors deal with the same logics, but in different ways. Insisting on the 'practical understanding' of the actors' agency, they revisit the purposive and effortful assumption on which most institutionalist academicians base their research. Zundel, Holt, and Cornelissen (2013) draw on Gregory Bateson to reconceptualize in a more processual and dynamic way the relationships between the individuals' backgrounds, experiences, and interpretations as well as the multiple ways in which institutions influence them. Alternatively, Granqvist and Gustafsson (2016) reconceptualize institutional research from a temporal perspective. They introduce the notion of 'temporal institutional work', which refers to 'how [actors] construct, navigate, and capitalize on timing norms in their attempts to change institutions' (Granqvist and Gustafsson, 2016, p. 1009).

In the past few years, institutional work research has endorsed new directions. Lawrence, Leca, and Zilber (2013) co-edited a special issue on institutional work that paved the way towards integrating a set of institutional streams such as institutional trajectories, institutional logics, and institutional entrepreneurs in research on institutional work. Following Smets and Jarzabkowski (2013), there is also a propensity to show the messiness and, perhaps more significantly, the distributed character of institutional work. Finally, recent research aims to uncover different forms and varieties of institutional work. In the aftermath of radical change proposed by the Fair Labor Association, which was intended to stabilize the code of conduct they had created with respect to working conditions in apparel factories, Mena and Suddaby (2016) studies the institutional work of 'theorization'.

In addition to those recent advances, emotions and materiality—two neglected topics in institutional research—have grown in popularity over the past few years and are likely to further develop in a near future. According to Voronov and Vince (2012), emotions as well as cognition act as key drivers of institutional work. Recently, Moisander, Hirsto, and Fahy (2016) identified diverse rhetorical strategies of emotional work allowing powerful institutional actors to influence others when creating emergent institutions. Wright and Nyberg (2017, p. 200) investigated moral emotions—'emotions linked to the interests of others'—of physicians and specialists working in emergency departments and showed how these emotions are intrinsic to the institutional work of maintaining their professional values. Looking at emotions in the constitution of institutional orders and at how institutions contribute to shape actor emotions improves our comprehension of the nature and dynamics of institutional work.

Throughout the institutionalist research programme, materiality has been mainly associated with structures as opposed to meanings. Some authors insist on the critical role of materiality and take into account the role of objects and artefacts as well of as temporality and space in institutional work. Monteiro and Nicolini (2014) show how ceremonial field-configuring events in the Italian public sector constitute an assemblage of human and material entities. Hence, institutional work researchers would need to explore the role of materiality at different phases of institutionalization to uncover if this role changes or not over time. More empirical research is also needed to better understand the distributed character of institutional work as a set of socio-material practices.

2.6 The greatness and misery of the institutional research programme

The role of institutions in organizational life has been a key concern in OTs over the past three decades. This research programme provided relevant answers to the call for bridging the old and the new institutionalism by integrating notions of change, interests, and agency in organizational institutionalism. It has also evolved towards a multi-level and interdisciplinary theory of institutional change. In this final section, I would like to tackle two issues related to the dazzling development of organizational institutionalism in OTs over the past 25 years. First, one is left wondering why organizational institutionalism has been and still is so popular in OTs. Second, there are concerns about the trajectory of this research programme. To wit, do changes observed in organizational institutionalism over the past 25 years bring institutionalists closer or further away from the core of their research programme? Or put differently, do those changes allow researchers 'to understand how organizational structures and processes acquire meaning and continuity beyond their technical goals' (Suddaby, 2010, p. 14)?

Several arguments can explain the successful institutionalization or diffusion of organizational institutionalism in OTs. As mentioned at the beginning of this chapter, organizational institutionalism provides a lens and a set of notions to explore crucial relations between business and society in our contemporaneous area. Beyond its empirical relevance, organizational institutionalism's conceptual nature justifies its popularity. Organizational institutionalism is simply a large interpretative framework aimed at exploring patterns and processes at the organizational or institutional field levels! Starting with this broad scope, this research programme is tying together the generic notion of 'institutional' with others such as legitimacy, pressures, complexities, logics, entrepreneurs, and work to put some coherence in the overall framework. These 'bridging' notions do not, however, offer any specific systems of ideas and relations to explain the patterns and processes of institutional order. This leaves a wide space for potential contributions, thus warranting the continued development of the institutional research programme.

As a consequence of this broad scope, institutional researchers integrated multiple organizational metaphors and theories to institutional explanations. If one looks closely at current institutional research, it is fairly easy to spot a large set of the contemporary notions and approaches in OTs. Organizational institutionalism has affinities with population ecology (e.g. when looking at institutional logics in different regions), transaction costs theory (e.g. when talking about organizational forms and structures), symbolic approaches (e.g. when discussing the essence of institutional logics and examining how actors interpret and make sense of them), and politics (e.g. by inferring resource dependence in institutional fields and prioritizing dominant institutional actors). Institutional researchers also focused on discursive approaches (e.g. referring to translation and theorization) and even on critical theories, as these approaches were the target of multiple calls for participating in the construction of the institutionalist research programme (Willmott, 2015). Therefore, the ability of organizational institutionalism to pull together competing theories around the commitment to generate explanations about the relationships between organizational structures and processes and the institutional environment partly explains why this research programme rapidly became popular and consolidated its dominant position in OTs. Indeed, I argue that organizational institutionalism has built its hegemony around conceptual heterogeneity rather than conceptual homogeneity.

Suddaby (2010) has compared organizational institutionalism to a Trojan Horse for other perspectives in OTs. Unsurprisingly, the heterogeneous nature of institutional explanations has given rise to considerable flexibility and variation in the way they are empirically constructed and diffused. Compounding this is that owing to the popularity of the institutional framework, other OTs are increasingly borrowing its terminology. This further blurs the institutionalist research agenda and renders its research programme less distinctive and more fragmented than ever. While the project of reconciling the old and the new institutionalism has been largely fruitful, it nevertheless brought the institutionalists into territories such as agencies and change, which are the points of entry for many other perspectives and research programmes.

Consequently, over the past few years, OTs scholars have increasingly been engaged in critical reflections and debates regarding the recent developments of organizational institutionalism and its future. Some researchers consider that the latest developments in organizational institutionalism have created new avenues for redirecting this research programme and that these should be pursued, while others think that organizational institutionalism has lost its way. The former makes organizations front and centre in the institutional explanations and insists on emphasizing their active role in the way organizations contribute to shaping the institutional patterns and processes that in turn constraint them. After all, Greenwood, Hinings, and Whetten (2014, p. 1206) said: 'the most important institution in modern society is the organization'. And thus, organizational researchers' efforts should be centred on the comparative analysis of how organizations are structured and managed instead of looking at what is happening at the organization-field level. The latter consider that the central object of organizational institutionalism is the institutions and the institutional processes that shape, and are in turn shaped by, organizations. For them, it is clear that inquiries in organizational institutionalism should begin with organizational practices at the field level, rather than the reverse. For Meyer and Höllerer (2014), the distinctiveness of organizational institutionalism resides in its capacity to explain typical patterns and similarities. Despite the need to integrate change in the argument, the distinguishing contribution of organizational institutionalism remains its capacity to explain the occurrence and nature of institutional processes that structure organizational meanings and continuity. Note that the first position is conveyed by North American institutionalist researchers who have a closer affinity with change and agency, while the second one is supported by European institutionalist researchers who have historically developed a strong sociological sensibility.

Despite all the efforts by the 'gatekeepers' in journals and academic associations to monitor and control what is published under the institutionalist lens, it seemed that at the end of this decade (2010s), the institutionalist research programme had reached a crossroads. In 1987, in an early appraisal, Scott described institutional theory as struggling through the *sturm und drang* of its adolescence. Twenty years later, the same author observes substantial signs of increasing maturation and claims that institutional theories are approaching adulthood (Scott, 2008). Yet, if organizational institutionalism is empirically relevant, it must be said that after maturation, any 'institution' (such as, for example, an organizational research programme) will at one moment or another enter into a phase of decline! According to Alvesson and Spicer (2019), this research programme has reached a mid-life crisis.

References

Alvesson, M. & Spicer, A. 2019. Neo-Institutional Theory and Organization Studies: A Mid-Life Crisis? *Organization Studies*, 40, 199–218.

Battilana, J., Leca, B., & Boxenbaum, E. 2009. How Actors Change Institutions: Towards a Theory of Institutional Entrepreneurship. *Academy of Management Annals*, 3, 65–107.

Beckert, J. 1999. Agency, Entrepreneurs, and Institutional Change. The Role of Strategic Choice and Institutionalized Practices in Organizations. *Organization Studies*, 20, 777–799.

Boxenbaum, E. & Pedersen, J. S. 2009. Scandinavian Institutionalism—A Case of Institutional Work. *In*: Lawrence, T. B., Suddaby, R., & Leca, B. (eds) *Institutional Work: Actors and Agency in Institutional Studies of Organizations*, pp. 178–204. New York, Cambridge University Press.

Clark, B. R. 1956. Organizational Adaptation and Precarious Values. *American Sociological Review*, 21, 327–336.

Czarniawska, B. & Sevón, G. 1996. *Translating Organizational Change*. Berlin, de Gruyter.

Dacin, M. T., Goodstein, J., & Scott, R. W. 2002. Institutional Theory and Institutional Change: Introduction to the Special Research Forum. *The Academy of Management Journal*, 45, 45–56.

Daudigeos, T. 2013. In their Profession's Service: How Staff Professionals Exert Influence in their Organization. *Journal of Management Studies*, 50, 722–749.

David, R. J., Sine, W. D., & Haveman, H. A. 2013. Seizing Opportunity in Emerging Fields: How Institutional Entrepreneurs Legitimated the Professional Form of Management Consulting. *Organization Science*, 24, 356–377.

De Holan, P. M. & Phillips, N. 2002. Managing in Transition: A Case Study of Institutional Management and Organizational Change. *Journal of Management Inquiry*, 11, 68–83.

DiMaggio, P. J. 1988. Interest and Agency in Institutional Theory. *In*: Zucker, G. L. (ed.) *Institutional Patterns and Organizations: Culture and Environment*, pp. 3–21. Cambridge, MA, Ballinger.

Dimaggio, P. J. & Powell, W. W. 1983. The Iron Cage Revisited: Institutional Isomorphism and Collective Rationality in Organizational Fields. *American Sociological Review*, 48, 147–160.

Durand, R. & Jourdan, J. 2012. Jules or Jim: Alternative Conformity to Minority Logics. *Academy of Management Journal*, 55, 1295–1315.

Friedland, R. & Alford, R. 1991. Bringing Society Back in: Symbols, Practices, and Institutional Contradictions. *In*: Powell, G. N. & Dimaggio, P. J. (eds) *New Institutionalism in Organizational Analysis*, pp. 232–263. Chicago, IL, University of Chigaco Press.

Glynn, M. A. 2017. Theorizing the Identity-Institution Relationship: Considering Identity as Antecedent to, Consequence of, and Mechanism for, Processes of Institutional Change. In: Greenwood, R., Oliver, C., Lawrence, T. B., & Meyer, R. E. (eds) The Sage Handbook of Organizational Institutionalism, pp. 243–257. London, Sage.

Granqvist, N. & Gustafsson, R. 2016. Temporal Institutional Work. *Academy of Management Journal*, 59, 1009–1035.

Greenwood, R. & Hinings, C. R. 1996. Understanding Radical Organizational Change: Bringing Together the Old and the New Institutionalism. *The Academy of Management Review*, 21, 4, 1022–1054.

Greenwood, R., Díaz, A. M., Li, S. X., & Lorente, J. C. 2010. The Multiplicity of Institutional Logics and the Heterogeneity of Organizational Responses. *Organization Science*, 21, 521–539.

Greenwood, R., Raynard, M., Kodeih, F., Micelotta, E. R., & Lounsbury, M. 2011. Institutional Complexity and Organizational Responses. *Academy of Management Annals*, 5, 317–371.

Greenwood, R., Oliver, C., Lawrence, T. B. & Meyer, R. E. (eds) 2017. *The Sage Handbook of Organizational Institutionalism*. London, Sage.

Harnon, D. J., Green, S. E., & Goodnight, G. T. 2015. A Model of Rhetorical Legitimation: the Structure of Communication and Cognition Underlying Institutional Maintenance and Change. *Academy of Management Review*, 40, 76–95.

Hirsch, P. M. & Lounsbury, M. 1997. Ending the Family Quarrel: Towards a Reconciliation of 'Old' and 'New' Institutionalism. *The American Behavioral Scientist*, 40, 406–418.

Jackall, R. 1988. *Moral Mazes, the World of Corporate Managers*. New York, University Press.

Latour, B. 1986. The Power of Association. *In*: Law, J. & Kegan, P. (eds) *Power, Action and Belief*, pp. 264–280. London, Routledge.

Lawrence, T. B. & Suddaby, R. 2006. Institutions and Institutional Work *In*: Clegg, S. R., Hardy, C., Lawrence, T. B., & Nord, W. T. (eds) *The Sage Handbook of Organization Studies*, pp. 215–254. London, Sage.

Lawrence, T. B., Suddaby, R., & Leca, B. 2009. *Institutional Work: Actors and Agency in Institutional Studies of Organizations*. Cambridge, UK, Cambridge University Press.

Lawrence, T. B., Suddaby, R., & Leca, B. 2011. Institutional Work: Refocusing Institutional Studies of Organization. *Journal of Management Inquiry*, 20, 52–58.

Lawrence, T. B., Leca, B., & Zilber, T. B. 2013. Institutional Work: Current Research, New Directions and Overlooked Issues. *Organization Studies*, 34, 1023–1033.

Lockett, A., Currie, G., Waring, J., Finn, R., & Martin, G. 2012. The Role of Institutional Entrepreneurs in Reforming Healthcare. *Social Science & Medicine*, 74, 356.

Lounsbury, M. 2001. Institutional Sources of Practice Variation: Staffing College and University Recycling Programs. *Administrative Science Quarterly*, 46, 25–96.

Lounsbury, M. 2007. A Tale of Two Cities: Competing Logics and Practice Variation in the Professionalizing of Mutual Funds. *The Academy of Management Journal*, 50, 289–307.

Lounsbury, M. 2008. Institutional Rationality and Practice Variation: New Directions in the Institutional Analysis of Practice. *Accounting, Organizations and Society*, 33, 349–361.

Maguire, S. & Hardy, C. 2009. Discourse and Deinstitutionalization: The Decline of DDT. *The Academy of Management Journal*, 2009, 148–178.

Maguire, S., Hardy, C., & Lawrence, T. B. 2004. Institutional Entrepreneurship in Emerging Fields: HIV/AIDS Treatment Advocacy in Canada . *Academy of Management Journal*, 47, 657–679.

Martí, I. & Fernández, P. 2013. The Institutional Work of Oppression and Resistance: Learning from the Holocaust. *Organization Studies*, 34, 1195–1223.

Mena, S. & Suddaby, R. 2016. Theorization as Institutional Work: The Dynamics of Roles and Practices. *Human Relations*, 69, 1669–1708.

Meyer, J. W. & Rowan, B. 1977. Institutionalized Organizations: Formal Structure as Myth and Ceremony. *The American Journal of Sociology*, 38, 340–363.

Meyer, J. W., Scott, R. W., & Strang, D. 1987. Centralization, Fragmentation, and School District Complexity. *Administrative Science Quarterly*, 32, 186–201.

Meyer, R. E. & Höllerer, M. A. 2014. Does Institutional Theory Need Redirecting? *Journal of Management Studies*, 51, 1221–1233.

Moisander, J. K., Hirsto, H., & Fahy, K. M. 2016. Emotions in Institutional Work: A Discursive Perspective. *Organization Studies*, 37, 963–990.

Monteiro, P. & Nicolini, D. 2014. Recovering Materiality in Institutional Work. *Journal of Management Inquiry*, 24, 61–81.

Oliver, C. 1991. Strategic Responses to Institutional Processes. *The Academy of Management Review*, 16, 145–179.

Olsen, T. D. 2017. Rethinking Collective Action: The Co-evolution of the State and Institutional Entrepreneurs in Emerging Economies. *Organization Studies*, 38, 31–52.

Perkmann, M. & Schildt, H. 2015. Open Data Partnerships Between Firms and Universities: The Role of Boundary Organizations. *Research Policy*, 44, 1133–1143.

Perkmann, M. & Spicer, A. 2008. How are Management Fashions Institutionalized? The Role of Institutional Work. *Human Relations*, 61, 811–844.

Rao, H., Monin, P., & Durand, R. 2003. Institutional Change in Toque Ville: Nouvelle Cuisine as an Identity Movement in French Gastronomy. *American Journal of Sociology* 108, 795–843.

Sahlin, K. & Wedlin, L. 2008. Circulating ideas: Imitation, translation and editing. *In*: Greenwood, R., Oliver, C., Suddaby, R., & Sahlin, K. (eds) *Organizational institutionalism*, pp. 218–242. London, Sage.

Scott, R. W. 1987. *Organizations: Rational, Natural, and Open Systems*. Hoboken, NJ, Prentice Hall.

Scott, R. W. 2008. Approaching Adulthood: the Maturing of Institutional Theory. *Theory & Society*, 37, 427–442.

Scott, R. W. 2014. *Institutions and Organizations. Ideas, Interests, and Identities.* Thousand Oaks, CA, Sage.

Selznick, P. 1949. *T.V.A. and the Grass Roots.* Berkeley, CA, University of California Press.

Selznick, P. 1957. *Leadership in Administration.* New York, Harper and Row.

Selznick, P. 1996. Institutionalism 'Old' and 'New'. *Administrative Science Quarterly*, 41, 270–277.

Seo, M.-G. & Creed, D. W. E. 2002. Institutional Contradictions, Praxis, and Institutional Change: A Dialectical Perspective. *The Academy of Management Review*, 27, 222–247.

Sharma, U., Lawrence, S., & Lowe, A. 2014. Accountants as Institutional Entrepreneurs: Changing Routines in a Telecommunications Company. *Qualitative Research in Accounting & Management*, 11, 190–214.

Smets, M. & Jarzabkowski, P. 2013. Reconstructing Institutional Complexity in Practice: A Relational Model of Institutional Work and Complexity. *Human Relations*, 66, 1279–1309.

Smets, M., Jarzabkowski, P., Burke, G. T., & Spee, P. 2015. Reinsurance Trading in Lloyd's of London: Balancing Conflicting-yet-Complementary Logics in Practice. *Academy of Management Journal*, 58, 932–970.

Suddaby, R. 2010. Challenges for Institutional Theory. *Journal of Management Inquiry*, 19, 14–20.

Suddaby, R. & Viale, T. 2011. Professionals and Field-Level Change: Institutional Work and the Professional Project. *Current Sociology*, 59, 423–442.

Thornton, P. H. 2004. *Markets from Culture, Institutional Logic and Organizational Decisions in Higher Education Publishing*. Stanford, CA, Stanford University Press.

Thornton, P. H., Ocasio, W., & Lounsbury, M. 2012. *The Institutional Logics Perspective: A New Approach to Culture, Structure, and Process*. Oxford, UK, Oxford University Press.

Tolbert, P. S. & Zucker, L. G. 1983. Institutional Sources of Change in the Formal Structure of Organizations: The Diffusion of Civil Service Reform, 1880–1935. *Administrative Science Quarterly*, 28, 22–39.

Townley, B. 1997. The Institutional Logic of Performance Appraisal. *Organization Studies*, 18, 261–285.

Tracey, P., Phillips, N., & Jarvis, O. 2011. Bridging Institutional Entrepreneurship and the Creation of New Organizational Forms: A Multilevel Model. *Organization Science*, 22, 60–80.

Vermeulen, P., Zietsma, C., Greenwood, R., & Langley, A. 2016. Strategic responses to institutional complexity. *Strategic Organization*, 14, 277–286.

Voronov, M. & Vince, R. 2012. Integrating Emotions into the Analysis of Institutional Work. *Academy of Management Review*, 37, 58–81.

Weik, E. 2012. Introducing 'The Creativity of Action' Into Institutionalist Theory. *M@n@gement*, 15, 563–581.

Westphal, J. D. & Zajac, E. J. 1994. Substance and Symbolism in CEOs' Long-Term Incentive Plans. *Administrative Science Quarterly*, 39, 367–390.

Willmott, H. 2015. Why Institutional Theory Cannot Be Critical. *Journal of Management Inquiry*, 24, 105–111.

Wright, C. & Nyberg, D. 2017. An Inconvenient Truth: How Organizations Translate Climate Change into Business as Usual. *Academy of Management Journal*, 60, 1633–1661.

Zald, M. N. & Denton, P. 1963. From Evangelism to General Service: The Transformation of the YMCA. *Administrative Science Quarterly*, 8, 214–234.

Zundel, M., Holt, R., & Cornelissen, J. P. 2013. Institutional Work in the Wire. *Journal of Management Inquiry*, 22, 102–120.

3

Convention Analysis

The analysis of contemporary societies frequently draws on economic value, which subsequently downplays the role of moral judgement in economy—even though economic value is interpreted and constructed through a set of coexisting and competing sociocultural frames. Organizations are pluralistic contexts in which individuals and groups have divergent interests. For decades, organizational researchers and practitioners have acknowledged that tensions between competing frames are at play within and outside organizational settings. Nevertheless, organizational goals are achieved and shared without having recourse to violence. From an economic point of view, how is this possible? According to some scholars, part of the answer is found in the notion of convention, which renews the traditional view of economic value and coordination.

Convention analysis, or what has also been referred to as the French Convention School, is a transdisciplinary project that brings together economists, sociologists, and management scientists, among others. The conventionalist perspective innovates by adopting a pragmatic approach to economic rationality and coordination. As any theoretical framework in organizational or institutional economics (e.g. transaction cost analysis and agency theory), convention analysis calls into question the separation between market and hierarchy or between individuals and the collective. The strengths of convention analysis lie in its attempts to introduce sociological thoughts into the field of economics.

Convention analysis seeks to understand how agents in situations of radical uncertainty make choices and adjust their behaviour in relation to one another in spite of their divergent interests. Grounded in the heterodox economics school of thought, the conventionalist research programme renews the economic view of rationality and coordination by introducing the notions of values and judgement. As we will see in this chapter, convention theory is based on a dense network of concepts developed by influential French economists and sociologists such as Gomez, Favereau, Orléan, Thévenot, and Boltanski, who all aimed to shed new light on economic and social coordination.

Organization Theories in the Making. Linda Rouleau, Oxford University Press.
© Linda Rouleau (2022). DOI: 10.1093/oso/9780198792024.003.0004

In organizational economics, convention analysis has been at the forefront of efforts to unify economics and sociology. Although it has been around for 25 years, the fact that its main proponents are French speakers explains why it has only recently managed to carve out its place in the Anglophone research community. However, despite its slow progression through the organization theories (OTs), its innovative research programme has been steadily gaining ground and is becoming increasingly used in OTs all over the world. Interestingly, the diffusion of this perspective finds resonance with organizational institutionalism and thus opens up multiple possibilities for the future.

This chapter is structured as follows. First, convention analysis is situated within the field of organizational economics. Then, the notion of convention is introduced, followed by a summary of the basic ideas of the economy of worth (EW) framework. A review of papers grounded in the concept of competing orders of worth in OTs completes the description of this perspective. Finally, this chapter ends on a discussion of the challenges and opportunities present in efforts to expand convention analysis in the OTs.

3.1 From standard to heterodox economics

Organizational economics is a vast field of research comprising many sub-areas, ranging from industrial economics (e.g. Porter, 1980) to regulation theory (e.g. Aglietta, 1976; Boyer, 1986). Between both ends of this spectrum, we find diverse forms of organizational economic analysis, such as the evolutionary theory of the firm (e.g. Nelson and Winter, 1982), propriety rights theory (e.g. Alchian and Demsetz, 1972), the resource-based view of the firm and dynamic capabilities (e.g. Barney, 1991; Teece, 2009), agency theory (e.g. Jensen and Meckling, 1976), and transaction cost analysis (e.g. Williamson, 1985), to name a few. These research programmes all have something in common: contrary to classical and neoclassical economic theories, they are interested in both markets and firms as ways of coordinating economic activities. Put differently, they all promote, in one way or another, the project of unifying an economic view with a sociological view.

So what distinctions are there between convention analysis, classical economic theory, and organizational economics? An economic theory (Table 3.1) essentially rests on two foundational postulates: one concerns the nature of agents' behaviour (the motives under which agents make economic choices), and the other concerns the coordination mechanisms at play between them (how free agents coordinate their transactions). For instance, classical and neoclassical economic theories posit that rationality

Table 3.1 Foundations of economic theories

Economic theory	Agent behaviour	Coordination mechanism(s)
Classical and neoclassical economics	Rationality and bounded rationality	Market (supply and demand/prices)
Organizational economics (e.g. agency theory and transaction cost analysis)	Bounded rationality Opportunism	Market and hierarchy (asset specificity)
Convention analysis	Procedural rationality Justification	Conventions (common values)

and bounded rationality, respectively, are the behavioural premises that explain what motivates economic agents as they make choices. According to classical economics, rational agents make choices in order to 'maximize' their utility based on the assessment of their preferences in a context of perfect information. Neoclassical economic theory revises this postulate: given agents' cognitive limits and the non-availability of perfect information, agents rather seek a 'satisficing' solution as they make choices. This has led Simon (1995) to come up with the notion of 'bounded rationality' as the core assumption of economic behaviour. Additionally, classical and neoclassical economics consider the market as the sole coordination mechanism, as reflected in the pricing system that results from supply and demand.

Organizational economics has enriched our understanding of the agent's behaviour and the coordination mechanisms regulating economic activities. Organizational economics theorists consider the rationality of economic agents to be not only bounded but also opportunistic, meaning that agents are driven by self-interest. Regarding the coordination of economic activities, transaction cost analysis proposes two ways of explaining the coordination of transactions. Similarly to orthodox economics, transaction cost analysis considers that the market is central to the coordination of transactions between economic agents. However, according to transaction cost analysis, the firm (or 'the hierarchy') also constitutes a way to ensure the coordination of transactions. The decision to rely on one or the other depends on the specificity of the transactions: the more specific the transaction, the more preferable it is to opt for the hierarchy as a coordination mechanism, and vice versa.

Convention analysis revisits the behavioural postulate underlying agent motivations in transaction cost analysis and agency theories and suggests another mechanism to coordinate economic activities by proposing behavioural hypotheses that take into account collective and subjective elements. First, rather than promoting the notion of rationality, convention analysts are concerned with the rationalization process. As such, convention analysis is based on the postulate of procedural rationality. According to procedural rationality, a decision is rational when the process leading to it is acknowledged by actors with divergent interests as being rational or intersubjectively shared. Therefore, they acknowledge the coexistence of a plurality of rationalities in organizations. In other words, being rational implies that agents are able to coordinate themselves with others who have divergent interests.

Second, convention analysis posits that justification is the other behavioural characteristic of individuals. Justification postulates that individuals are capable of appraising or valuing the quality of objects and persons. The judgement about the quality of objects and persons stands on their value systems. As a result, the most efficient way to coordinate in a context of divergent interests and, therefore, to demonstrate procedural rationality, whether individually or collectively, is to follow a common system of values. Embedded in a variety of principles, these common values are the building blocks upon which collective action and social order are produced. Instead of being centred on competition, convention theory is driven by valuation in which public criticism plays a central role.

According to convention analysis, coordination between agents is achieved through organizational and social conventions. Between market and hierarchy are other mechanisms by which individuals coordinate their activities; these mechanisms correspond to multiple formal and informal conventions. Organizational and social conventions refer to the system of rules, accepted beliefs, or common frameworks that guide agents as they make choices. According to transaction cost analysis and agency theory, the organization is a set of contractual relationships; according to convention theory, the organization is the result of multiple conventions between agents. Therefore, heterodox economics considers that coordination mechanisms oscillate from market to non-market; that is, other institutional forms of coordination such as hierarchy and conventions.

To summarize, convention analysis aims to understand how economic agents rationalize and justify their choices and behaviours rather than how they make rational choices and decisions. To do so, they draw on a set of social and organizational conventions based on common values and norms. While recognizing that economic choice has a moral component, convention analysis is concerned with the fundamental problem of valuation (i.e. judgement about the quality of objects and persons). Therefore, convention analysis explores mundane valuation processes and activities involved in economic coordination and social cooperation by addressing the issues of conventions and their underlying common values. Before further exploring these common values, we will examine the nature of conventions.

3.2 On the nature of convention

According to heterodox economist Pierre-Yves Gomez (2006), convention analysis originally revisits the notion of information. Thus, it offers a broader view of the nature of economic human behaviour, which proves helpful in reconsidering the standard conceptions of market and hierarchy. Classical and organizational economists see information as transmitted through signals, messages, and data. Acting as transmitters or receivers, individuals and firms communicate with each other through information flows. Markets are thus seen as networks of information transfers about goods and individuals and where rational and satisficing choices are made. This standard view of information supposes that it is complete, transparent, and, above all, independent from individuals and firms who are passively transmitting it. Nevertheless, when firms advertise their products, the information communicated to their clients is far from complete, transparent, and neutral. Rather, embedded within advertisements are emotions, symbols, and sensible words that strive to convince targeted clients that they will be happier owning their products. Hence, according to convention analysis, while information is often incomplete and not always transparent, most of the time, it is actively interpreted by individual and/or collective economic agents. Based on these assumptions, convention analysts propose to look at the notion of information in terms of a 'screen' (Gomez, 2006).

Put differently, convention analysts take seriously the meaning that individuals and firms convey through their message when they communicate or share information with others. For them, there is no single interpretation of information—contrary to what classical and organizational economists generally assume. Any piece of information is interpreted according to the social universe in which it is shaped, as this social universe provides the system of rules allowing individuals and firms to interpret the information they gather, package, and transmit. Instead of examining how individuals and firms exchange or use this information, convention analysis is concerned with understanding the 'screen' or the system of rules that individuals and firms use to interpret information circulating around them. As such, a choice or a decision is far from being individual; it only makes sense according to the system of rules in which it is made or implemented. Such a system of rules is called 'convention' by heterodox economists.

As mentioned above, conventions allow individuals to align their judgement or agree on the quality of objects and persons, and in so doing coordinate themselves. Conventions are characterized by a system of rules and mutual expectations between individuals, which they draw on when they must make choices and coordinate among themselves. As Schelling (1960) explains, the fact of driving left or right is the result of a convention established between drivers rather than any objective criteria. If each driver had to decide on which side of the road they drove, traffic would take on apocalyptic qualities. Traffic lights are also a good example of the notion of convention. In themselves, the red, green, and yellow colours mean nothing if not associated with traffic lights; however, they allow pedestrians, motorists, cyclists, motorcyclists, and others to mutually expect specific behaviours from each other. Conventions are akin to 'collective cognitive tools' acting as a system of information based on a set of practices, materials, and immaterial devices (e.g. objects, persons, brands) that individuals draw on in their interactions in order to coordinate.

Conventions exist only because they have been collectively built, accepted, and shared. It is precisely because underlying beliefs are taken for granted that individuals can use conventions for coordination purposes. The effectiveness of conventions depends on the degree of shared acceptance and stability. Although the stability of conventions becomes reinforced when agents forget about their origins, conventions can nonetheless change over time. A convention can always be challenged by dissonant interpretations and discourses circulating in an organization. According to Isaac (2003), a convention can evolve in three ways: resistance, displacement, and breakdown. A convention will endure despite alternative interpretations if its power of conviction is stronger than the doubt cast upon the convention. If this doubt is strong, the scope of the convention can shift or be displaced in favour of a new purpose. Also, a convention can collapse if it becomes insufficiently convincing for the individuals adhering to its principles, allowing alternatives to take root. It is worth noting that the relationship between conventions and individuals is co-constituted rather than causal or constraining. Conventions do not precede nor are they separate from individuals' actions and behaviours; in fact, they cannot exist if individuals do not adopt them. In that sense, convention analysts maintain that the economic and the social are co-constructed.

Organizations are therefore the result of complex arrangements of conventions taking multiple forms. Conventions can be written or unwritten, codified or not. For instance, strategic plans, accounting devices, and human resources policies are all seen as conventions, as are habits of long working hours, eating with or without teammates or colleagues, playing tricks on newcomers, and so on. Conventions differ from contracts and institutions as they appear to be founded principally on a set of accepted and commonly held beliefs within the organization that make sense for individuals when they have to evaluate and choose between alternatives (as opposed to some sort of objective rationality). Even though conventions sometimes appear to be arbitrary and unsanctioned, they nevertheless provide useful rationalizations that do not require justification as they are commonly accepted. This does not mean that conventions cannot be questioned or reinterpreted by actors. For instance, some pedestrians cross the street without respecting the 'don't walk' sign, although most of the time they do respect traffic lights. Human behaviour is not predictable; also, there is always a possibility that a convention will not be endorsed. This is what convention analysts call 'radical uncertainty'.

Convention analysis also revisits the conception of market and hierarchy put forth by organizational economics. Hence, as per convention analysis, markets appear to be defined in terms of conventions of quality. Convention analysis calls on us to consider social and informal conventions other than price mechanisms that contribute to regulating the relative economic values of production factors or consumer goods. According to these researchers, the evaluation of quality in the marketplace constitutes an important dimension of transaction coordination. Defining markets this way implies approaching transactions in terms of their social dynamics by considering the ethical and normative context by which actors are making and justifying their quality claims.

Convention analysis also proposes to consider the firm as a 'convention of efforts' (hierarchy) between a variety of stakeholders (e.g. owners, managers, employees, clients). Each stakeholder pursues specific goals. Owners want a return on their investments, managers want to be promoted, employees want to keep their jobs, and clients want to get the best product or service. However, there needs to be trust, as the only way they can get what they want is by depending on one another. Owners might not realize short-term capital growth if managers strive to expand business by developing new markets, just as employees might not have good jobs and salaries if owners do not properly invest in the future of the organization. To solve this problem, agency theory suggests reducing the agent's potential loss by designing contracts preventing opportunistic behaviours in order to advance shared goals within the organization. According to convention analysis, maximizing individual interest by minimizing agency costs is not the solution. Rather, convention analysis suggests looking at formal and informal conventional rules that allow each stakeholder to invest the necessary effort to ensure the organization's common goals. In each organization, there are multiple rules shaped through the conventions that inform each party about the efforts they are expected to make.

In the logic of convention analysis, market and hierarchy are not mutually exclusive; rather, they are two complementary sets of conventions (qualification and effort) that stand as intermediaries between contracts and institutions. Moreover, they are neither purely intentional nor unintentional. They are socially constructed and mobilized by individuals as they act in a market or organization. Nevertheless, given the interpretive nature of all rules, whether or not they are perceived as conventional may give rise to interpretations, which may threaten coordination. How are these conventions drawn up? According to what principles? The EW framework proposes an answer to these central questions.

3.3 Economies of worth framework

The EW framework was born of a desire to distance the socioeconomic research programme from the structuralist sociology of power relations. Sociologist Luc Boltanski, both disciple and critic of Bourdieu, joined economist Laurent Thévenot to propose a pluralist view of conflict resolution around collective issues. They wrote a theoretical essay providing 'a grammar' to explain how competent actors justify their actions within different spheres of social life. The result was the release of a book[1] in 1987, which was translated into English more than 15 years later and titled *On Justification. Economies of Worth*. Also called the sociology of convention, EW proposes a typology of competing rationales based on the historical analysis of core values emerging from western political philosophy. The focus of the EW framework is on the dynamics involved in local and contextual conventions based on values that would appear as acceptable and appropriate when a dispute or a controversy about these values emerges.

As previously mentioned, in order to coordinate their activities, individuals refer to common principles to agree on the quality of goods and persons. When criticizing, justifying, and evaluating goods and persons, competent actors assign to them some degree of worth, as defined by a set of common values or principles. These values or principles rest on a system of shared equivalence, labelled by Boltanski and Thévenot as 'worlds'.

---

[1] First published in France in 1987 and edited in a much-revised form in 1991 (Boltanski and Thévenot).

Modern societies consist of a plurality of orders of worth or forms of justice following different values and norms that are invoked in dispute or controversy. Boltanski and Thévenot (1991, 2006) rely on canonical texts of French philosophers to identify six 'worlds' or constitutive value frameworks that structure social arrangements: 'market'; 'fame'; 'industrial'; 'inspired'; 'domestic'; and 'civic' (see Table 3.2). Boltanski and Chiapello (1999) introduced the 'network' world to describe the 'new' spirit of capitalism, and Thévenot, Moody, and Lafaye (2000) proposed the 'green' world in support of environmental conflicts and disputes.

As Table 3.2 shows, each world is characterized by a set of dimensions, which are in turn based on a higher-order principle that specifies what needs to be valued or respected in any social situation. This common higher-order principle provides the grounds for judging the quality of goods and persons, or for evaluating their deficiency (or 'state of unworthiness') against what is normally valued in this world (lower-order principle). Between these opposite states of worth, each world is characterized by privileged subjects and objects showing attributes substantiating the higher-order principle. When there is a dispute, each world proposes a worthiness test ('*épreuve*') that is considered to be fair in order to determine or restore legitimacy within a given world. There are also other dimensions in the EW framework, though they are less frequently referred to (e.g. investment formula, common dignity, harmonious figure, common good, and principle of differentiation).

Inspired by a Smithian philosophy, the 'market' world is driven by the interests of competing actors who take part in a commercial game in order to achieve their personal goals. While in this world, worth is defined in terms of money, success, and gain, its state of deficiency appears to be expressed in the notions of being slaves to money, and failures. According to the higher-order principle of this world, the representative figures are businesses or rational actors looking for opportunities and promoting competitive behaviours to achieve their own interests. The worthiness test in this world consists of being able to strike a deal or sign a contract, as completing an economic transaction reaffirms the legitimacy of both parties.

The world of 'fame' or 'opinion' values the achievement of public recognition, reputation, and prestige. This world is based on a Hobbesian vision of human nature that is led by a deep desire for 'honour and fame after death'. Governed by recognition in public space, this world vigorously demeans indifference from others and banality in life. Successful and prestigious individuals are constantly seeking recognition from others. In our contemporary society, this world characterizes the field of communications and the regime of information and social media. Receiving recognition, winning a prize,

Table 3.2 Orders of worth

	Market	Fame	Industrial	Inspired	Domestic	Civic	Network	Green
Common higher-order principle	Competition	Public opinion	Efficiency	Inspiration	Tradition	Collectives	Flexible connectivity	Sustainability
State of worthiness	Desirable, valued	Fame	Efficient	Inexpressible, ethereal	Hierarchal superiority	Representative	Flexibility	Sustainable
Subjects	Competitors	Stars and their fans	Professionals	Visionaries	Superiors and inferiors	Collective and their leaders	Partners and brokers	Inhabitants
Objects	Wealth	Names in the media	Means	Waking dream	Rules of etiquette	Legal forms	Projects	Nature
Test(s) of worthiness	Deal	Event (press, inauguration, demonstration, etc.)	Trial	Adventure, quest, lived experience	Family ceremonies, social events	Demonstration of a just cause	Mobilization of network	Greening
Common lower-order principle	Enslavement to money, looser	Indifference, banality	Instrumental action	Temptation to come down to earth	Lack of inhibition	Division	Bondage	Pollution

* Adapted from Reinecke et al. (2017).

being featured in the news, and so on are the privileged worthiness tests in the world of 'fame'.

The 'industrial' world is driven by the search for efficiency and standardization. Influenced by the Saint-Simonian philosophy of scientific progress, in this world, rationality and technology are seen to be powerful tools in the service of industrial development. Scientists, engineers, and medical and law experts are examples of harmonious figures of this world, where work and performance are highly valued and instrumental action is not. Formal testing procedures for judging products and work methods are mechanisms by which the industrial world shows its efficiency.

Boltanski and Thévenot draw on St Augustine's 'City of God' to define the 'inspired' world. This world refers to the legitimacy of the artist's grace, creativity, and imagination. Highly individualistic, the inspired world rests on unpredictability, passion, and eccentricity, and depreciates everything that is down to earth. The great artist will be someone who constantly takes risks and experiences the loneliness and trauma of introspective adventures.

The 'domestic' world is a world of tradition ruled by the principles of loyalty and the respect of authority based on assigned roles, statuses, and duties among individuals. In this world inspired by Bossuet, the actor is *homo hierarchicus*, as superiors (such as fathers, kings, chief executives, professors, and so on) are worthy, and inferiors (such as children, subjects, employees, students, and so on) are worthless. The judgements that the former make about the latter are critical in this world. As the main figure of the domestic world, the patriarch or the superior will show wisdom and benevolence and will demonstrate a deep sense of duty. In the domestic world, family, and even social and organizational ceremonies, restore the weight of tradition, as the rules of etiquette are legitimate signs.

The 'civic' world values civic duties and the suppression of particular interests in the pursuit of the common good. This world is based on the romantic Rousseauist view of human nature. Pursing an ideal of justice and solidarity, civic heroes will promote solidarity and genuine collaboration in order to advance humankind. Conflicts, war, and misunderstandings are forbidden in this world. In the civic world, public demonstrations in favour of moral or humanitarian causes are appreciated as well as changes in policy and laws based on principles of equality.

Rather than stemming from the sphere of social justification, the 'network' world proposed by Boltanski and Chiapello (1999) originated from the reading of management literature. According to these authors, because the capitalist spirit was renewed in keeping with flexible and distributed forms of organization, this economic regime has demonstrated the capacity to adapt from its critics. Ideals of connectivity, partnerships, and brokerage are valued in this world, to the detriment of opportunistic networking, bondage, and isolation. Being able to mobilize multiple actors around a common project or a temporary organization is worthy.

Finally, the 'green' world is based on a general concern for the survival of human beings and the planet. According to Lafaye and Thévenot (2017), the existing orders of worth are constantly challenged by the justifications provided around environmental concerns. In the green world, sustainability appears to be the distinct common higher-order principle. Ecological actors (inhabitants and even natural elements such as water, air, climate, and so on) act in accordance with concerns for environmental protection. Any act of pollution is considered an unworthy behaviour in this world. However, given the fallibility of instruments and tools used to establish equivalences of pollution, the test of worthiness remains vulnerable. Such tools should incorporate accessibility to all and the ability to link local decisions to the common good.

According to Boltanski and Thévenot (2006, p. 18), organizations are 'composite assemblages that include arrangements deriving from different worlds'. All organizational contexts are characterized by multiple orders of worth, even though we can sometimes recognize that some units (e.g. departments, groups, individuals) present more affinities with a specific world. For example, marketing departments carry the values of the market world, while production departments convey the industrial world. However, it is important to note that these orders of worth are not strictly linked to their very representative domains, such as business, the arts, markets, or others. Moreover, they are considered to be symmetrical, which means that there is no supremacy of one world over the other. The prevalence of one order of worth over another depends solely on the context in which the actors are situated while debating a common good. The EW framework assumes that socially competent actors justify their position, evaluate objects and persons, and develop criticism by mobilizing these sets of values. In any given situation, such values can be invoked by anyone in order to fuel a dispute or reach an agreement.

These worlds constitute realms of argumentation and justification that individuals mobilize in public when engaged in mundane disputes or controversies. For example, the debate around free university tuition involves myriad justifications, and hence belongs to several worlds concomitantly. Students will argue that free tuition favours equality of opportunity (civic world), while associations of employers might defend the need to increase the specialization of work (industrial world). For other groups, education is a merit good (domestic world), whereas the opportunity costs of tuition fees at university are higher than those for lower vocational training (market). During a meeting or in any other public place or arena where individuals express their points of view concerning an organizational or social issue, they refer to general arguments exceeding their personal needs and interests. This is the only way to act in a public place. In such a debate, if you want to tip the scales in your favour, you must pull out arguments related to the common good or to defensible justification logics in order to look for agreement or compromise.

These worlds therefore form a theoretical framework recognizing multiple and contradictory orders in the dynamic of collective action that coexist together and are often confronted with each other in social conflicts. The EW framework provides normative solutions for reconciling different orders of worth: clarification in one world, or local arrangement and compromise between two or three worlds (Jagd, 2011). When a dispute or a controversy arises within a single world, it is relatively easy to reach an agreement. *Tests* are used to reach an agreement on the distribution of states of worth among social agents. Moreover, if a world is dominant, clarification thus prioritizes the test characteristic of this world at the expense of the others. In both cases, tests are used to draw on appropriate evidence that worth can be weighed within and across worlds. For instance, in the industrial world—which can be considered to include, for instance, universities—numbers, data, and scientific evidence constitute legitimate arguments for referring to the common good. Hence, when members of a university department have a dispute pertaining to the profile of a tenure-track position, one of the best ways to resolve this dispute is to invoke the numbers relative to our capacity to teach a greater diversity of courses.

If any dispute occurs between two or three worlds, the EW framework proposes to rely on a mix of the different worlds by creating either a local or a temporary arrangement and/or by developing a durable compromise. When a dispute occurs between heterogeneous worlds, social agents may prefer a short-term compromise such as creating a committee with social agents representing the main values at play. In a university, it is usual to have working groups composed of research-oriented, teaching-oriented, and administration-oriented professors. Local arrangements are a contingent agreement between parties striving for mutual satisfaction as opposed to the achievement of a higher level of common good. Yet social agents may prefer to negotiate durable agreements by developing an object reflecting multiple conventions that acts as an acceptable compromise between competing value frameworks in a specific context. An object of convention can take the shape of a tool, a text, or an artefact. For example, a quality improvement policy in a non-profit organization contributes to building synergy between the merchant, the industrial, and even the civic world (Michaud, 2014). Guidelines for medical practitioners bridge the industrial world of evidence-based medicine data and the domestic world, where developing close relationships with patients is important (Moreira, 2005). Issuing a Protected Designation of Origin certification for a cheese product or a regional or local farm-raised meat constitutes a compromise between the domestic and industrial worlds (Boisard and Letablier, 1989).

Of course, such local arrangements or compromises can give rise to tension and be subject to criticism. If people feel that some fundamental principles associated with an arrangement or a compromise are not respected, they may dispute or 'critique' its legitimacy. In so doing, they are acting as potential agents of change. In organizations and society, the need to secure local arrangements and acceptable compromises between the various worlds that compete for legitimacy constitute a fertile ground for the development of conventions.

In the past 25 years, convention analysis has been applied to study a diversity of objects in the OTs. As demonstrated in Table 3.3, we can find four research streams belonging to convention analysis that all refer to the EW framework. However, each research stream has different goals: (i) describing how coordination is achieved through conventions (economics of convention); (ii) reconsidering valuation and evaluation processes in markets (valuation studies); (iii) opening the black box of controversies in pluralistic contexts (controversies analysis); and (iv) paying attention to the processes through which a normative order gains or maintains legitimacy (justification studies). The two first goals provide explanations that are more compatible with the economic side of convention analysis, while the other two goals, at first glance, are more compatible with the sociological side of convention analysis. I will therefore introduce these research streams according to their main disciplinary affinity.

3.4 Economics of convention and valuation studies

The economics of convention and valuation studies both aim to explain the collective constructions in and between markets by which economic actors make decisions and resolve complex problems of coordination. While the former focuses on the conventions of coordination between economic production, distribution, and consumption, the latter examines the qualification rules and criteria that are socially constructed in diverse marketplaces. Put differently, economics of convention focuses mainly on economic coordination in and between markets, and valuation studies are concerned with the collective assignment of value to products and services. They both assume the

Table 3.3 Synoptic overview of convention analysis

	Economics of convention	Valuation studies	Controversies analysis	Justification studies
Definition	The coordination between economic production, distribution, and consumption through conventions (systems of rules and mutual expectations)	The qualification rules, criteria, or categories by which the value of objects, actions, and persons is assessed, negotiated, or contested	The way contradictions, tensions, and disagreements between different worlds are managed in pluralistic contexts	The purposeful efforts at creating, solidifying, repairing, and criticizing compromises
Research question	How is coordination collectively constructed by actors in and between markets?	How do individuals align their judgement or agree on the quality of objects and persons?	How are compromises achieved between actors with divergent views and interests?	How do actors justify their arguments and actions in keeping with the 'common good'?
Organization	Compromising device between several modes of coordination	Conventions of quality between a variety of stakeholders	Composite assemblage of compromises between orders of worth	Composite assemblage of compromises between orders of worth
Influences	Salais and Thévenot (1986); Dupuy et al. (1989); Storper and Salais (1997)	Desrosières et al. (1983)	Boltanski and Thévenot (2006)	Boltanski and Thévenot (2006)

Continued

Table 3.3 Continued

	Economics of convention	Valuation studies	Controversies analysis	Justification studies
Topics	Goods, labour, and financial markets (economics and finances studies)	Labour classification, management control system, categorization (socio-technical studies, critical accounting)	Pluralistic contexts, paradox, inter-organizational collaboration (management studies)	Corporate social responsibility, multi-stakeholders' contexts (management/social studies)
Conceptual resources	Radical uncertainty, quality conventions, worlds of production	Equivalence, investments in forms, quantification, calculability	Types of conflicts resolution; responses to paradoxes of moral legitimacy	Regimes of justification; justification–power framework; legitimacy maintenance/repair
Methods	Quantitative/qualitative analysis of conventional rules	Quantitative/qualitative analysis of values of objects, actions, and persons	Textual analysis of diverse medias (semantic descriptors)	Systematic content analysis of documents (e.g. public hearings/press articles)
Exemplars	Gomez (2006); Diaz-Bone et al. (2015); Migliore et al. (2015); Ponte (2016)	Huault and Rainelli-Weiss (2011); Strauß (2018); Barbe and Hussler (2019); Mercier-Roy and Mailhot (2019)	Cloutier (2009); Lehtimäki et al. (2011); Reinecke et al. (2017b); Barros and Michaud (2020)	Patriotta et al. (2011); Gond et al. (2016); Demers and Gond (2019)

existence of 'capable actors, a plurality of conventions and different forms of rationality' (Diaz-Bone, 2011, p. 43).

The scholars associated with the economics of convention (e.g. Dupuy, Eymard-Duvernay, Favereau, Orlena, Salais, and Thévenot) put forth a notion of coordination that is open to radical uncertainty. These authors claim that if there exists uncertainty about the quality of a product in a market, agents should develop coordination mechanisms between economic production, distribution, and consumption other than those generally used involving formal market criteria. Migliore, Schifani, and Cembalo (2015) studied farmers' markets specialized in certified organic products and observed that informal criteria lead to conventions of quality that differed from the prevailing formal market criteria of prices and certification. Conventions of quality in such emerging markets are then shaped through systems of rules and mutual expectations negotiated by the actors.

Eymard-Duvernay (1989) was one of first scholars to formulate a framework dedicated to better understanding the diversity of coordination forms (e.g. standard, non-market, partnership) or conventions to evaluate the quality of goods in markets. These conventions of qualities are often referred to in terms of the EW (e.g. domestic/market conventions of quality). Later on, Storper and Salais (1997) developed a typology of 'worlds of production' (industrial, network market, Marshallian market, and innovation worlds) underpinning a combination of technologies, markets factors, economic resources, and patterns of decision-making. According to Ponte (2016), the literature on the agro-food sector based on economics of convention has developed along two lines of analysis: conventions of quality to analyse the forms of governance coordination in global value chains; and worlds of production to explain the emergence of alternative food markets.

Scholars in economics of convention examine how coordination is collectively constructed by actors in and between markets. In recent years, these scholars have paid attention to the financial system and financial crisis. By outlining an alternative theory of value and revisiting the role of money, Orléan (2014) suggests that the 2008 financial crisis was not really the result of mistaken individual assessments of company profitability; rather, it resulted from the conventional constructions of market participants (e.g. about the potential growth of communication technology) that funnelled investments into the creation of financial bubbles. Scholars in economics of convention are also interested in studying the forms of conventions that take shape in the political economy surrounding privatization, the creation of flexible productive systems, the role of the state, and so on. Diaz-Bone (2016, p. 219) insists on the need to 'integrate the analysis of (economic) law, quantification, and economic discourses' in order to better understand the conventions and justifications that support the dissemination of neo-liberal ideas and practices.

Closely related but quite distinct, valuation studies comprise a burgeoning set of transdisciplinary studies that focus on valuation and evaluation within and across organizations that draw on the notion of convention to provide a pragmatic understanding of quantification and calculation going beyond mainstream economics. In a paper exploring the historical development of valuation studies, Thévenot (2016) identifies the roots of this stream of research as residing in the notions of 'investments in forms' (ways of making objects and relations worthy) and Desrosières' idea of 'forms of equivalence' (equal value). These notions come from the seminal work of Desrosières et al. (1983). Since then, valuation studies have been influenced by socio-technical studies and critical accounting. In the past decades, valuation studies have been concerned with any social practice that establishes criteria by which the value of objects, actions, and persons are assessed, negotiated, or contested. Therefore, it is not surprising to see the EW framework associated with this stream of research, given that assessing 'worth' is central to Boltanski and Thévenot's research programme. Most of these studies use the EW framework to uncover the forms of worth underlying antecedents, dynamics, and outcomes of processes of valuation or evaluation. Put differently, they use the EW to identify values or moral principles and how they manifest themselves in practices, tools, and applications.

These studies are particularly relevant for investigating the social construction of goods and new markets, such as prices in fair trade markets (Reinecke, 2010), risk in the climate market (Huault and Rainelli-Weiss, 2011), value creation in artistic organizations (Strauß, 2018), and the dynamic pricing devices in shared economy platforms (Mercier-Roy and Mailhot, 2019). Recent studies using the EW framework highlight how criteria for valuing objects or persons are chosen during public controversies. For instance, Annisette et al. (2017) show how accounting is used to justify actions and decisions in diverse situations. Barbe and Hussler (2019) studied the role of decentralized evaluation systems in supporting/solving the coexistence and/or competition of several conceptions of worth in market organizations of the sharing economy. Dionne, Mailhot, and Langley (2019) look at the role of the evaluation processes in the evolution of a controversy around a public debate. By applying the EW framework to qualitative and sometimes quantitative empirical studies, these works show promise for developing the situated stance of valuation studies, thereby enhancing the way we look at relationships between economy and society.

3.5 Controversies analysis and justification studies

Controversies analysis and justification studies mainly investigate how individuals navigate between different orders of worth to achieve compromises and resolve moral contradictions. While controversies studies open the black box of disputes in pluralistic contexts, justification studies pay attention to the processes through which a normative order gains or maintains legitimacy. Both are largely influenced by the Boltanski and Thévenot (2006) EW framework. Research in these substreams is generally produced by scholars in management and social studies.

One of the major applications of the EW framework in organizational studies has been to explain how to manage the tensions between different worlds in pluralistic contexts (Denis, Langley, and Rouleau, 2007). It is by identifying coexisting orders of worth, especially in public or non-profit settings, that organizational researchers explain how to navigate such contexts. For example, Hervieux, Gedajlovic, and Turcotte (2007) analyse various expressions of social entrepreneurship and show how they entail a synthesis of commercial and civic orders of worth. They provide insights for scholars and practitioners about the sources of success and tension in social and sustainable projects. According to Stark (2009), the coexistence of multiple orders of worth in organizations can be a source of innovation and adaptability—as long as they are well managed. In the same vein, some researchers have shown how organizational members mobilize different orders of worth to resist (Fronda and Moriceau, 2008) or facilitate change (Gagnon and Séguin, 2010). Other researchers using the EW framework have also examined how actors resolve conflicts and how they respond to pluralism. For example, Cloutier (2009) studied relationships with funders in non-profit organizations. Drawing on paradox literature, she described four different ways of resolving conflicts between divergent orders of worth: *buy-in* (clarification in one world); *cycling between values* spatially or temporally; *firewalling* or assigning responsibility for each value to different institutional structures (arrangements between competing worlds); and *building a hybrid arrangement* by introducing new terms (compromise). More recently Reinecke et al. (2017) studied how moral legitimacy, or what is perceived as just or unjust, can be co-achieved through dialogue with various audiences. They propose a process model of moral legitimacy in which three responses can be negotiated: transcendence; compromise; and antagonism.

In order to examine the coexistence of multiple orders of worth, previous studies were mainly conducted with fieldwork data based on interviews and observations. However, some organizational researchers have employed textual analysis of diverse media to better understand how to communicate with stakeholders and various audiences in a context of divergent views or orders of worth. Rousselière and Vézina (2009) investigated the annual reports of a financial cooperative in the cultural sector. Performing a statistical analysis of text chunks, they analysed how a compromise between cultural and financial projects was reached in order to present a specific identity to stakeholders and members. Daigle and Rouleau (2010) examined strategic plans of three artistic organizations and show the coexistence of two forms of agreements. While clarification in the industrial world was predominant, the qualitative textual analysis through diverse linguistic markers demonstrates the existence of multiple micro-agreements between arts and management. Lehtimäki, Kujala, and Heikkinen (2011) studied press releases in the controversial situation of a foreign investment, whereas Barros and Michaud (2020) examined texts posted on social media (online forums, blogs, Facebook, and Twitter) showing that they constitute new spaces for debating governance issues. While the former explains how the use of language in press releases by dominant actors mobilizes certain stakeholders and reassures others, the latter demonstrate how consumer-members of a large financial cooperative resist the attempt of board members to change its governance rules.

Jagd (2011) concluded his literature review on the use of the EW framework by inviting researchers to focus on 'justification work' as a promising avenue for future research. Organizational researchers responded to this call by looking at moral complexity (Reinecke, van Bommel, and Spicer, 2017), injustice (Ramirez, 2013), and the legitimation process (Patriotta, Gond, and Schultz, 2011; Gond and Leca, 2012; Reinecke, Manning, and von Hagen, 2012). Justification work refers to the use of 'discursive and material resources to justify the moral worthiness of their claims in relation to specific situations, objects or persons' (Demers and Gond, 2019, p. 5). Put differently, it corresponds to the purposeful efforts aimed at creating, solidifying, repairing, and criticizing compromises. Taupin (2012) identifies different forms of justification that financial rating agencies engaged with after the 2008 financial crisis in order to restore and maintain their institutional legitimacy. Oldenhof, Postma, and Putters (2014) looked at how justification work is constituted in practice through objects, behaviour, and rhetoric by studying the solidification of compromises during times of public change where managers face contradictory stakeholder pressures.

Jean-Pascal Gond and colleagues have played a leading role in advancing knowledge in this research stream with their work on sustainability issues. Patriotta, Gond, and Schultz (2011) studied a controversy emerging from a nuclear accident involving a large European energy company. Relying on the press coverage of this controversy, they analysed the stakeholder justifications, as presented to a public audience. They showed how the process of recovering and maintaining legitimacy required robust justifications based on multiple modalities and forms of agreement. Some years later, Gond and other colleagues studied how multiple stakeholders (government, civil society, and industry) mobilized diverse modes of justification and forms of power aimed at influencing the moral legitimacy of fracking technology during a controversy surrounding shale gas exploration in Quebec (Gond et al., 2016). Finally, Demers and Gond (2019) rely on the notion of justification work to explore the moral micro-foundations of institutional complexity. Drawing on interviews with corporate members of an oil sand organization, they identify four distinct types of justification work—sheltering, solidifying, fragilizing, and deconstructing—by combining different worlds and related objects used to respond to a new sustainability strategy. It is noteworthy to mention that two of these papers propose a systematic content analysis of the newspaper articles gathered around the controversy examined (Patriotta, Gond, and Schultz, 2011; Gond et al., 2016). To conduct the analysis, they refer to a list of semantic descriptors based on Boltanski and Thévenot (2006) schematic account of common worlds (see Patriotta, Gond, and Schultz, 2011), allowing them to qualitatively identify the common worlds but to also quantify their usages throughout the material analysed.

3.6 Where is convention analysis heading?

Before we answer this question, we must first consider the contributions of convention analysis and the EW framework to organizational economy, as well as its limitations. Undoubtedly, convention analysis advances the project of building explanations that take into account both the economic and social aspects of organizations. According to this analysis, agents are not completely free to behave of their own volition in order to compete in a perfect and universal market, as economists too often assume; nor are they constrained by the environment, as sociologists too often assume. They are able to accomplish complex operations of cultural adjustments and evaluation when facing situations of economic uncertainty. Convention analysis supposes that individuals have the freedom to work out compromises between pre-existing and competing logics. Thus, coordination among actors where there is a plurality of divergent views and interests largely results from the recourse to common 'frames' or 'conventions' that relate to their ability to justify their reasoning and, more broadly, to their sense of justice.

Convention analysis constitutes a general research programme on coordination and interaction (between individuals and objects) that provides a highly engaging, stimulating, and theoretically useful contribution to current debates in organizational economics and, more generally, in organization studies. It provides a particularly significant contribution to the study of 'public arguments' as it outlines a roadmap of argumentation registers most commonly used in disputes. The research programme is also insightful because it accounts for the 'real world' in the sense that compromises between different worlds need to be materialized through objects and tools during worthiness tests (Barbe and Hussler, 2019; Dionne, Mailhot, and Langley, 2019).

Another major contribution of convention analysis to organizational economy consists in revisiting the rationality postulate. Previous economic frameworks consider the nature of rationality as given or obvious. Convention analysis expands our understanding of this notion. Indeed, assuming that rationality is socially constructed implies that human behaviours are unique and thus unpredictable, even though they are conventionally driven. Such a view of rationality implies a rather radical vision of uncertainty, as it admits that it is impossible to know or to predict the result of an action. Needless to say, convention analysis constitutes a major innovation to push further the agenda of organizational economics as it integrates the collective dimension into economic behaviour analysis. However, we should remember that it is a moderate form of constructionism, as we still know little about the origin of conventions; that is, the conditions of their emergence.

However, convention analysis has also been widely criticized for not taking into account power dynamics, even though some authors have begun to address this gap (e.g. Gond et al., 2016; Wright and Nyberg, 2017). This framework proposes a consensual vision of social reality. It explains how individuals cooperate, reconcile their different values, and achieve compromises in spite of divergent interests. The framework is based on the principle of equivalence between the different worlds. Yet, such equivalence is neither natural nor obvious. The convention analysis framework expresses ideal forms of socio-political order and focuses on the morality of actors—morality that seems to be indifferent to social determinants (e.g. gender, ethnicity, class, age) and free of motivational and historical backgrounds. Although individuals are critical of unfair situations, they are conceived as honest, serious, and in constant search of the common good. However, in our western society, they are also opportunists and rather individualists. Therefore, intentionally or not, they might have been motivated to act for one reason, yet claim to have acted for another. Taking EW's logic further, its framework might serve as a normative tool about the right way to handle an argumentation in a dispute. It is, however, noteworthy to mention that some authors have begun to address the power gap.

Although the EW framework is based on a very impressive theoretical reflection, it nevertheless stands on a complex theoretical architecture and a loose methodological account. Terms such as 'world', 'test', 'justification', 'dispute', 'worth', 'compromise', 'higher common principle', and 'investment form' are very specific to this framework. Boltanski and Thévenot make an obvious effort to distance themselves from their social sciences and organization studies colleagues by developing a unique vocabulary rather than by advancing conceptual frameworks developed by their predecessors. Such theoretical isolationism has long prevented the dissemination of their framework. On the methodological side, the difficulty of locating the worlds in discourse due to a lack of methodological points of reference has also proved to be a limitation when seeking to be published in high-ranked journals. However, the situation has evolved, and we can now find robust ways of analysing data based on the EW framework (Patriotta, Gond, and Schultz, 2011; Gond et al., 2016).

In organizational economics, convention analysis is one of the research streams that has most advanced the heterodox project of bridging the economic and the social to explain choices in uncertain situations. That said, this project remains incomplete and difficult to achieve, as the divide between the economic and social persists in spite of the efforts to integrate them. On the one hand, what is called the economics of convention looks at how individuals draw on diverse conventions of quality and effort (e.g. quality of goods, business models, recruitment, financial operations) to perform complex operations of adjustment and coordination in contexts of economic uncertainty. On the other hand, the sociology of justification based on the EW framework relies on individuals' sense of justice to better understand how they resolve their differences in pluralistic contexts. Still, there remains much work to be done to overcome this foundational divide between economics and sociology. Until now, economic convention analysis has not succeeded in finding its niche in organizational economics.

That said, the future of the sociology of justification or of the EW framework is more promising than ever. In the past few years, many international scholars, in particular Francophones, have attempted to promote this theoretical option (Cloutier, Gond, and Leca, 2017). One way of doing this has been by advocating the complementarity between the EW framework and organizational institutionalism (Dequech, 2008; Cloutier and Langley, 2013; Boxenbaum, 2014; Pernkopf-Konhäusner, 2014; Westenholz, 2017). This has proved very helpful, as several recent studies positioned themselves as alternatives to refine diverse aspects of institutional theory, such as the micro-foundations of institutional complexity (Demers and Gond, 2019), institutional logics in the context of financial market regulation (Munzer, 2019), the role of material devices for maintaining institutional logics (Barbe and Hussler, 2019), the way legitimacy and institutional work are co-constructed (Richards, Zellweger, and Gond, 2017), and so on. However, neo-institutional theorists themselves do not seem to demonstrate the same interest for convention analysis as its promotors. This remains a major challenge for the dissemination of this perspective within the OTs.

In addition to this mingling with organizational institutionalism, it is important to acknowledge the evolution of empirical studies that rely on the EW framework. Until recently, this framework was mainly employed as a methodological tool for identifying a plurality of logics, views, or discourses and thus to advance the microanalysis of compromise-making around diverse issues in organization studies, such as sustainability, paradoxes, materiality, categorization, morality, and so on. While convention analysis is open and flexible, it nevertheless constitutes a self-organized system of thoughts, making it very difficult to push further. Of course, it is always possible to identify worlds or forms of justification other than those currently making up the framework. But aside from this, the potential for contributions aimed at advancing the EW is rather weak. A few researchers have nevertheless begun to introduce various hybridization strategies to further what we know on various organizational topics. In so doing, they are able to publish in high-ranking academic journals. For example, in a paper published in the *Journal of Management Studies*, Gond et al. (2016) combine Boltanski and Thévenot's EW framework with Lukes' concept of power and develop a process model of what they call a 'justification–power framework'. Barros and Michaud (2020) draw on the EW framework and critical discourse analysis in a paper demonstrating the importance of alternative discursive arenas or spaces of dissent to regenerate organizational democracy. In a paper published in *Journal of Business Ethics*, Mercier-Roy and Mailhot (2019) draw on the work of Boltanski and Thévenot and the notion of *agencement* to show how a compromise can be solidified. The future of the EW framework in the OTs depends on the capacity of organizational researchers to find ways to develop strong contributions in order to make breakthroughs in high-ranking journals, in both Europe and North America.

References

Aglietta, M. 1976. Monnaie et inflation: quelques leçons de l'expérience américaine des dix dernières années. *Economie et statistique*, 77, 49–71.

Alchian, A. A. & Demsetz, H. 1972. Production, Information Costs and Economic Organization. *American Economic Review*, 62, 777–795.

Annisette, M., Vesty, G, & Amslem, T. 2017. Accounting Values, Controversies, and Compromises in Tests of Worth. *In*: Cloutier, C., Gond, J.-P., & Leca, B. (eds) *Justification, Evaluation and Critique in the Study of Organizations: Contributions from French Pragmatist Sociology*, pp. 209–239. Bingley, UK, Emerald Publishing Limited.

Barbe, A.-S. & Hussler, C. 2019. The War of the Worlds Won't Occur: Decentralized Evaluation Systems and Orders of Worth in Market Organizations of the Sharing Economy. *Technological Forecasting and Social Change*, 143, 64–75.

Barney, J. 1991. Firm Resources and Sustained Competitive Advantage. *Journal of Management*, 17, 99–120.

Barros, M. & Michaud, V. 2020. Worlds, Words, and Spaces of Resistance: Democracy and Social Media in Consumer Coops. *Organization*, 27, 578–612.

Boisard, P. & Letablier, M.-T. 1989. Un compromis d'innovation entre tradition et standardisation dans l'industrie laitière. *In*: Boltanski, L. & Thévenot, L. (eds) *Justesse et justice dans le travail*, pp. 209–218. Paris, Presses Universitaires de France.

Boltanski, L., Thévenot, L. (1991). *De la justification : les économies de la grandeur,* Paris : Gallimard.

Boltanski, L. & Chiapello, E. 1999. *Le nouvel esprit du capitalisme*. Paris, Gallimard.

Boltanski, L. & Thévenot, L. 2006. *On Justification. The Economies of Worth*. Princeton, NJ, Princeton University Press.

Boxenbaum, E. 2014. Toward a Situated Stance in Organizational Institutionalism. *Journal of Management Inquiry*, 23, 319–323.

Boyer, R. 1986. *La théorie de la régulation: une analyse critique*. Paris, La Découverte.

Cloutier, C. 2009. Managing Opportunity, Managing Power and Managing Difference: How Nonprofits Strategically *Manage Their Relations With Funder*. PhD thesis, HEC Montréal.

Cloutier, C. & Langley, A. 2013. The Logic of Institutional Logics. *Journal of Management Inquiry*, 22, 360–380.

Cloutier, C., Gond, J.-P., & Leca, B. 2017. Justification, Evaluation and Critique in the Study of Organizations: An Introduction to the Volume. *In*: Cloutier, C., Gond, J.-P., & Leca, B. (eds) *Justification, Evaluation and Critique in the Study of Organizations*, pp. 3–29. Bingley, UK, Emerald Publishing.

Daigle, P. & Rouleau, L. 2010. Strategic Plans in Arts Organizations: A Tool of Compromise Between Artistic and Managerial Values. *International Journal of Arts Management*, 12, 13–30.

Demers, C. & Gond, J.-P. 2019. The Moral Microfoundations of Institutional Complexity: Sustainability Implementation as Compromise-Making at an Oil Sands Company. *Organization Studies*, 41, 563–586.

Denis, J.-L., Langley, A., & Rouleau, L. 2007. Strategizing in Pluralistic Contexts: Rethinking Theoretical Frames. *Human Relations*, 60, 179–215.

Dequech, D. 2008. Logics of Justification and Logics of Action. *Journal of Economic Issues*, 42, 527.

Desrosières, A., Goy, A., & Thévenot, L. 1983. L'identité sociale dans le travail statistique: la nouvelle nomenclature des professions et catégories socioprofessionnelles. *Économie et statistique*, 152, 55–81.

Diaz-Bone, R. 2011. The Methodological Standpoint of the 'économie des conventions'. Historical Social Research. *Historical Social Research*, 36, 43–63.

Diaz-Bone, R. 2016. Convention Theory and Neoliberalism. *Journal of Cultural Economy*, 9, 214–220.

Diaz-Bone, R., Didry, C., & Salais, R. 2015. Conventionalist's Perspectives on the Political Economy of Law. An Introduction. *Historical Social Research*, 40, 7–22.

Dionne, K.-E., Mailhot, C., & Langley, A. 2019. Modeling the Evaluation Process in a Public Controversy. *Organization Studies*, 40, 651–679.

Dupuy, J.-P., Eymard-Duvernay, F., Favereau, O., Orlean, A., Salais, R., & Thévenot, L. 1989. Introduction. *Revue économique*, 40, 141–145.

Eymard-Duvernay, F. 1989. Conventions de qualité et formes de coordination. Revue économique, 40, 2, 329–359.

Fronda, Y. & Moriceau, J. L. 2008. I Am Not Your Hero: Change Management and Culture Shocks in a Public Sector Corporation. *Journal of Organizational Change Management*, 21, 589–609.

Gagnon, S. & Séguin, F. 2010. Institution and Change: Possible Coexistence. *Canadian Journal of Administrative Sciences/Revue Canadienne des Sciences de l'Administration*, 27, 136–147.

Gomez, P.-Y. 2006. Information et conventions. Le cadre du modèle général. *Revue Française de Gestion*, 32, 217–240.

Gond, J.-P. & Leca, B. 2012. Theorizing Change in a Pluralistic Institutional Context: What Can Economies of Worth and New-Institutionalism Learn From Each Other? *Lille: Document de travail du LEM*, 15, 1–52.

Gond, J.-P., Barin Cruz, L., Raufflet, E., & Charron, M. 2016. To Frack or Not to Frack? The Interaction of Justification and Power in a Sustainability Controversy. *Journal of Management Studies*, 53, 330–363.

Hervieux, C., Gedajlovic, E., & Turcotte, M.-F. 2007. Social Entrepreneurship: A Synthesis of Civic and Commercial Logics. Academy of Management Annual Conference, 3–8 August, Philadelphia, PA.

Huault, I. & Rainelli-Weiss, H. 2011. A Market for Weather Risk? Conflicting Metrics, Attempts at Compromise, and Limits to Commensuration. *Organization Studies*, 32, 1395–1419.

Isaac, H. 2003. Paradoxes et conventions. *In*: Perret, V. & Josserand, E. (eds) *Le paradoxe: Penser et gérer autrement les organisations*, pp. 147–163. Paris, Éditions Ellipses.

Jagd, S. 2011. Pragmatic Sociology and Competing Orders of Worth in Organizations. *European Journal of Social Theory*, 14, 343–359.

Jensen, M. C. & Meckling, W. H. 1976. Theory of the Firm: Managerial Behavior, Agency Costs and Ownership Structure. *Journal of Financial Economics*, 3, 305–360.

Lafaye, C. & Thévenot, L. 2017. An Ecological Justification? Conflicts in the Development of Nature: Contributions from French Pragmatist Sociology. *In*: Cloutier, C., Gond, J.-P., & Leca, B. (eds) Justification, Evaluation and Critique in the Study of Organizations, Bingley, UK, Emerald Publishing, 273-300.

Lehtimäki, H., Kujala, J., & Heikkinen, A. 2011. Corporate Responsibility in Communication. *Business Communication Quarterly*, 74, 432–449.

Mercier-Roy, M. & Mailhot, C. 2019. What's in an App? Investigating the Moral Struggles Behind a Sharing Economy Device. *Journal of Business Ethics*, 159, 977–996.

Michaud, V. 2014. Mediating the Paradoxes of Organizational Governance Through Numbers. *Organization Studies*, 35, 75–101.

Migliore, G., Schifani, G., & Cembalo, L. 2015. Opening the Black Box of Food Quality in the Short Supply Chain: Effects of Conventions of Quality on Consumer Choice. *Food Quality and Preference*, 39, 141–146.

Moreira, T. 2005. Diversity in Clinical Guidelines: The Role of Repertoires of Evaluation. *Social Science & Medicine*, 60, 1975–1985.

Munzer, M. 2019. Justifying the Logic of Regulatory Post-Crisis Decision-Making—The Case of the French Structural Banking Reform. *Critical Perspectives on Accounting*, 60, 44–64.

Nelson, R. R. & Winter, S. G. 1982. *An Evolutionary Theory of Economic Change*. Cambridge, MA, Belknap Press of Harvard University Press.

Oldenhof, L., Postma, J., & Putters, K. 2014. On Justification Work: How Compromising Enables Public Managers to Deal with Conflicting Values. *Public Administrative Review*, 74, 52–63.

Orléan, A. 2014. *The Empire of Value. A New Foundation for Economics*. Cambridge, MA, MIT Press.

Patriotta, G., Gond, J.-P., & Schultz, F. 2011. Maintaining Legitimacy: Controversies, Orders of Worth, and Public Justifications. *Journal of Management Studies*, 48, 1804–1836.

Pernkopf-Konhäusner, K. 2014. The Competent Actor. *Journal of Management Inquiry*, 23, 333–337.

Ponte, S. 2016. Convention Theory in the Anglophone Agro-Food Literature: Past, Present and Future. *Journal of Rural Studies*, 55, 12–23.

Porter, M. E. 1980. *Competitive Strategy: Techniques for Analyzing Industries and Competitors*. New York, Free Press.

Ramirez, C. 2013. 'We are being Pilloried for Something, We Did Not Even Know We Had Done Wrong!' Quality Control and Orders of Worth in the British Audit Profession. *Journal of Management Studies*, 50, 845–869.

Reinecke, J. 2010. Beyond a Subjective Theory of Value and Towards a 'Fair Price': An Organizational Perspective on Fairtrade Minimum Price Setting. *Organization*, 17, 563–581.

Reinecke, J., Manning, S., & Von Hagen, O. 2012. The Emergence of a Standards Market: Multiplicity of Sustainability Standards in the Global Coffee Industry. *Organization Studies*, 33, 791–814.

Reinecke, J., Van Bommel, K., & Spicer, A. 2017. When Orders of Worth Clash: Negotiating Legitimacy in Situations of Moral Multiplexity. *In*: Cloutier, C., Gond, J.-P., & Leca, B. (eds.) *Justification, Evaluation and Critique in the Study of Organizations*, pp. 33–72. Bingley, UK, Emerald Publishing.

Richards, M., Zellweger, T., & Gond, J.-P. 2017. Maintaining Moral Legitimacy through Worlds and Words: An Explanation of Firms' Investment in Sustainability Certification. *Journal of Management Studies*, 54, 676–710.

Rousselière, D. & Vézina, M. 2009. Constructing the Legitimacy of a Financial Cooperative in the Cultural Sector: A Case Study Using Textual Analysis. *International Review of Sociology*, 19, 241–261.

Salais, R. & Thévenot, L. 1986. *Le travail. Marchés, règles, conventions*. Paris, Economica.

Schelling, T. C. 1960. *The Strategy of Conflict*. Cambridge, MA, Harvard University Press.

Simon, H. A. 1995. A Behavioral Model of Rational Choice. *The Quarterly Journal of Economics*, 69, 99–118.

Stark, D. 2009. *The Sense of Dissonance: Accounts of Worth in Economic Life*. Princeton, NJ, Princeton University Press.

Storper, M. & Salais, R. 1997. *Worlds of Production*. Cambridge, MA, Harvard University.

Strauß, A. 2018. Value-Creation Processes in Artistic Interventions and Beyond: Engaging Conflicting Orders of Worth. *Journal of Business Research*, 85, 540–545.

Taupin, B. 2012. The More Things Change... Institutional Maintenance as Justification Work in the Credit Rating Industry. *M@n@gement*, 15, 528–562.

Teece, J. D. 2009. *Dynamic Capabilities and Strategic Management: Organizing for Innovation and Growth*. Oxford, UK, Oxford University Press.

Thévenot, L. 2016. From Social Coding to Economics of Convention: A Thirty-Year Perspective on the Analysis of Qualification and Quantification Investments. *Historical Social Research*, 41, 96–117.

Thévenot, L., Moody, M., & Lafaye, C. 2000. Forms of Valuing Nature: Arguments and Modes of Justification in French and American Environmental Disputes. *In*: Lamont, M. & Thévenot, L. (eds) *Rethinking Comparative Cultural Sociology: Repertoires of Evaluation in France and the United States*, pp. 229–272. Cambridge, Cambridge University Press.

Westenholz, A. 2017. Conventions and Institutional Logics: Invitation to a Dialogue Between Two Theoretical Approaches Research. *In*: Krücken, G., Mazza, C., Meyer, R. E., & Walgenbach, P. (eds) *New Themes in Institutional Analysis*, pp. 77–103. Cheltenham, UK, Edward Elgar Publishing.

Williamson, O. E. 1985. *The Economic Institutions of Capitalism*. New York, Free Press.

Wright, C. & Nyberg, D. 2017. An Inconvenient Truth: How Organizations Translate Climate Change into Business as Usual. *Academy of Management Journal*, 60, 1633–1661.

4

Network Analysis

As Manuel Castells suggests in his book *The Rise of Network Society*, we are living in—you guessed it!—a network society! The new forms of competition generated by globalization have transformed the way organizations are connected to one another. In this global economy, the dominant organizational model is no longer the hierarchical firm, but rather a plethora of lateral and horizontal connections between suppliers, distributors, and even competitors. The hierarchical control dominating traditional businesses has been replaced by a constant search for increasing flexibility and collaboration in the way sellers, providers, clients, and partners operate. Of course, without the recent technological developments in the manufacturing and telecommunications sectors, the development of distributed organizational forms, such as networks, would not have been possible. Organization theories (OTs) scholars have demonstrated great interest in advancing our understanding of how networks are developed, maintained, and transformed—and it is no wonder, given that we live in a world in which the transfer of innovation, creativity, and information is key to firm performance.

In our network society, social life is no longer solely the result of a series of rights and obligations towards a community or business. Individuals belong to several social groups (e.g. family, sports associations, political parties, work teams, circles of friends), which may have little to no overlap. Moreover, members of the new generation of workers are likely to be exposed to up to seven or eight organizations during their working life, including periods of self-employment. Indeed, in today's world, connections between individuals are temporary but continuous; rather than requiring careful maintenance, they can be renewed as needed, regardless of geographical, professional, or even cultural distances. As a result, there has been a multiplication of meetings between individuals, which has exploded the size of social and organizational networks.

Unsurprisingly, organization theorists have witnessed a proliferation of network studies in their domain. Network researchers in OTs often use expressions like 'network paradigm' or 'network theory'. However, network analysis can hardly be considered a unified domain of research. Rather, it is

Organization Theories in the Making. Linda Rouleau, Oxford University Press.
© Linda Rouleau (2022). DOI: 10.1093/oso/9780198792024.003.0005

constituted of an eclectic set of studies influenced by a wide variety of disciplines and based on diverse methods and ontological representations of reality. Nevertheless, all forms of network analysis share familiar grounds and exhibit specific characteristics: they highlight the 'relations' between entities as a unity of analysis and have developed a set of concepts for understanding network patterns, features, and properties.

This chapter will review four different forms of network analysis, each of which produces knowledge around a specific type of network. First, social network analysis (SNA) examines the pattern of social connections between individuals. Second, interfirm network analysis (INA) investigates the network structure of the firm. Third, the socioeconomic perspective of network analysis (SENA) is dedicated to understanding networks as an organizational form. Fourth, the chain of socio-technical relations is the object of the newest network analysis; that is, actor–network theory (ANT). After briefly introducing the history and the terminology of network studies, this chapter will chart the diverse forms of network analysis in OTs. It will end by discussing why, in terms of knowledge production, network analysis is so popular today, and will propose avenues for pushing this research agenda forward.

4.1 A long tradition of network analysis

Until the beginning of the 2000s, organization theorists largely ignored networks; the seminal article by Walter Powell (1990) was an exception. However, network analysis is hardly a new perspective. Some authors trace its origins to the classical works of Machiavelli and Hobbes. The former highlights the coalitions formed in Italian society, while the latter puts forth the famous maxim 'to have friends is power'. Yet, according to Mercklé (2011, p. 3), Georg Simmel (1858–1918) appears to be the legitimate pioneer of network analysis as he investigated social forms in terms of 'relations' and reciprocity between individuals.

During the twentieth century, network analysis became popular and expanded into several disciplines, such as anthropology, sociology, and even mathematics. According to Kilduff and Tsai (2012), three types of works gave rise to network analysis in the social sciences. First, in the 1920s and 1930s, researchers such as Lewin, Heider, and Moreno used this type of analysis to study interpersonal influence during interactions. Over the same period, Harvard researchers drew on network analysis to study interactions in what would later be widely known as the Hawthorne studies (Roethlisberger and Dickson, 1939). In fact, this is where the first sociograms came from.

The psychotherapist Jack L. Moreno (1889–1974), who co-founded sociometry with Helen Hall Jennings, developed a systematic method to graphically represent individuals as points (or 'nodes') and the relationships between them.

Second, structural anthropology (in the 1930s and 1940s) and the Manchester School (in the 1950s and 1960s) used network analysis to understand primitive and urban groupings based on ethnographic studies (Mercklé, 2011, pp. 8–10). Radcliffe-Brown (1940, p. 2), in a conference before the Royal Anthropological Society, affirmed that 'human beings are connected by a complex network of social relations'. Barnes (1954) was one of the first anthropologists to use a network approach to understand the formation of community and class in Norway. Early network-based ethnographies studied bounded social groups such as systems of households, kinships, communities, and so on. In doing so, they explained how latent phenomena were embedded in the structural forms of social life. For instance, Barnes (1954) shows how 'class inequalities emerged despite the fact that people living in a Norwegian parish emphasized social equality in their relations with one another' (Knox, Savage, and Harvey, 2006, p. 122).

While the anthropologists were busy adopting the idea of networks to expand their theoretical repertoires for fieldwork, during the 1950s, mathematicians and related scientists started to develop graphs and statistical models to address issues of relatedness in social groups. That decade saw the development of sophisticated mathematical models aimed at network analysis and the reinforcement of a structural approach to networks. Concomitantly, according to Knox et al. (2006), there was a growing lack of interest in the notion of networks on the part of anthropologists, who became, some decades later, fascinated about qualitative accounts of power, meaning, and agency rather than depicting latent issues related to connectedness in social life.

Third, over the 1960s and 1970s, sociologists took over anthropologists' interest in networks and began studying interlocked directorships and ownerships (one or more persons sitting on the board of directors or owning shares simultaneously of at least two firms). According to Galaskiewicz (2007), this development can be seen as a counter-reaction to survey research focused on individual behaviours that used to be popular in social sciences. These sociologists studied the interorganizational cooptation elite in large organizations. Using a network approach enabled them to better understand how and why organizations select partners (Levine, 1972; Allen, 1974). Researchers suggest that interlocks are an important way of reinforcing cohesion among the elite, as executives and owners who socialize in the same elite social group will also share strong ties when sitting on the same board (for a review, see Lamb and Roundy, 2016).

It is not until recently that OTs researchers developed an interest in network analysis. At the beginning of the 2000s, Borgatti (2003, p. 991) reviewed and analysed empirical research published in what he called 'the emerging network paradigm in organizational research'. Then, American journals dedicated special issues (see the *Academy of Management Journal* (47, 6, 2004) and the *Academy of Management Review* (31, 3, 2006)) to the network approach for diverse OTs circles. Interest in network analysis in OTs, and therefore in networks, has grown significantly over the past decades, as evidenced by the sheer number of communications at conferences and published articles that make direct reference to networks in their titles.

This rise in interest in researching networks in OTs has been commensurate with the growing importance of networks in social life and organizations over the past two decades. Today, the notion of network implies new ways of belonging to and understanding the world and corresponds to the breakdown of social and organizational life. The advances in information and communication technologies also contributed to the dissemination of network studies in OTs. As a result, we can currently find software (e.g. UCINET, NetDraw, and EgoNet) and journals (e.g. *Journal of Network and System Management, Journal of Historical Network Research, Applied Network Science, International Journal of Networking, and Virtual Organizations*) dedicated to network analysis.

For those not familiar with network analysis, let me first introduce the basic vocabulary required to understand the constitutive meaning of this research perspective. A large part of network analysis originates from Granovetter (1973, 1985), who invited researchers to pay more attention to the embeddedness of the economic actor in organizational analysis. According to this author, economic behaviour, whether on the individual or organizational level, is far from context free, but is rather embedded in social relations (e.g. family, friendships, acquaintances, teams, partnerships). These social relations are organized into networks, meaning that a set of actors or units of analysis (e.g. persons, teams, work units, organizations, or even more abstract things such as concepts) are connected through strong or weak ties, which in turn has consequences for the maintenance of social and organizational life.

Instead of focusing on the actors and their attributes, network analysis targets the relations connecting individuals, firms, and other units in order to better understand the relationships or ties between these different entities. These ties have direction and diverse properties that determine how a network takes shape. Centrality, density, distance between entities, and flows of information and communication figure among the most important properties investigated by network researchers. Most of the time, networks are visualized or mapped through graphs containing nodes (actors, individuals, firms, or other units of analysis) and ties. Nodes are represented as points, and ties are represented as lines. These visualizations provide a means of assessing networks by varying the visual representation of their nodes and ties to reflect properties of interest.

As will be demonstrated, the multiplicity of origins and approaches to network analysis contribute to the eclecticism of this perspective in OTs (see Table 4.1). According to network studies, actors (interindividual, intergroup, and interorganizational) are embedded in interconnected relationships that provide opportunities and constraints. The next section describes the four different substreams of network analysis that have been developed over the past 25 years in OTs.

4.2 Social network analysis

SNA has long been the bread and butter of network studies in OTs. Historically, SNA has been the dominant prerogative of American quantitative social scientists, especially sociologists. Applied to OTs, SNA is about connections and the mapping of relationships between colleagues, workers, and friends in organizational settings. Social networks can exhibit dense clusters of actors that provide conduits for information flows. In organizational settings, people are bounded together by proximity (offices on the same floor or in the same building), shared characteristics (age, language, and gender) and common goals (specific projects, skills, and capabilities). Also, when entering a new social environment, such as an organization, individuals are generally motivated to get a global picture of the group and find out about subgroups as well as their own position within these groups. This is where SNA provides a relevant tool for answering questions such as: Who shares information with whom? Who trusts whom? Who is in conflicts with whom? Who are the leaders? Who is the most popular actor, and who resides at the margins?

SNA aims to depict the structural patterns created by and reflected in social relations. To accurately describe the pattern of a social network, researchers use graphs generally built on a binary matrix (Yang, Keller, and Zheng, 2017). Figure 4.1a represents the archetypal form of a social network. For instance, such a social network could be a friendship network in a PhD classroom. As a set of close relations among a group of people, a classroom can indeed be studied as a network—similarly to any other type of group, such as a

Table 4.1 Synoptic overview of network analysis

	Social network analysis (SNA)	Interfirm network analysis (INA)	Socioeconomic network analysis (SENA)	Actor–network theory (ANT)
Definition	Relations between individuals (e.g. managers and employees)	Relations between different firms, where one firm constitutes a hub or the focal organization	Multilateral relationships between three or more organizations aimed at achieving a common goal	Socio-technical relations between actors and actants (human and non-human entities)
Research question	Who shares information with whom? Who is the most popular actor?	How do the ties-related properties between the firms influence their performance and efficiency?	How are the common goals set achieved by the interorganizational network?	How are innovations produced, disseminated, and how do they become socially accepted?
Level of analysis	Individual (ego network) or group (social network)	The network of the firm (Network 'in itself'; Raab and Kenis, 2009)	The whole interorganizational network (Network 'for itself'; Raab and Kenis, 2009)	Chain of translation of the interests and identities of network's members
Organization	The set of cliques, friendships, or teams	The interfirm network	The network organization as a form of governance	The actor–network

Continued

Table 4.1 *Continued*

	Social network analysis (SNA)	Interfirm network analysis (INA)	Socioeconomic network analysis (SENA)	Actor–network theory (ANT)
Influences	Sociology and mathematics (Granovetter, 1973, 1985; Coleman, 1990; Burt, 1992)	Strategic management literature, e.g. resource-based view/dynamic capabilities (Powell, 1990)	Organizational economics, e.g. transaction cost theory and social theory (Giddens, 1984; Williamson, 1985)	Science and technology studies (Callon, 1986; Latour, 1987, 2005)
Conceptual resources	Density, centrality, distance, structural holes, and social capital	Antecedents, network structure and dynamics, and outcomes	Governance structure and processes (e.g. evaluation, identity, membership, and leadership)	Translation (problematization, interessement, enrolment, and mobilization) and obligatory passage points
Type of analysis	Structural and explicative (realism)	Causal and normative (realism)	Descriptive and comprehensive (soft constructionism)	Descriptive and comprehensive (radical constructionism)
Methods	Quantitative social network analysis (mathematical)	Quantitative analysis (statistical)	Longitudinal case studies	Organizational ethnography
Exemplars	Kilduff and Tsai (2012); Greenberg and Fernandez (2016); Monaghan Lavelle, and Gunnigle (2017); Tasselli and Kilduff (2018)	Galaskiewicz and Zaheer (1999); Zaheer and Bell (2005); Tatarynowicz et al. (2016); Mazzola et al. (2018); Kumar and Zaheer (2019)	Sydow and Windeler (1998); Rometsch and Sydow (2006); Müller-Seitz and Sydow (2012); Moretti and Zirpoli (2016); Sydow and Müller-Seitz (2020)	Attila (2005); Czarniawska and Hernes (2005); Akrich, Callon, and Latour (2006); Lamine (2017); Bilodeau and Potvin (2018)

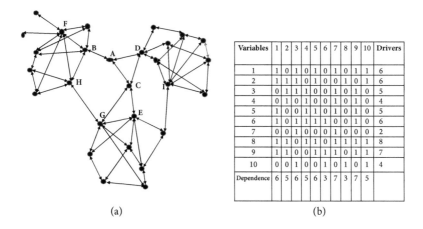

Variables	1	2	3	4	5	6	7	8	9	10	Drivers
1	1	0	1	0	1	0	1	0	1	1	6
2	1	1	1	0	1	0	0	1	0	1	6
3	0	1	1	1	0	0	1	0	1	0	5
4	0	1	0	1	0	0	1	0	1	0	4
5	1	0	0	1	1	0	1	0	1	0	5
6	1	0	1	1	1	1	0	0	1	0	6
7	0	0	1	0	0	0	1	0	0	0	2
8	1	1	0	1	1	0	1	1	1	1	8
9	1	1	0	0	1	1	1	0	1	1	7
10	0	0	1	0	0	1	0	1	0	1	4
Dependence	6	5	6	5	6	3	7	3	7	5	

(a)   (b)

Figure 4.1 Social network (a) and binary matrix (b)

family, a neighbourhood, a work team, an organizational unit, and so on. A social network graph can be drawn from a binary network matrix (see Figure 4.1b) in which respondents are asked to indicate '1' to identify the persons with whom they are friends, and '0' for those with whom they are not. Binary data are widely used in network analysis to develop graph methods and algorithms to measure networks. Of course, other mathematical measures (e.g. ordinal, interval) can be used to analyse the structural pattern of a social network. Moreover, data from social networks can also be exploited to test hypotheses that are grounded in statistical methods. Drawing on mathematical and statistical measures to study network patterns allows social network researchers to systematically describe the patterns of relationships they are observing. Such structural descriptions *a posteriori* should highlight unsuspected findings related to the collective aspect of social life.

The analysis of network data consists of describing the properties of the network or the connections (or clustering) and distances between actors (betweenness) in order to assess the cohesion between social actors (density), the intensity of their relations (reciprocity), their network positions or the exercise of influence (centrality), the roles they play in a group (equivalence), and so on. For an exhaustive understanding of network properties, one should not forget the notions of 'social capital' and 'structural holes', which often come together and play an important role in SNA (Kilduff and Tsai, 2012). According to Coleman (1990), strong connections (identified as network closure) facilitate the acquisition of social capital, which refers to the set of material (e.g., faster promotions and higher salaries), informational (e.g., breadth of information, timing, and arbitrage), and symbolic resources (e.g., positive evaluation and recognition) that comes with membership to a specific network (Burt, Kilduff, and Tasselli, 2013). Consider the diverse forms of support provided by your partner, your parents, your friends, and even neighbours during your PhD studies (e.g. money, food, moral support, contacts for finding fieldwork)—key resources to make the already arduous PhD journey a little less lonely and difficult! But the source of social capital can also come from one's network position. For instance, Burt (1992) demonstrated that some people occupy 'structural holes'. Structural holes (or an absence of ties) are types of 'empty spaces' through which information is transmitted between networks. Such a bridging or brokering position provides an advantage to the one occupying it only because it connects people across networks—especially in our society, where information is highly valued!

The most researched topics in SNA within organization studies include job search processes, friendships, small worlds, and brokering roles, to name a few. The studies focusing on job search processes are based on Granovetter (1973)'s seminal work on this topic. His research on employees in the Boston area shows that people looking for jobs were better placed if they had a wide range of 'weak' contacts (acquaintances or colleagues) rather than a smaller number of 'strong' contacts (relatives or close friends). The idea behind the 'strength of weak ties' is that weak ties (e.g. social media such as Facebook) are diversified and thus provide job seekers with new information, while strong ties provide information that job seekers already know, as they are strongly connected with them. Granovetter's findings are still widely used in job search studies that adopt an SNA lens. For instance, Greenberg and Fernandez (2016) examined job searches among an MBA student population. Even though jobs found through strong ties (e.g. search based on personal contacts) are better paid, MBA students are more likely to accept job offers via weak ties (e.g. search based on business schools recruiting channels). The authors explain that they do so because they think they will have more potential to develop their career and qualify for non-monetary incentives. The authors conclude that business schools' recruiting services provide job offers in specific sectors that are otherwise difficult to access (e.g. finance, consulting) as well as information related to work opportunities that are often not available. In light of these results, the authors conclude that Granovetter (1973) was correct to stress the importance of the value of the information that derives from weak ties in the job search process.

Nevertheless, recent studies on job searches on online platforms such as LinkedIn (Garg and Telang, 2018) and Facebook (Gee, Jones, and Burke, 2017) arrived at different results. These studies show that strong ties have more positive outcomes (e.g. job leads, job interviews, and offers) than weak ties. However, Gee et al. (2017) propose a more nuanced conclusion. According to these authors, 'most people are helped through one of their numerous weak ties but a single stronger tie is significantly more valuable at the margin' (Gee et al., 2017, p. 485). In addition to the job search process, SNA is also used to explore the role of strong and weak ties in diverse types of settings and professions (e.g. healthcare, technology, finance). Right in our wheelhouse, Seibert et al. (2017 p. 1103) studied the networks of researchers and their publication productivity. They show that 'the number of strong ties in the focal author's professional support network is positively related to his or her total citation count, independent of the number and quality of publications'.

Are we living in an individualist society? According to SNA, the answer is 'no'. Rather, it suggests that we are living in a 'small world'—an important topic that was developed by Milgram and colleagues in the early 1970s (Korte and Milgram, 1970). To test this concept, individuals chosen from large populations were asked to mail a folder directly to a person. When they did not know this person, they were asked to target an intermediate person who would be more likely to know the target. They found that the mean number of intermediaries for completing the chain was 5.2. It is one foundational story that leads people to exclaim: 'We are living in a small world'. Recent research on 'small worlds' has explored this phenomenon by paying attention to friendship patterns in organizations. Kilduff et al. (2008) demonstrate that people are likely to perceive more clustering of colleagues and friends than actually exists. By analysing 'perceived' friendship networks and comparing them to 'real' friendship networks in four different organizations, they show that 'these perceived networks exhibited greater small world properties than the actual friendship networks' (Kilduff et al., 2008, p. 15). Such counterintuitive findings about smallworldedness give way to intriguing issues that could push further our knowledge of organizational friendship relationships. In this vein, Pillemer and Rothbard (2018) explore the dark side of friendship networks at work for individuals, groups, and organizations. They highlight how the introduction of social media in the workplace affects friendship emergence, development, and tension.

In accordance with friendship research, the concept of brokers (individuals who link disconnected individuals within the network) is currently an attractive research topic in SNA. It has been largely recognized that brokers have more social capital, as they have the opportunity to access a wide array of information. Network research is promoting the investigation of other levels of analysis to advance this topic. For example, Stea and Pedersen (2017) surveyed employees in a Danish knowledge firm and proposed a contingency explanation. More precisely, they show that brokers acting in a more stable context have a higher level of creativity than those whose tasks are related to research and development. For their part, Tasselli and Kilduff (2018) opt for what they call a 'personality–network fit' perspective to study the personality of an individual who is managing two sets of friends (cliques or networks) who are not friends with one another. Such a broker is called a simmelean broker and is a relatively common phenomenon (Burt, 2016). According to these authors, simmelean brokers present a diplomatic personality style involving a high self-monitoring orientation and a low propensity to speak about everything. Today, these studies on friendship ties and brokers are of critical importance for organizations, which are increasingly based on project teams and must build alliances across groups, departments, and divisions.

4.3 Interfirm network analysis

The application of SNA at the interorganizational level paved the way to a growing field of research in OTs called interfirm network analysis (INA). These network studies focus on the ties between different organizations in which one firm constitutes a hub or a focal organization. Such networks result from 'a collection of more than two firms that pursue repeated exchange relationships with one another but lack a legitimate organizational authority to manage the exchange process' (Fowler and Reisenwitz, 2013, p. 53). Largely influenced by strategic management literature, INA looks at the cooperative relationships dedicated to strengthening firms' competitive advantage and improving their efficiency and effectiveness as well as their chances of survival (Vandaie and Zaheer, 2014). Such cooperative relationships can be with suppliers, customers, competitors, and other organizational actors. Examples of such networks mainly include diverse forms of long-term partnerships, strategic alliances, outsourcing, and so on.

Figure 4.2 represents the archetypal form of an interfirm network. Such a network remains hierarchical, as there is most often a focal organization that monitors the relationships with its partners. Interfirm networks are generally created for a specific duration and they are dissolved or renegotiated after reaching the goals set prior to their formation. Nevertheless, interfirm network configurations can be adjusted or changed over time according to the environmental constraints they are facing (Kumar and Zaheer, 2019). Such networks generally emerge as a way to share research and development costs, gain access to new markets, capital, skills, and information or to speed up the introduction of new products and processes. In these networks, issues are typically resolved through reciprocated rules negotiated formally or informally between the partners (Powell, 1990).

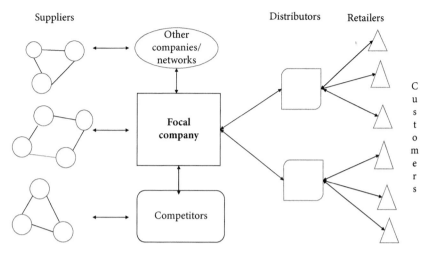

Figure 4.2 Interfirm network

INA is based on two complementary assumptions. First, the importance of networks stems from a locus of resources (e.g. technology, information, and legitimacy). While in economics, firms are seen as autonomous actors, the interfirm network perspective holds that firms gain access to resources and capabilities through their linkages between one another. Second, it assumes that the embeddedness of firms in strategic relations with other external firms impacts their actions and the outcome of such actions. Also, the embeddedness of the firm in a network of relations with other firms explains how and why firms behave strategically. Research on interfirm networks explores how the relational characteristics (e.g. centrality, reciprocity, trust, closure, brokerage, and other ties-related properties) between the firms influence their performance and efficiency. Researchers aim to shed light on the strengths and weaknesses of connectivity patterns characterizing these networks. They seek to identify the interfirm network's structural factors on which firms create or recreate connections and assess the characteristics of optimal network configurations to foster innovation.

INA is grounded in systematic empirical research on the antecedents or origins of interfirm networks, their structure, and the outcomes of such networks. Research on the antecedents of interfirm networks examines what motivates firms to enter and maintain their network of relationships (Fowler and Reisenwitz, 2013). The most frequent antecedents identified by the literature are related to the firm's need to increase its capabilities and resources as well as to acquire legitimacy and reinforce its social capital.

For example, Tatarynowicz, Sytch, and Gulati (2016) investigate why structures of organizational networks vary across industries. According to these authors, such variation is explained by differences in the industry's technological dynamism and in the value creation that stems from the network. Firms in dynamic industries generally develop wider and more open networks in order to facilitate knowledge transfer and innovation, while firms in stable industries tend to value closer networks in order to build reliable collaboration and preserve existing resources.

INA also pays a great deal of attention to the structure of interfirm networks. Far from being static, a network structure has its own dynamics. Additionally, a network's structure is likelier to evolve and transform owing to changes in its environment rather than as a result of the agency of network members. Thus, in an introduction to a special issue on interfirm networks in *Organization Science*, Ahuja, Soda, and Zaheer (2012) invite organization scholars to seriously consider network dynamics and changes in network structure over time. For example, Mazzola, Perrone, and Handfield (2018) examined the role of networks' dynamic positioning over time in the pharmaceutical industry. They show that these firms dynamically shift their positioning over time within their interfirm networks from central positions to structural holes (and vice-versa). This shifting dynamic allows pharmaceutical firms to develop new products. Yet the authors also found that such strategy must be carefully managed, because if applied too often, it can have the opposite effect (i.e. harming its capability to develop such products).

Finally, INA focuses on the effectiveness or outcomes of interfirm networks. More specifically, it examines the relationship between a firm's membership in an interfirm network and the different factors that could affect the network performance (e.g., strategic choices of firm members, knowledge creation and transfer, innovation). Interfirm network effectiveness is often explained by the capacity of firms to innovate and learn from their partners as a result of their collaborative endeavours. For instance, Zaheer and Bell (2005) examined the effect of a network's structure on the performance of firms in the Canadian insurance industry. They suggest that firms with superior network structures and internal innovation capabilities are better at developing new products. Building on network research and dynamic capabilities, Zaheer and Bell (2005, p. 820) put forth the notion of 'network-enabled capabilities', a concept that corresponds to the 'capability of an innovative firm to exploit a favourable network of structural position'.

Anchored in a realist onto-epistemology, INA assumes that organizations, though embedded in relations, are economic actors making rational choices in the context of bounded rationality and opportunism. Most of these studies use large sets of data (e.g. panel data sample, cross-sectional data sample) to test hypotheses. Researchers aim to replicate data on interfirm networks in order to develop mid-range theories about their antecedents, dynamics, and outcomes. After being criticized about the fact that knowledge on social ties cannot be applied at the organizational level, interfirm network research now also considers the impact of individual actors on network dynamics (Gulati and Srivastava, 2014). Current research also focuses on interfirm networks involving multi-level embeddedness (Brass et al., 2004; Ahuja et al., 2012).

4.4 Socioeconomic network analysis

The previous section proposes a firm-centric perspective on how a single firm can benefit from being part of a network. This section explores SENA; that is, interfirm networks as constituting a form of governance 'for itself' (Raab and Kenis, 2009). Such networks consist of three or more organizations linked through multilateral ties that facilitate the achievement of a common goal. Sydow and Windeler (1998, p. 265) define this type of interfirm network as 'an institutional arrangement among distinct but related for-profit organizations which are characterized by a special kind of network relationship, a certain degree of flexibility, and a logic of exchange that operates differently from that of markets and hierarchies'. These network organizations are often, but not always, developed by large corporations in industries where organizations face extreme technological uncertainty (e.g. biopharmaceutical, semi-conductor, automotive, electronics, financial services, and even film).

Figure 4.3 represents the archetypal form of a network organization. Such a network is characterized by repetitive exchanges among semi-autonomous organizations aimed at reducing transaction costs (Williamson, 1985). In the context of open innovation, firms act as agents of innovation and change while simultaneously being subjected to these forces. As a result, markets and hierarchies have become less effective at coordinating the R&D processes of firms engaged in related activities. The network organization thus balances 'the flexibility of markets with the predictability of traditional hierarchies' (Borgatti, 2003, p. 995). Neither market nor hierarchy, this hybrid organizational form is heterarchical; that is, 'no one organization formally presides over the network or has any formal quasi-hierarchical control' (Sydow and Müller-Seitz, 2020, p. 2). While members share substantial autonomy, a network organization is governed by contractual structures often involving a dedicated administrative unit formally established to coordinate the whole

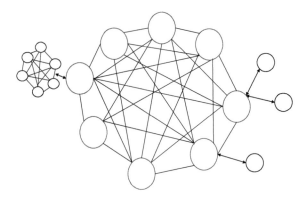

Figure 4.3 Network organization

network (Provan and Kenis, 2008). SENA studies how the advantages of being organized as a network are exploited in order to develop and maintain shared governance between distinct but related for-profit organizations that still have separate identities (Rometsch and Sydow, 2006).

SENA refers to some of the traditional vocabulary used in network research, but not exclusively. Researchers study the relationships or ties between the network members and how those members achieve the common goals set by the network 'as a whole'. More specifically, SENA focuses on the governance structures and processes of the entire network rather than on the organizations that compose the network (Provan, Fish, and Sydow, 2007). Therefore, this stream of network analysis often borrows concepts and approaches from social theory as it aims to understand the emergence, reproduction, and transformation of the interorganizational network governance and effectiveness (e.g. identity, leadership, framing, power). For example, Sydow and Windeler (1998) use Giddens' structuration theory to propose a framework to study managers organizing and evaluating practices as they monitor and coordinate the organization of a network. Although the network's economic environment imposes certain criteria and procedures for effectiveness, managers knowledgeably interpret, reproduce, and even transform these according to the institutional constraints and opportunities they face. Dagnino, Levanti, and Mocciaro (2016, p. 349) refer to network research and complexity science to come up with 'a multilevel interpretive framework that clarifies the role and scope of intentional agency at different structural levels of interorganizational networks'.

Empirical works in SENA draw mainly on longitudinal single case studies to shed light on how network managers ensure that all network members contribute to optimizing the network's resources and effectiveness in spite of their inability to guarantee an equal benefit to all members. For example, Sydow (2004) relied on a 10-years longitudinal study of a network of industrial insurance brokers to examine the effectiveness of their governance structures and processes. From 2003 to 2010, he also studied, with a colleague, the leadership of Intel in the Sematech network within the semi-conductor industry (Müller-Seitz and Sydow, 2012). They show how Intel skilfully 'manoeuvre[s] between networks' (its own interfirm network and the Sematech network) to exercise leadership in Sematech while taking advantage of its position by guiding technology development along its own supply chain. In a recent paper, these authors draw on two longitudinal case studies (2004–2010; 2010–2013) of network organizations in the semi-conductor industry (respectively, Sematech and International Technology Roadmap for Semi-conductors). They examine how open innovation is managed in these network organizations in the face of technological discontinuity (Sydow and Müller-Seitz, 2020).

Generally speaking, most research in network studies emphasizes positive network functionalities and outcomes, while placing a special focus on effectiveness. SENA is no exception. Yet, some recent studies take a different viewpoint by looking at the failure of collaborative efforts in network organizations. For example, Moretti and Zirpoli (2016) examine the Venice Film Festival and its local hospitality network. They found that 'the presence of two competing frames for network coordination initiated several processes of mobilization and coalition-building affecting the network's evolution' (Moretti and Zirpoli, 2016, p. 628). Based on this case study, they propose a 'theory of network failure'. In the same vein, Fortwengel and Sydow (2020) studied a network that originally consisted of seven small- and medium-sized enterprises but then accepted a very large multinational firm as a new member. Subsequently, the coordination of the network began to deteriorate. These studies invite researchers to pay closer attention to network micro-dynamics, that is, to individuals' actions and agency, as the actions of network actors can have important consequences for the network's development.

4.5 Actor–network theory

In the 1980s, Michel Callon (1986) and Bruno Latour (1987), from the Paris Group of Science and Technology Studies, focused on an important aspect of the contemporary world neglected in social sciences: scientific and technological innovation. How are they produced, disseminated, and socially accepted? According to Law (1986), Callon and Latour's works gave birth to a new way of understanding the world called the actor–network theory (ANT), or the sociology of translation. Unlike previous forms of network analysis—which are closer to a realist onto-epistemology—ANT is based on a constructionist onto-epistemology. Still, ANT belongs to the network analysis family as it emphasizes the way relationships are mutually constitutive of networks. These relationships consist of, and link, both human (actors) and non-human (actants) entities in a chain of translation.

Within ANT's framework, actors can be individuals, groups, and even objects (ranging from texts to technological objects and artefacts) that all have agency (hence the name 'actants'). According to ANT researchers, the social and the technical cannot be dissociated from one another. Human entities (e.g. individuals, groups, and organizations) and non-human entities (e.g. knowledge, material and financial resources, policies, programmes, reports) are mutually constitutive and actively involved in the making of organizational worlds. Because they are part of a network association or an 'action-net' (Czarniawska and Hernes, 2005), human and non-human entities help to define the network and the network recursively influences who they are and what they do. Of course, only human entities can put non-human entities in circulation in a network. However, when making up a network, a non-human entity is necessarily vested with agency. It has the capacity to make others do things that they would not ordinarily do. This symmetrical approach between human and non-human entities is central to the earliest ANT case studies. Such is the case of Callon's (1986) famous essay on the domestication of scallops in St. Brieuc Bay or Latour's search for 'who has killed Aramis'.

Rather than exploring network properties (e.g. density, distance, network position, reciprocity, membership, trust), ANT proposes an attractive set of concepts mixing networks, technology, innovation, translation, and so on, which is perfectly aligned with the network society we partake in. Take for instance the innovation process. Such a process starts with an original idea put forward by various stakeholders and is then materialized by a team of engineers and technicians. From the idea of the new product or service to the innovation per se, there is a chain of actors that need to align their divergent interests and translate them into a common language. The actor–network around an innovation is thus constructed gradually from the moment where the central actors (called translators or spokespersons) mobilize other participants and non-human entities as supporters of their idea, while simultaneously participating in redefining this idea in a way that will maintain this support. In this translation process, translators are supported by 'mediators' (actors having the capacity to create new connections, displace others, and transform the network), and 'intermediaries' (entities that stabilize the network such as agreements, devices, plans, prototypes, and so on). The success of the 'translation' process is based on the cooperation of all actors concerned with building the actor–network.

This brings us to our next point: what is meant by the chain of translation? ANT proposes four moments of translation: problematization, interessement, enrolment, and mobilization. Problematization starts when translators face complex organizing issues (e.g. how could the decline in the population of scallops in St. Brieux Bay be reduced (Callon, 1986)? How could someone get a start-up off the ground in the aerospace industry when they have only recently graduated from university (Lamine, 2017)? How can the complexity of public health interventions be managed (Bilodeau and Potvin, 2018)?). To solve these issues, there is a need to reformulate or literally 'translate' them such that they will appear acceptable or manageable by diverse actors or groups having divergent interests. When an issue is reformulated, allies from diverse horizons must be recruited and appropriate tools and artefacts (actants) developed. This is the interessement moment where the translators attempt to attach specific identities to key actors (e.g. scientists, industrials, activists) to ensure they support the way the issue has been reformulated. If the interessement is successful, actors and actants become enrolled in the network. Simply put, actors start playing their roles (e.g. designing an experiment, developing a prototype, or adopting rules and structures of governance) as defined through prior negotiations, and align their interests. Finally, translators invite the representative of the main groups of actors involved around the issue to build alliances. Therefore, in the mobilization moment, the network is said to have achieved an 'obligatory point of passage'. More specifically, it marks the partial achievement of complex organizing, as a point of no return has been agreed upon and become irreversible. The network has thus reached a level of stabilization through which all actors must pass to obtain what they need and to be part of the network.

These translation moments are hardly linear; nor are they necessarily slated to succeed. Indeed, it is not always easy to create different and mutually compatible meanings in order to 'interest', 'enrol', and 'mobilize' a group of actors to solve complex and sometimes controversial issues. A way to achieve this is for the translators to accomplish multiple displacements or to 'draft' the controversy in several distinct smaller parts to induce small wins that will eventually lead to some irreversible gains. Each translation (or displacement) contributes to extending the actor–network beyond the initial group. For example, Lamine (2017) studied the start-up project of a young entrepreneur driven by the development of a nanosatellite in aerospace. To deal with the technical uncertainties around the new technology and his lack of experience and resources, the young entrepreneur (the spokesperson of the new technology) had to translate his project three times. In order to cope with technical difficulties, he enlisted the help of lecturers, international researchers, and engineering students nearing the end of their studies and he went from developing nanosatellites to developing picosatellites. Then, rather trying to sell the satellite, which was risky at the time, he offered a certification and made a prototype. This was made possible by enrolling new partners such as aerospace local firms and incubators. Finally, to gain the interest of investors who had initially withheld their endorsement for project, he entered negotiations with three international launching stations simultaneously. By displacing the initial issue three times, the young entrepreneur eventually succeeded in weaving a network around his project and in developing an irreversible innovation; that is, a start-up that generated sales and revenues one year after its creation. Still, one must remember that the stability of a network is always temporary. Translation is in constant flux, subject to negotiation, compromise, subversion, and revolution. As a result, there is always a possibility that the outcome of a translation process will lead to unintended consequences.

At first sight, ANT reminds us of the strategic model in which strategic actors with bounded rationality build alliances and align their interests with others around a negotiated definition of the world. However, this would be a reductionist interpretation of ANT (Alcadipani and Hassard, 2010). The expression 'actor–network' implies that the actors themselves (human and non-human) are the network. Put differently, agency in ANT is not the privilege of a single strategic actor but that of a network of humans and non-humans bound together in action. Contrarily to what the strategic model traditionally assumed, translators do not precede networks; rather, they *perform* networks through their connections with others. All actors/actants contribute to the definition of the identities and roles of other actors/actants. It is their associations or their connections with others that confer to them the possibility to act.

According to ANT, phenomena such as organization, innovation, and change are viewed as the assemblage of the heterogeneous human and non-human entities that make them up (Attila, 2005). ANT proposes a distributed and performative view of organizing by focusing the actions of assembling that bring a network into being. Its emphasis on non-human entities has significantly impacted OTs over the past 25 years. While the symmetrical approach between human and non-human entities was at first provocative when ANT emerged as a new stream of research, it is now largely accepted that matter matters in organizing (see Chapter 7, Section 7.4).

4.6 What makes network studies so popular in OTs?

From social networks to interorganizational networks and beyond, network studies have carved out a growing niche in OTs over the past 25 years. They have expanded across disciplines and generated diverse, varied, and somewhat contradictory empirical findings. What are the consequences of taking such a turn in OTs? What made network studies so popular and attractive?

Of note, network studies can be credited for allowing OTs to take a 'relational turn'. Taking a relational turn brings a new level of analysis to organization studies; that is, relationships between entities or actors (e.g. individuals, groups, firms, technologies). By assuming that actors' behaviours are a result of their relationships, network analysis invites researchers to reject the substantive or entitative view of organizational action in favour of a relational approach. Indeed, according to a network studies perspective, it is no longer the institution (i.e. the organization), the group, or the individuals that are the focus of attention, but rather the relations between them. For instance, a middle manager or a human entity does not exist per se outside their relationships. Managers exist and behave as managers only through their interactions with superiors and subordinates. The same logic applies to their superiors and subordinates.

Taking a relational turn also sheds new light on core debates in OTs. First, most network studies reject the modern dualism between the micro and macro levels of analysis. Network thinking predisposes the researcher to focus on multiple levels of analysis as they simultaneously see both the individuals' embeddedness within structures and the emergence of structure from the micro-relations between individuals. In network analysis, 'actors are part of their relationships and relationships are made up of actors' (Galaskiewicz, 2007, p. 5). The researcher freely circulates between the micro and the macro instead of being concerned with one level at a time only. Second, network studies provide a different perspective on power as constructed through associations of weaknesses. As a matter of fact, the balance of power resides in the aggregation of weak ties or the capacity to establish obligatory points of passage. Third, network analysis proposes a different way of seeing the contextuality of organizational or social events. Each node (or obligatory point of passage in ANT) is contextualized through the set of ties it has established with other nodes. Therefore, the context exists only through the moving and fluid reticular texture of ties. According to Latour (2005), network studies open the door to a 'flat' ontology of organizing. Fourth, relational thinking also rejects the distinction between society and nature while it takes into account non-human interactants. While this principle is far from being shared by all types of network analysis, it nevertheless should be mentioned as it is an important principle of relational thinking in OTs as well as in sociology.

Yet as Galaskiewicz (2007) claimed some years ago, network studies still haven't delivered on their promises. Most of network analysis continues to rely heavily on grounded empirical analysis that examines how resources are distributed between actors as well as the latent structures of relationships between them. Network analysis belongs to two different worldviews. On the one hand, structural network approaches (SNA and INA, which are used predominantly by American quantitative social scientists) have been widely criticized for not taking into account either individual motivation and cognition or the embeddedness of networks in a larger cultural, ecological, or societal context. On the other hand, the poststructuralist network approaches (SENA and ANT, which are used predominantly by European qualitative researchers) emerged as a way to renew network studies. However, these two poststructuralist streams of research remain marginal and have been criticized for their dismissal of the social structure and the political context at play in network governance and stabilization. In fact, there is very little dialogue between the different network analysis traditions, which compromises network analysis's ability to deliver on its promises, despite its prodigious expansion.

Network studies have been very popular over the past 25 years, and this popularity will not vanish in the future—not least because we are living in a network society! Two epistemological rationales explain the popularity of network analysis. First, the concept of network is a powerful 'loose' metaphor for building knowledge about contemporaneous organizations. The network metaphor enables researchers to move from local actors' behaviours to broader questions of embeddedness and connectivity between individuals or organizations. It also supports multiple characteristics to describe organizational dynamics such as mobility, distribution, self-organization, complexity, fragmentation, and so on. It can also take on multiple forms of interconnections (e.g. web, action-net, discursive networks). Furthermore, network analysis reminds us of the analytical structure of general system theory in OTs. As systemic analysis is based on a set of properties (e.g. interaction, retroaction, interdependence, and equifinality), network analysis is also working on the existence of a specific set of network properties (centrality, density, membership, and obligatory passage points). Systemic analysis pervaded the twentieth century, and there is little doubt that network analysis will continue to spread its influence in the twenty-first century.

Second, network analysis shares diverse sets of methodological devices that make it possible to study relatedness issues around organizing. More than a theory or a paradigm, network analysis is first and foremost a set of methodological tools ranging from a diversity of epistemological positions. This is what explains the popularity of this vibrant research programme! For instance, SNA offers mathematical concepts, graph technics, and software packages to rigorously describe how nodes connect through ties. Conversely, ANT is a descriptive tool that enables to retrace connections and associations between heterogeneous entities. As Latour (2005, p. 61) suggests in *Reassembling the Social*, you have to 'follow the actors themselves'. In between both ends of this spectrum, Berthod, Grothe-Hammer, and Sydow (2017) propose a mixed-method approach called 'network ethnography', which consists of drawing on both SNA and a set of techniques of organizational ethnography to research interorganizational networks.

The emergence and development of network studies in the past two decades helped us to take a relational turn in OTs. Up to now, we have learnt much about their patterns, antecedents, and outcomes. However, much is still unknown about how they are formed, how they evolve, and how to manage them. Over the past ten years, we have witnessed important calls for the need to go beyond a structuralist view of network analysis in order to better understand their dynamics, their transformative capacity, and their cross-level interactions and outcomes. Cross-fertilization between diverse forms of network analysis, disciplines, and methods is thus welcome as a way to improve our 'understanding of the transformative impact of network dynamics on organizations and society' (Clegg et al., 2016, p. 277).

References

Ahuja, G., Soda, G., & Zaheer, A. 2012. The Genesis and Dynamics of Organizational Networks. *Organization Science*, 23, 434–448.

Akrich, M., Callon, M., & Latour, B. 2006. *Sociologie de la traduction. Textes fondateurs*. Paris, Presses des Mines de Paris.

Alcadipani, R. & Hassard, J. 2010. Actor-Network Theory, Organizations and Critique: Towards a Politics of Organizing. *Organization*, 17, 419–435.

Allen, M. P. 1974. The Structure of Interorganizational Elite Cooptation: Interlocking Corporate Directorates. *American Sociological Review*, 39, 393–406.

Attila, B. 2005. Shadowing Software and Clinical Records: On the Ethnography of Non-Humans and Heterogeneous Contexts. *Organization*, 12, 357–378.

Barnes, J. 1954. Class and Committees in a Norwegian Island Parish. *Human Relations*, 7, 39–58.

Berthod, O., Grothe-Hammer, M., & Sydow, J. 2017. Network Ethnography. *Organizational Research Methods*, 20, 299–323.

Bilodeau, A. & Potvin, L. 2018. Unpacking Complexity in Public Health Interventions with the Actor-Network Theory. *Health Promotion International*, 33, 173–181.

Borgatti, S. P. 2003. The Network Paradigm in Organizational Research: A Review and Typology. *Journal of Management*, 29, 991–1013.

Brass, D. J., Galaskiewicz, J., Greve, H. R., & Tsai, W. 2004. Taking Stock of Networks and Organizations: A Multilevel Perspective. *The Academy of Management Journal*, 47, 795–817.

Burt, R. S. 1992. *Structural Holes. The Social Structure of Competition*. Cambridge, MA, Harvard University Press.

Burt, R. S. 2016. Integrating Brokerage and Closure as Social Capital. Intra-Organizational Network Conference, Lexington, University of Kentucky, 23–24 April.

Burt, R. S., Kilduff, M., & Tasselli, S. 2013. Social Network Analysis: Foundations and Frontiers on Advantage. *Annual Review of Psychology*, 64, 527–547.

Callon, M. 1986. Some Elements of a Sociology of Translation: Domestication of the Scallops and the Fishermen of St Brieuc Bay. *In*: Law, J. (ed.) *Power, Action and Belief: A New Sociology of Knowledge?* London, Routledge & Kegan-Paul, 196–233.

Clegg, S., Josserand, E., Mehra, A., & Pitsis, T. S. 2016. The Transformative Power of Network Dynamics: A Research Agenda. *Organization Studies*, 37, 277–291.

Coleman, J. 1990. *Foundations of Social Theory*. Cambridge, MA, The Belknap Press.

Czarniawska, B. & Hernes, T. 2005. *Actor-Network Theory and Organizing*. Malmo, Sweden, Liber and Copenhagen Business School Press.

Dagnino, G. B., Levanti, G., & Mocciaro, L.D.A. 2016. Structural Dynamics and Intentional Governance in Strategic Interorganizational Network Evolution: A Multilevel Approach. *Organization Studies*, 37, 349–373.

Fortwengel, J. & Sydow, J. 2020. When Many Davids Collaborate with One Goliath: How Inter-organizational Networks (Fail to) Manage Size Differentials. *British Journal of Management*, 31, 403–420.

Fowler, J. G. & Reisenwitz, T. H. 2013. A Review of Interfirm Network: A Deeper Understanding of the Relationships Paradigm. *Journal of Business Strategies*, 30, 52–95.

Galaskiewicz, J. 2007. Has a Network Theory of Organizational Behaviour Lived Up to Its Promises? *Management and Organization Review*, 3, 1–18.

Galaskiewicz, J. & Zaheer, A. 1999. Networks of Competitive Advantage. *Research in the Sociology of Organizations*, 16, 237–261.

Garg, R. & Telang, R. 2018. To Be or Not to Be Linked: Online Social Networks and Job Search by Unemployed Workforce. *Management Science*, 64, 3926–3941.

Gee, L., Jones, J., & Burke, M. 2017. Social Networks and Labor Markets: How Strong Ties Relate to Job Finding on Facebook's Social Network. *Journal of Labour Economics*, 35, 485–518.

Giddens, A. 1984. *The Constitution of Society*. Cambridge, UK, Polity.

Granovetter, M. S. 1973. The Strength of Weak Ties. *American Journal of Sociology*, 6, 1360–1380.

Granovetter, M. S. 1985. Economic Action and Social Structure: The Problem of Embeddedness. *American Journal of Sociology*, 3, 481–510.

Greenberg, J. & Fernandez, R. 2016. The Strength of Weak Ties in MBA Job Search: A Within-Person Test. *Sociological Science*, 3, 296–316.

Gulati, R. & Srivastava, S. B. 2014. Bringing Agency Back into Network Research: Constrained Agency and Network Action. *In*: Brass, D.J. Labianca, G. Mehra, A. Halgin, D.S. Borgatti, SP (eds.) *Contemporary Perspectives on Organizational Social Networks*. Bingley: Emerald Publishing, 73–93.

Kilduff, M. & Tsai, W. 2012. *Social Networks and Organization*. London, Sage.

Kilduff, M., Crossland, C., Tsai, W., & Krackhardt, D. 2008. Organizational Network Perceptions versus Reality: A Small World After All? *Organizational Behavior and Human Decision Processes*, 107, 15–28.

Knox, H., Savage, M., & Harvey, P. 2006. Social Networks and the Study of Relations: Networks as Method, Metaphor and Form. *Economy and Society*, 35, 113–140.

Korte, C. & Milgram, S. 1970. Acquaintance Networks Between Racial Groups: Application of the Small World Method. *Journal of Personality and Social Psychology*, 15, 101–108.

Kumar, P. & Zaheer, A. 2019. Ego-Network Stability and Innovation in Alliances. *Academy of Management Journal*, 62, 691–716.

Lamb, N. H. & Roundy, P. 2016. The 'Ties That Bind' Board Interlocks Research: A Systematic Review. *Management Research Review*, 39, 1516–1542.

Lamine, W. 2017. The Social Network and Entrepreneurial Process: A Sociotechnical Approach. *Thunderbird International Business Review*, 59, 623–663.

Latour, B. 1987. *Science in Action: How to Follow Scientists and Engineers Through Society*. Cambridge, MA, Harvard University Press.

Latour, B. 2005. *Reassembling the Social: An Introduction to Actor-Network Theory*. Oxford, UK, Oxford University Press.

Law, J. 1986. *Power, Action and Belief. A New Sociology of Knowledge?* Keele, UK, Sociological Review Monograph.

Levine, J. 1972. The Sphere of Influence. *American Sociological Review*, 37, 14–27.

Mazzola, E., Perrone, G., & Handfield, R. 2018. Change Is Good, But Not Too Much: Dynamic Positioning in the Interfirm Network and New Product Development. *Journal of Product Innovation Management*, 35, 960–982.

Mercklé, P. 2011. *Sociologie des réseaux sociaux*. Paris, La Découverte.

Monaghan, S., Lavelle, J., & Gunnigle, P. 2017. Mapping Networks: Exploring the Utility of Social Network Analysis in Management Research and Practice. *Journal of Business Research*, 76, 136–144.

Moretti, A. & Zirpoli, F. 2016. A Dynamic Theory of Network Failure: The Case of the Venice Film Festival and the Local Hospitality System. *Organization Studies*, 37, 607–633.

Müller-Seitz, G. & Sydow, J. 2012. Maneuvering between Networks to Lead—A Longitudinal Case Study in the Semiconductor Industry. *Long Range Planning*, 45, 105–135.

Pillemer, J. & Rothbard, N. P. 2018. Friends without Benefits: Understanding the Dark Sides of Workplace Friendship. *Academy of Management Review*, 43, 635–660.

Powell, W. W. 1990. Neither Market Nor Hierarchy: Network Forms of Organization. *Research in Organizational Behavior*, 12, 295–336.

Provan, K. G. & Kenis, P. 2008. Modes of Network Governance: Structure, Management, and Effectiveness. *Journal of Public Administration Research and Theory: J-PART*, 18, 229–252.

Provan, K. G., Fish, A., & Sydow, J. 2007. Interorganizational Networks at the Network Level: A Review of the Empirical Literature on Whole Networks. *Journal of Management*, 33, 479–516.

Raab, J. & Kenis, P. 2009. Heading toward a Society of Networks Empirical Developments and Theoretical Challenges. *Journal of Management Inquiry*, 18, 198–210.

Radcliffe-Brown, A. R. 1940. On Social Structure. *Journal of the Royal Anthropological Institute*, 70, 1–12.

Roethlisberger, F. J. & Dickson, W. J. 1939. *Management and the Worker*. Cambridge, MA, Harvard University Press.

Rometsch, M. & Sydow, J. 2006. On Identities of Networks and Organizations—The Case of Franchising. *In*: Kornberger, M. & Gudergan, S. (eds) *Only Connect: Neat Words, Networks and Identities*, pp. 19–47. Copenhagen, Copenhagen Business School Press.

Seibert, S. E., Kacmar, K. M., Kraimer, M. L., Downes, P. E., & Noble, D. 2017. The Role of Research Strategies and Professional Networks in Management Scholars' Productivity. *Journal of Management*, 43, 1103–1130.

Stea, D. & Pedersen, T. 2017. Not All Brokers Are Alike: Creative Implications of Brokering Networks in Different Work Functions. *Human Relations*, 70, 668–693.

Sydow, J. 2004. Network Development by Means of Network Evaluation? Explorative Insights from a Case in the Financial Services Industry. *Human Relations*, 57, 201–220.

Sydow, J. & Müller-Seitz, G. 2020. Open Innovation at the Interorganizational Network Level—Stretching Practices to Face Technological Discontinuities in the Semiconductor Industry. *Technological Forecasting and Social Change*, 155, 1–12.

Sydow, J. & Windeler, A. 1998. Organizing and Evaluating Interfirm Networks: A Structurationist Perspective on Network Processes and Effectiveness. *Organization Science*, 9, 265–284.

Tasselli, S. & Kilduff, M. 2018. When Brokerage between Friendship Cliques Endangers Trust: A Personality–Network Fit Perspective. *Academy of Management Journal*, 61, 802–825.

Tatarynowicz, A., Sytch, M., & Gulati, R. 2016. Environmental Demands and the Emergence of Social Structure: Technological Dynamism and Interorganizational Network Forms. *Administrative Science Quarterly*, 61, 52–86.

Vandaie, R. & Zaheer, A. 2014. Surviving Bear Hugs: Firm Capability, Larger Partner Alliances, and Growth. *Strategic Management Journal*, 35, 566–577.

Williamson, O. E. 1985. *The Economic Institutions of Capitalism*. New York, Free Press.

Yang, S., Keller, F. B., & Zheng, L. 2017. *Social Network Analysis. Methods and Examples*. New York, Sage.

Zaheer, A. & Bell, G. G. 2005. Benefiting From Network Position: Firm Capabilities, Structural Holes, and Performance. *Strategic Management Journal*, 26, 809–825.

5

Knowledge Studies

In Chapter 4, we saw that globalization and the development of information technologies fostered the rapid expansion of network studies in organization theories (OTs). These same factors also explain the popularity of knowledge-based studies, which has been steadily rising since the 1990s. An enormous body of work on knowledge, competence and capabilities, learning, and knowing has emerged over the past few decades. All together, they reflect the assumption that organizations today mobilize the cognitive capabilities of individuals, teams, and communities to maintain their competitive edge. Such studies deepen our understanding of what is commonly called 'the knowledge economy', which is radically changing the way organizations produce, manage, and transfer knowledge. Initially, the increasingly rapid growth of intangible capital—knowledge-driven activities (e.g. R&D, training, and skilled jobs)—have given rise to knowledge studies. Subsequently, then, the technological revolution led to a rapid increase in production gains, as well as to the emergence of new industries whose activities relied explicitly on knowledge (e.g. multimedia, electronic commerce). As a result, knowledge studies are now shedding new light on current organizational innovations and trends and have far-reaching impacts on the expansion of OTs.

Knowledge studies are interested in how knowledge in organizations is acquired, maintained, extended, and sometimes lost or forgotten. They raise fundamental questions about the nature of knowledge: Can we transform tacit knowledge into explicit knowledge? How do organizations learn? Is knowledge an individual or a collective phenomenon? These questions are not new in themselves; indeed, they have been key to the emergence and development of OTs. However, it is only in the past 25 years that OTs have considered them seriously. In order to answer those questions, knowledge studies bring together different research disciplines that are interested in the creation, sharing, and dissemination of knowledge across a variety of work settings, organizational levels, and contexts. More specifically, knowledge studies are the cornerstone of four research disciplines in OTs: human resource management; strategic management; organizational change; and innovation research.

Organization Theories in the Making. Linda Rouleau, Oxford University Press.
© Linda Rouleau (2022). DOI: 10.1093/oso/9780198792024.003.0006

OTs emerged at the beginning of the twentieth century with Taylorism, which proposed a redefinition of productive knowledge that bifurcated the concepts of planning and execution into two separate tasks. Taylor was convinced that simplifying jobs and deskilling industrial workers via scientific management principles would improve individual work performance, which would in turn benefit the firm. One century later, organizations are endorsing a completely different discourse about knowledge, and are promoting the development of the skills and cognitive capacities of bright, educated workers. In the context of the new economy, does this discourse help restore the autonomy and discretion of what is now generally referred to as the 'knowledge worker'? Are knowledge managers the 'Taylors' of the new century? These questions set the stage for the present chapter.

This chapter will first explore the historical development of what has been coined the 'indeterminacy of knowledge' in OTs. Then, it will review four streams of knowledge studies that have emerged since the end of the 1990s in OTs: knowledge management; dynamic capabilities; organizational learning; and organizational knowing. Each of these research streams on knowledge is inspired by diverse sets of theories and disciplines and is undergirded by different views of knowledge: knowledge as a commodity; knowledge as an intangible asset; knowledge as a mental structure; and knowledge as a situated activity. Finally, the chapter will discuss unresolved paradoxes underlying knowledge studies.

5.1 The indeterminacy of knowledge

One of the most longstanding issues in OTs concerns the central problem of enhancing the work performance of individuals, teams, and groups within and around organizations. This critical issue was first addressed by Frederick Winslow Taylor in his famous book *The Principle of Scientific Management* (1911). According to Taylor, the main reason behind the apparent inefficiency of many organizations was that skilled workers were able to control the use of their craft and experiential knowledge because their employers ignored what was the most efficient way to perform those tasks. Taylor's solution was to separate planning from execution. He was convinced that for each task there was 'one best way' to accomplish it, which could be uncovered only through time and motion studies based on scientific principles. According to Taylor, the only way to increase workers' performance, and thus industrial efficiency, was to let engineers or methods officers 'scientifically' determine the best way to accomplish each of the workers' tasks. Based on scientific facts, managers could design systematic training and development activities to enhance worker productivity. However, a fundamental issue remained: 'How do we ensure that employees do as managers say?' (Sewell, 2005, p. 688). Labour process theorists called this uncertainty 'the indeterminacy of labour'.

Some decades later, Friedrich Hayek, an economist who is well known for his paper titled 'The use of knowledge in society' (Hayek, 1945), endorsed the opposite position. In his paper, he argued that scientific knowledge had only a limited impact on increasing the performance of individuals and organizations. Rather, he claimed that 'decisions must be left to the people who are familiar with [the particular] circumstances [of time and place], who know directly of the relevant changes and of the resources immediately available to meet them' (Hayek, 1945, p. 524). In other words, because individuals' practical knowledge of local and specific circumstances is central to work and economic performance, it is almost impossible to centralize and accumulate knowledge about how tasks should be performed. Indeed, in this view, this knowledge resides within each and every individual worker.

At present, the issue surrounding the separation of task planning from task execution, or the centralization of worker knowledge in organizations, is still front and centre—as though it never went away. Since the beginning of the twenty-first century, the uncertainty surrounding the conversion of physical efforts into profitable work has now been replaced by what is called 'the indeterminacy of knowledge' (Sewell, 2005). Managers now develop programmes and procedures to help employees achieve their full potential as a means of ensuring that organizations get the full benefit of their 'cognitive' capacities or competencies. Drawing on the assumption that organizations have shifted from natural resources to intellectual assets, the *modus operandi* of the knowledge economy stands on the conversion of knowledge work into value creation and competitiveness.

There are indeed new conditions underlying the use of knowledge in organizations. In the globalization context that has characterized the past 25 years, competitive pressures on organizations have greatly increased. Advances in communication and technology, as well as the global transformation of the value chain, have given rise to a far more competitive business environment. In addition to the need to compress product life cycles, organizations are now facing constant demand for product and service innovation. As a result, more and more knowledge-intensive organizations are able to provide knowledge-intensive support for the business processes of other organizations. The emergence of new sectors around social media, cultural industries, and the artificial intelligence industry also contributes to making knowledge a key and central feature of contemporaneous organizations. Furthermore, organizations are merging, restructuring, and constantly looking for new forms of organizational structures that will enable them to extract and mobilize knowledge. It is in this context that we are witnessing an increased salience of knowledge management and multiple forms of knowledge work.

Overall, the aim of knowledge studies is to better understand the characteristics of knowledge that have critical implications for organizations and management. In so doing, knowledge studies have developed a set of constructs related to knowledge, such as competence, capabilities, expertise, and skills, to name a few. Knowledge studies also zoom in on various dimensions of knowledge, such as tacit/explicit knowledge, individual/organizational knowledge, and exploration/exploitation of knowledge. In the following sections, we will explore how four research streams in knowledge studies conceptualize and investigate why and how they can help us to better understand knowledge in modern organizations (see Table 5.1).

5.2 Knowledge management

Today, all organizations and managers need more and more information to be instantaneously captured and diffused as precisely and accurately as possible. In this context of information abundance, collaborative information technologies appear to be the 'Holy Grail' for many managers; in other words, more information has become synonymous with better organizing! This is the credo of the knowledge management stream, also referred to as the 'commodity' school (McIver et al., 2012). In this research stream, researchers consider knowledge as residing in information or in any facts systematically organized around a specific issue. Understanding knowledge in terms of information is not without consequences. It entails that similarly to any other artefact or object, knowledge can be 'possessed, stored, and transferred, though its cognitive location can create challenges for its retrieval and use' (Kuhn and Jackson, 2008, p. 455). Consequently, researchers of the commodity school generally try to identify the various types of knowledge found within an organization and to understand how they impact other organizational phenomena, such as innovation, alliance formation, and performance (McIver et al., 2012).

Based on their work on the capacity of Japanese companies to use and produce new knowledge to develop successful products and technologies, Nonaka and Takeuchi (1995) led scholarly efforts to develop the commodity view of knowledge. In their best-selling book, *The Knowledge-creating*

Table 5.1 Synoptic overview of knowledge studies

	Knowledge management	Dynamic capabilities	Organizational learning	Organizational knowing
Definition (views of knowledge)	Information that can be codified, stored, and distributed (knowledge as a commodity)	Intangible resources that can be estimated, quantified, accumulated, and valued (knowledge as intangible assets)	Process(es) by which organizations modify their mental representations of reality (knowledge as a mental structure)	Knowing is performed via participation in social activity (knowledge as a situated activity)
Research question	How do tacit and explicit knowledge interact along a continuum?	How does organizational knowledge contribute to the competitive advantage of the firm?	How do organizations learn, forget, and remember?	How is knowledge skilfully performed through interactions?
Locus of knowledge	Individuals and information technologies	Organizations and their routines	Organizational and individuals	Situated in social relations
Organization	A socio-technical system of knowledge (project and information system)	A set of integrated organizational capabilities, competencies, and routines	Ability to process new and unexpected information and solve a variety of problems	A network of community practices

Influences	Nonaka and Takeuchi (1995); Nonaka and von Krogh (2009)	Barney (1991); Teece et al. (1997)	Cyert and March (1963); Argyris and Schön (1978); March (1991)	Brown and Duguid (1991); Lave and Wenger (1991)
Disciplines	Knowledge management (information technology and human resources management)	Resource-based view (RBV) and dynamic capability (DC) (strategic management)	Learning theories (organizational change)	Communities of practice and performative approaches (innovation)
Conceptual resources	Knowledge creation and conversion, explicit and tacit knowledge, task competencies	Resources, capabilities and competencies, knowledge accumulation, integration, utilization, and reconfiguration	Single- and double-loop learning, exploitation/exploration, memory, and ambidexterity	Communities of practice, communicative knowledge, skilful performance, knowledgeability
Methods	Quantitative and case studies	Firms' data sets and surveys	Qualitative studies (interviews)	Qualitative studies (ethnography)
Exemplars	Kimble et al. (2016); Mariano and Awazu (2017); Powell and Ambrosini (2017)	Helfat and Peteraf (2003); Dosi et al. (2008); Eriksson (2014); Riviere and Bass (2019)	Easterby-Smith and Lyles (2011); O'Reilly and Tushman (2013); Miller and Martignoni (2016); Argote and Hora (2017);	Gherardi (2009, 2016); Pyrko et al. (2017); Sandberg et al. (2017)

Company: How Japanese Companies Create the Dynamics of Innovation, they introduced the 'knowledge creation theory'. Their overall aim was to show that the superior performance of Japanese companies, compared with most European and US companies at the time, was due to their ability 'to create new knowledge, disseminate it throughout the organization, and embody it in products, services, and systems' (Nonaka and Takeuchi, 1995, p. viii). With the right incentives, knowledge can be produced, codified, shared, and managed just as any other manufactured goods. According to these authors, there are three models of knowledge management. The first one is a top-down model, where leaders or managers create new knowledge, which they can then leverage to manage the coordinated action of many actors in the form of guidelines and handbooks. The second model is bottom-up and considers knowledge as created individually and entrepreneurially. Here, leaders play the role of sponsors by selecting individually produced knowledge and promoting it by channelling additional resources to its continued development and creation. Lastly, the 'middle-up-down' model assumes that knowledge is created by self-organizing teams. Here, leaders play two roles: that of catalysts who influence and facilitate knowledge creation; and that of evaluators who screen knowledge by assessing its quality or by assigning it some value.

Later on, Nonaka and von Krogh (2009, p. 635) defined the process of knowledge creation as consisted of two consecutive steps: (i) knowledge emergence (making available and amplifying knowledge created by individuals); followed by (ii) knowledge formalization (crystallizing knowledge and connecting it to an organization's knowledge system). They also articulated the two foundational premises of knowledge creation theory; that is, 'tacit and explicit knowledge can be conceptually distinguished along a continuum, and knowledge conversion explains the interaction between tacit and explicit knowledge' (Nonaka and von Krogh, 2009, p. 636). Explicit knowledge refers to knowledge transmittable in formal, systematic language found in manuals, procedures, and so on. Tacit knowledge refers to knowledge acquired by individuals through their experiences, which makes it difficult to formalize and communicate (e.g. knowledge about writing papers, wine-tasting, competitive swimming). For instance, this book, *OTs in the Making*, comprises a myriad of explicit knowledge about OTs that was disseminated through papers, books, websites, conferences, and so on. However, interpreting this information and putting it together in order to get a whole picture of the field is a whole other ballgame. The 'spirit' of this book—the way research programmes are introduced and described—comes from my own 'knowledge' of the field, a knowledge that I have built over time through my teaching and research experiences. Whenever I teach OTs to my students, I transfer to them my tacit knowledge of this field of study.

The distinction between explicit and tacit knowledge is central to Nonaka and Takeuchi's (1995) book, where they posit their SECI model of knowledge creation (socialization, externalization, combination, and internalization; see Figure 5.1). Socialization allows the transfer of tacit knowledge through guidance, imitation, and observation. Externalization is the conversion mechanism from tacit to explicit knowledge through codification. Combination refers to the knowledge conversion mechanism whereby codified information is recombined to create new knowledge. As explicit knowledge is used and learned, the new knowledge is internalized in a way that modifies the user's existing tacit knowledge. The SECI model should be seen as a series of dynamic and sequential processes through which knowledge becomes converted from tacit to explicit knowledge. According to this model, knowledge is continually converted and created. The relationships between tacit knowledge and explicit knowledge—or documented and undocumented knowledge (Powell and Ambrosini, 2017)—remain central to the efforts of knowledge management researchers.

There are two generations of studies associated with knowledge management (Kimble, De Vasconcelos, and Rocha, 2016). The first generation (2000–2010) predominantly focused on how organizations capture explicit knowledge and store it in information technology systems. The idea was to codify individual knowledge such that each piece of coded information would be interpreted in the same way throughout the organization.

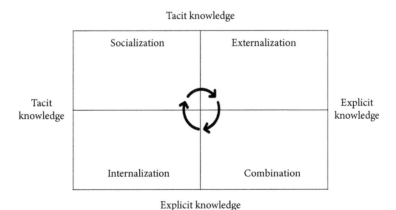

Figure 5.1 SECI model*
*Adapted from Nonaka and Takeuchi, 1995, p. 62.

For example, Dhanaraj et al. (2004) studied knowledge transfer in international joint ventures and showed the complementary nature between explicit knowledge (written knowledge gained in the area of technology and management and the transfer of it in procedural manuals) and tacit knowledge (managerial techniques, marketing expertise, knowledge of foreign cultures, and consumer tastes transferred to international joint ventures by the parent organization). They also showed that the transfer of tacit knowledge facilitates the explanation of explicit knowledge and that the influence of tacit knowledge on international joint venture performance depends primarily on the transfer of explicit knowledge. Choi et al. (2008) examined the relationships between knowledge management strategies (tacit–internal oriented versus explicit–external oriented) developed by organizations and their impacts on performance and innovation. Using statistical analysis, Birkinshaw, Nobel, and Ridderstråle (2002) demonstrated that knowledge appears to be a contingency variable in organizational structure.

The second generation of studies in knowledge management (2010 and after) distance themselves from the explicit and tacit knowledge debate. Researchers shift away from knowledge codification through information systems to focus rather on how knowledge is transmitted in small groups. They rely on the notion of competency (i.e. sets of skills and abilities related to task activities) to study knowledge-sharing strategies. Drawing on interviews, Powell and Ambrosini (2017) examined knowledge-sharing strategies (via social network contact, a colleague identified through a knowledge map, and knowledge management tools) that managers and consultants generally favour in knowledge-intensive firms. Their findings show that managers and consultants used different knowledge-sharing strategies. While managers prefer sharing knowledge via codified tools, consultants give more value to knowledge shared via personalization strategies. Mariano and Awazu (2017) build a literature review on artefacts in knowledge management research, and invite researchers to pay attention to the role and effects of human factors (e.g. motivation, teamwork, organizational culture) in the knowledge creation processes involving information artefacts, such as mailing lists, issue trackers, and software versioning tools. Nevertheless, even if open innovation systems give more room to human competency, the fundamental objective still revolves around controlling or managing knowledge.

Regardless of the school they subscribed to, knowledge management researchers were widely criticized for their 'one-size-fits-all' vision of knowledge as information (Brown and Duguid, 2001; Tsoukas, 2005; Gourlay, 2006). Nevertheless, the knowledge management research stream still conceptualizes the organization as an institution where individual knowledge integration can take place. According to this stream of research, individuals are the holders of the knowledge that they share with others, and knowledge managers ensure that the organization keeps traces of it.

5.3 Dynamic capabilities

According to the resource-based view (RBV) of the firm, knowledge is seen as one of the most strategically significant intangible organizational resources (Barney, 1991). Associated with organizational economics, RBV suggests that each firm is the result of a set of physical resources (e.g. equipment and raw materials), human resources (e.g. training and expertise of individual workers and managers), and organizational resources (e.g. control and planning systems) acquired from past experiences. Largely used in strategic management, RBV's attention focuses on organizations' internal tangible and intangible resources as a source of sustainable competitive advantage—so long as these resources are valuable, rare, imperfectly imitable, and not substitutable (note that this framework is commonly referred to as the VRIN model; Barney, 1991).

Initially, RBV struggled to distinguish resources from dynamic capabilities. Teece, Pisano, and Shuen (1997, p. 516) eventually presented a clear distinction between these two notions. Resources are 'firm-specific assets that are difficult if not impossible to imitate', whereas dynamic capabilities correspond to the 'firm's ability to integrate, build, and reconfigure internal and external competences to address rapidly changing environment'. More specifically, dynamic capabilities correspond to the organizational and managerial processes and routines that coordinate, develop, and reconfigure the firm's resources and competences in order to renew its competitive advantage. While organizational knowledge as a resource is defined in terms of 'assets', organizational knowledge as a dynamic capability is associated with 'what the firms do more effectively than their rivals' (e.g. distinct skills, procedures, routines, rules). The organizational economics stream of research in knowledge studies considers organizational knowledge either an 'asset' or something with 'economic value'. Therefore, it assumes that knowledge can be estimated, quantified, and accumulated or capitalized.

For proponents of RBV and dynamic capabilities, 'firms know how to do things' (Dosi, Faillo, and Marengo, 2008, p. 1165). Organizational knowledge is merely incorporated in the minds of organizational members, as it is primarily found in organizational routines, shared representations, and material artefacts that shape an organization. Paraphrasing Winter (1982), Dosi et al. (2008, p. 1171) argue that 'it is firms, not people [who] work in firms, that know how to make gasoline, automobiles, computers'. Indeed, according to RBV and dynamic capabilities researchers, organizational knowledge has a dimension that cannot be reduced to the capacities and skills of individuals. Rather, organizations coordinate a series of activities to produce gasoline, automobiles, computers, and so on. Moreover, it would probably be impossible, even for the most skilled and competent chemist, engineer, or informatician, to produce one of these goods by themselves. Indubitably, within the economic perspective, the locus of knowledge lies at the organizational level.

Teece (2007) proposes a framework specifying the foundations of capabilities in the context of open innovation and rapid change. Drawing on his previous work, the author comes up with three core micro-foundations of dynamic capabilities: 'sensing', 'seizing', and 'reconfiguring' (see Figure 5.2 for a simplified view of this framework). For her part, Eriksson (2014), in her synthesis of dynamic capabilities research, identifies four focal overlapping knowledge processes of dynamic capabilities: 'accumulation'; 'integration'; 'utilization'; and 'reconfiguration'. Knowledge 'accumulation', or what corresponds to 'sensing' in Teece's (2007) framework, is based on the assumption that the shaping of capabilities cannot be understood without looking at how knowledge accumulates through experience and over time. The challenge of knowledge accumulation revolves around the ability to balance between knowledge replication and renewal. Helfat and Peteraf (2003) came up with the notion of 'capability life cycle' to propose a long-term view of the different paths involved in the evolution of organizational capabilities (e.g. founding, development, and maturity). Riviere and Bass (2019) examined a sample of 94 multinational enterprises (MNEs) and investigated how diverse dimensions of internationalization (depth, breadth, and speed) shaped the MNE's renewal of its dynamic capabilities at different levels (within-MNE and between-MNE). They found diverse effects (positive and negative) across

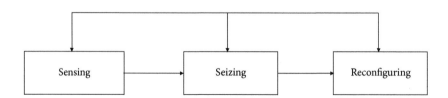

Figure 5.2 Dynamic capabilities*
*Adapted from Teece, 2007, p. 1342.

levels of internationalization. For instance, at the within-MNE level, internationalization breadth is negatively related to renewal capability, while, on the contrary, speed is positively related.

'Seizing' opportunities, the second micro-foundation of dynamic capabilities of the Teece (2007) framework, corresponds to knowledge 'integration' and 'utilization' in the Eriksson (2014) framework. To consolidate the renewal capability initiated by knowledge accumulation, firms use a variety of ways to integrate and embed new knowledge coming from external and internal sources. Also, Salunke, Weerawardena, and McColl-Kennedy (2019) put forth the notion of 'knowledge integration capabilities', which refer to the firm's capacity to synthesize and apply current and acquired knowledge with the aim of reinforcing its competitive advantage. Following interviews with senior managers from project-oriented service firms, the authors suggest that knowledge integration capabilities are strongly driven by entrepreneurial behaviours and client-focused tools. Furthermore, the authors mention that to reach optimal innovation performance in this type of firm, it is important to balance knowledge acquisition coming from external and internal sources.

Knowledge 'utilization'—according to Eriksson (2014)—brings us back to knowledge sharing and the conversion between tacit and explicit knowledge, as discussed in Section 5.2. According to RBV and dynamic capabilities, organizational knowledge grows the more it is used or elaborated (as opposed to other resources, which tend to get depleted with use). As such, to get the full benefits of organizational knowledge, managers must stimulate the use of knowledge and knowledge sharing. Drawing on a governance approach, Andersson, Buckley, and Dellestrand (2015) studied 169 innovation projects in multinational contexts and looked at knowledge transfer effectiveness (i.e. the use and adoption of knowledge). The results of their study suggest that 'hierarchical and formal governance tools are not positively related to transfer effectiveness, but that lateral relationships affect transfer effectiveness positively' (Andersson et al., 2015, p. 41). Put differently, headquarters have very little influence on the knowledge used by their subsidiaries, while knowledge transfer between subsidiaries happens to be much more beneficial for multinationals.

The knowledge 'reconfiguration' process, or 'reconfiguring' in the Teece (2007) framework, involves 'generating new combinations of existing knowledge or leveraging existing knowledge for new purposes or in new ways' (Eriksson, 2014, p. 71). Mention, Barlatier, and Josserand (2019) piloted a special issue in *Technological Forecasting and Social Change* about social media and innovation. Social media are more and more used by firms not only to communicate with a wide range of stakeholders but also for the purpose of enhancing innovation capabilities and generating new knowledge. According to the authors, the papers published in this special issue all show how firms recombine, or 'reconfigure', their dynamic capabilities by engaging in multiple knowledge sources and empowering internal human resources towards an open and collaborative culture.

As opposed to the knowledge management stream, where individuals are the holders of knowledge, the economic stream of research assumes knowledge resides in organizations and appears to be an essential asset endowed with economic value key to building firms' competitive advantage. As knowledge is embodied in organization systems and in the goods and services produced and sold by organizations, existing research essentially considers it as an independent variable influencing firms' performance. Hence, knowledge can be objectified through proxies and measures. As such, similarly to the commodity school, the resource-based and dynamic capabilities views consider that knowledge can indeed be accumulated, integrated, utilized, and reconfigured—much as one would an object.

5.4 Organizational learning

In knowledge studies, the ability of organizations to respond to environmental change is often associated with organizational learning. Following Cyert and March (1963), Argyris and Schön (1978, p. 16) advance this conversation with their notion of 'single- and double-loop learning', which suggests that organizational learning occurs when individuals 'experience a surprising mismatch between expected and actual results of action and respond to that mismatch through a process of thought and further action that lead them to modify their images of organization or their understandings of organizational phenomena'. According to Easterby-Smith and Lyles (2011), Argyris and Schön (1978) were the first authors to point out that organizations and individuals are not always willing to learn, as their actions are often inconsistent with the precepts of economic rationality.

Organizational learning emerged in OTs in the 1980s by proposing a set of notions for studying the phenomenon. Fiol and Lyles (1985) discussed the learning levels within an organization, while Argote and Epple (1990) introduced the idea of learning curves. In a highly influential paper, March (1991) described the dilemma of balancing exploitation (i.e. doing what is already known or what the organization is already good at) with exploration (i.e. looking for unknown and radical innovative opportunities). These pioneering works were very influential and set most of the research agenda for the following decades. In general, organizational learning research is based on the assumption that it is desirable to maximize the efficient use of knowledge in organizations. However, subsequent research showed that the relationship between organizational learning and performance is not always direct and often depends on contextual circumstances.

Despite the abundance and variety of definitions found in the literature, the nature of organizational learning remains rather enigmatic in the field of OTs. Organizational learning generally refers to a process whereby 'organizations understand and manage their experience' (Glynn, Lant, and Milliken, 1994, p. 45). Organizational learning is therefore associated with an organization's capability to process new and unexpected information and to solve diverse problems emerging in situations of change and innovation. More recently, Chiva, Ghauri, and Alegre (2014, p. 689) clarified the definition of organizational learning by arguing that it corresponds to the process by which 'organizations change or modify their mental models, rules, processes or knowledge, maintaining or improving their performance'. Thus, organizational learning refers to a cognitive structure and entails the learning of a collective subject.

Is there a distinction between organizational knowledge and organizational learning? As we saw in the above definitions, organizational learning is a 'process', while organizational knowledge is generally associated with the 'information' that an organization possesses. Although it remains the predominant view in knowledge studies, such an obvious dichotomy has to be nuanced according to the underlying epistemological position taken by researchers. It is also worth noting that recent literature reviews argue that it is becoming increasingly difficult to distinguish between organizational learning and knowledge management (Castaneda, Manrique, and Cuellar, 2018). Hence, these two notions are sometimes referred to by the acronym OLKM (organizational learning knowledge management). Moreover, organizational knowledge and knowledge management tend to use the same terminology to distinguish between the different processes of organizational learning. For instance, Argote and Hora (2017) include the processes of creating, retaining, and transferring knowledge in their definition of organizational learning.

Organizational learning studies are concerned about three central interrelated themes: learning and innovation; the interplay between knowledge exploitation and exploration; and knowledge remembering and forgetting. First, the links between learning and innovation are generally described through a firm's efforts to transform and recombine ideas and information into new insights or innovations and to share the resulting knowledge that is produced. Papers have been written about the capacity of organizations to 'absorb' or integrate both internal and external knowledge (see

Roper and Love, 2018). Originating from Cohen and Levinthal (1990), this broad notion of absorptive capacity is central in the literature on learning and innovation. The literature has also widely examined how learning and innovation take place during the process of inter-organizational knowledge transfer (Easterby-Smith Lyles, and Tsang, 2008; Ratten, Braga, and Marques 2018) and between clusters and networks (Giuliani, 2007).

A second theme around organizational learning takes a strategic perspective and examines the interplay between the exploitation of what is known and the exploration of what is unknown (Gupta, Tesluk, and Taylor, 2007; Lavie and Rosenkopf, 2007). The trade-off between exploration and exploitation is expressed in the idea of organizational ambidexterity (Birkinshaw and Gupta, 2013; O'Reilly and Tushman, 2013). Ambidextrous organizations exploit existing knowledge while simultaneously fostering efforts to innovate. Firms that balance exploitation and exploration are more likely to develop a robust competitive advantage and achieve higher performance—which is precisely what Campanella et al. (2020) demonstrate in their large-scale empirical study of banks across European countries.

Third, learning studies are also interested in organizational memory, generally defined as the persistent maintenance of organizational knowledge that has been built over the years. Recent work around organizational memory took a 'forgetting turn' (de Holan, Phillips, and Lawrence, 2004) that focuses on phenomena such as knowledge depreciation, knowledge loss, and the process of unlearning—with the latter point attracting particular scholarly attention. Whether organizational forgetting is intentional (e.g. getting rid of organizational knowledge) or accidental (e.g. failing to retain prior knowledge), it is an essential aspect of strategic renewal. Indeed, organizations, much like individuals, have limited memory capacity and are susceptible to forgetting, which limits their ability to adapt over the long term. Mariano, Casey, and Olivera (2018) conducted a literature review on the role of managers in organizational forgetting. Studying commemorative events, Cutcher, Dale, and Tyler (2019) investigate the process of 'remembering' rather than looking at organizational memory as an entity and thus consider the politics of how organizations remember and forget. Miller and Martignoni (2016), on their part, show that 'slow learning is not always better'.

Overall, the notion of organizational learning (as well as organizational forgetting) is 'excessively broad, encompassing merely all organizational change' (Wang and Ahmed, 2003, p. 8). Organizational learning is generally viewed as a mental or cognitive structure that is individual and/or collective in nature. Lastly, most studies on learning are based on the assumption that individuals and groups learn and can therefore change for the better.

5.5 Organizational knowing

The substreams of research in knowledge studies covered in the previous three sections focus on information codification and transfer as well as on the nature of learning. This entails a representational view of knowledge. Yet, for several researchers, knowledge is much more than information or a mental structure held by individuals and/or organizations. Rather than talking in terms of knowledge, these researchers propose a 'knowing' perspective. What does this refer to? Using the 'ing' form entails endorsing the idea that knowing is neither a substance nor a static capability, but rather a performance or an accomplishment. According to the 'knowing' stream of research, knowledge is performed instead of being transferred as a mere thing. Building on this, this stream posits that learning cannot be passed from person to person; rather, knowledge transfer takes place through social interactions and involves a renegotiation of meaning and experience. Instead of looking at 'what' is known, this stream of research is concerned about 'how' things become known.

Here, knowing is not only a cognitive activity: as individuals, our senses and our entire being contribute to it. Rather, it is a social activity that takes place as we connect with others. According to this view, knowledge is not in our heads, but situated in space and time through human interactions. In other words, knowledge is *situated*. This approach assumes that knowledge is produced and reproduced by 'knowers during those very acts of "knowing"' (Pyrko, Dorfler, and Eden, 2017, p. 395). Therefore, researchers who follow this approach seek to understand how knowledge is used, interpreted, unlearned, and relearned, and in what circumstances.

The knowing perspective has deep roots in the idea of Community of Practice (CoP), which has been around for more than 25 years in the field of OTs (Brown and Duguid, 1991, Orr, 1996; Wenger, 2010). A CoP includes practitioners from different contexts who learn from each other as they try to solve similar organizational or professional problems. For instance, digital technologies make it possible to bring together a large number of individuals from different geographic and time zones to share their experience and resolve shared issues (Faraj et al., 2016). Online communities are, in a way, the new form of CoP and structure that facilitates knowledge sharing and creation. The locus of knowledge is the community itself, which over time enacts and sustains a shared repertoire of practices through mutual engagement. It is the very participation (occasional, peripheral, or complete) of an individual in a community that provides them with competence and legitimacy within that community. By participating in a CoP, members learn to distinguish newcomers from practitioners, or outsiders from insiders (Lave and Wenger, 1991). For example, one becomes an organization theorist by taking courses in a department of management and organization studies, and this can forge their academic identity for ever. Transferring knowledge to a PhD student or a junior faculty involves more than transferring codified knowledge of organization theories. It involves working together on papers, developing common research projects, and so on. These newcomers must also join diverse communities of organization theorists. Being active members in local, national, and international conferences in management and organization studies, all of which are CoPs, is a privileged way of learning how to become an organization theorist.

Researchers ascribed to the knowing perspective in knowledge studies developed a variety of related concepts aimed at advancing our view of knowledge in OTs. Gherardi (2009, p. 353) defines knowledge 'as an activity, as a collective and distributed "doing," [which is] situated in time and space, and therefore as taking place in work practices'. Rennstam and Ashcraft (2014, p. 4) propose the notion 'communicative knowledge'; that is, 'situated and embodied knowledge about interaction that is also created and used in interaction'. In their book, which brings together a diverse range of traditions in knowledge studies, Sandberg et al. (2017) suggest the idea of 'skillful performance', referring to the multiple processes whereby individuals enact various forms of knowledge such as capabilities, competence, expertise, and learning when interacting with each other and practising their activities.

In the same vein, emerging streams of process- and practice-oriented research (see Chapter 7) have opened up new conversations and enquiries pertaining to knowing in OTs. For instance, researchers have started looking at how knowledge is embedded in various sociomaterial assemblages (Gherardi and Perrotta, 2014; Gherardi, 2016). To learn is therefore to be 'capable of participating with the requisite competence in the complex web of relationships among people, material artefacts, and activities' (Gherardi, 2008, p. 517). Knowing research has also taken the 'performative turn' (Spry, 2006), which focuses on the performative effects of knowledge discourses and accomplishments in shaping managerial, professional, and employees' subjectivities and identities (Simpson, Tracey, and Weston, 2018). Still, other recent conversations around 'activity theory' (Engeström, 2008) and the 'constitutive communication of organization' perspective (CCO, Kuhn, 2014; see Chapter 6) are being developed, thereby further pushing research on knowing.

The knowing perspective displaces the unit of analysis in knowledge studies from individuals to the practices of individuals. By highlighting activities rather than individuals as knowing agents, this perspective provides a different way of understanding the 'knowledgeability' or the 'social competence' of the agent (Giddens, 1984). It also renews our comprehension of what Schatzki (2002) calls the practical 'intelligibility' or 'understanding' that allows actors to recognize and act in keeping with the organizational rules that apply a specific context. Note, however, that the knowing perspective is hardly dominant in knowledge studies.

5.6 The unresolved knowledge paradox

Different communities of scholars concerned with knowledge studies—crossing the boundaries of scientific disciplines—have proliferated over the past 25 years in an attempt to address the challenges of the knowledge economy. Did this enormous body of work live up to its promise to respond to the challenges of innovation, creativity, and economic performance? Do we know much more today about what organizational knowledge is about than we did 25 years ago? Sadly, the quantity of papers published within knowledge studies seems to be inversely proportional to their quality. Why? Among other reasons, the underlying philosophical assumptions behind knowledge studies suffer from a strong bias, which is explained in the following paragraphs.

From an ontological point of view, knowledge studies generally question when, how, and by whom knowledge is produced. Although very diverse, the streams of research in knowledge studies tend to conceptualize knowledge (including its derivatives, e.g. competence, capability, and learning) as an entity characterized by specific attributes. For example, 'competence' is seen as being made up of a specific set of knowledge, skills, and personal traits, while 'capabilities' are approached as a unique bundle of knowledge and resources. Consequently, knowledge studies are mainly based on a realist ontology as though, in some way, knowledge exists independently from our experience as knowing subjects. In terms of epistemology, knowledge studies were built essentially on a controversy surrounding the locus of knowledge. Where is knowledge? Is it in the head of individuals, in organizational artefacts and work routines, or even in the beliefs at the heart of organizational culture? These questions are not inconsequential. Indeed, concepts, notions, and theories put forth by knowledge studies generally have limited external validity. As a matter of fact, research outcomes around dynamic capabilities, competences, learning, and so on can always be confuted by opposing points of views.

With respect to the methodology used, knowledge as a variable is generally captured through the rationalistic operationalization of observable characteristics. Yet, methodologically speaking, is it even possible to separate individual knowledge from collective or organizational knowledge? This may be very useful heuristically, but knowledge flows between levels and domains—including any attempt to distinguish such contradictory characteristics is purely arbitrary. Knowledge studies are therefore built on unresolved paradoxical assumptions. Furthermore, researchers observe knowledge from a position they claim is one of detachment. Hence, they do not take into account the fact that in so doing, they themselves are embedded in the process of knowledge production.

On the axiological level, knowledge studies present a very positive vision of human behaviour, notably when it comes to learning. In their thought-provoking paper on 'functional stupidity', Alvesson and Spicer (2012) consider that knowledge studies reinforce the need for contemporary organizations to enlist in a positive or smart way the cognitive capacities of workers in order to remain competitive. According to these authors, knowledge sharing and learning in organizations are also inhibited by hypocrisy, ignorance, incompetence, cheating, and mistrust. Knowledge, as Foucault brilliantly demonstrated, is intrinsically associated with power. Yet, the notion of power is generally missing from knowledge studies! It makes no sense to explore organizational knowledge without addressing how affective or motivational issues as well as power and politics constrain and enable the production of knowledge.

The rationalization project that pervades the OTs field is more present than ever in knowledge studies. Indeed, the classics in OTs explore tangible aspects of organizations (e.g. tasks, decision-making, structures) in an attempt to uncover how to rationalize them. However, as the saying goes, the more things change, the more they stay the same! By promoting the codification and storage of knowledge, knowledge studies rationalize what is in the minds of individuals that stands to benefit organizations. Therefore, knowledge studies are far from securing the autonomy and discretion of the 'knowledge worker'—the supposed ideological aim of the new economy. To put it bluntly, knowledge managers are, in a way, the 'Taylors' of the twenty-first century!

Overall, OTs have overestimated the potential of knowledge studies to manage and understand organizations. They are built on paradoxical assumptions (e.g. tacit/explicit, individual/collective, replication/renewal, internal/external) inherited from the classic managerial approach in OTs. The fact that these paradoxical assumptions have remained unresolved even now is haunting knowledge studies. For instance, it assumes we can translate what is tacit into something explicit and that the costs of this translation do not outweigh its benefits. Nonetheless, there is knowledge in both the tacit and the explicit; they are paradoxically inseparable. As Polanyi (1966, p. 4) said in *The Tacit Dimension*, 'We can know more than we can tell'. Knowledge studies aim to trigger a reflection and a debate on the notion of knowledge itself rather than building on contradictory features. A philosophical reflection on knowledge is clearly—and surprisingly!—missing, even though such a reflection could significantly advance our understanding of knowledge in organizations. To do so, there is a need to go back to the sources of the philosophy of knowledge and explore what Polanyi, Dewey, Ryles, Hutchins, and others have to teach us about 'knowledge and knowing'.

References

Alvesson, M. & Spicer, A. 2012. A Stupidity-Based Theory of Organizations. *Journal of Management Studies*, 49, 1194–1220.

Andersson, U., Buckley, P. J., & Dellestrand, H. 2015. In the Right Place at the Right Time!: The Influence of Knowledge Governance Tools on Knowledge Transfer and Utilization in MNEs. *Global Strategy Journal*, 5, 27–47.

Argote, L. & Epple, D. 1990. Learning Curves in Manufacturing. *Science*, 247, 920–924.

Argote, L. & Hora, M. 2017. Organizational Learning and Management of Technology. *Production and Operations Management*, 26, 579–590.

Argyris, C. & Schön, D. A. 1978. *Organizational Learning: A Theory in Action Perspective*. Reading, MA, Addison-Wesley.

Barney, J. 1991. Firm Resources and Sustained Competitive Advantage. *Journal of Management*, 17, 99–120.

Birkinshaw, J. & Gupta, K. 2013. Clarifying the Distinctive Contribution of Ambidexterity to the Field of Organization Studies. *Academy of Management Perspectives*, 27, 287–298.

Birkinshaw, J., Nobel, R., & Ridderstråle, J. 2002. Knowledge as a Contingency Variable: Do the Characteristics of Knowledge Predict Organization Structure? *Organization Science*, 13, 274–289.

Brown, J. S. & Duguid, P. 1991. Organizational Learning and Communities-of-Practice: Toward a Unified View of Working, Learning, and Innovation. *Organization Science*, 2, 40–57.

Brown, J. S. & Duguid, P. 2001. Knowledge and Organization: A Social-Practice Perspective. *Organization Science*, 12, 198–213.

Campanella, F., Del Giudice, M., Thrassou, A., & Vrontis, D. 2020. Ambidextrous Organizations in the Banking Sector: An Empirical Verification of Banks' Performance and Conceptual Development. *The International Journal of Human Resource Management*, 31, 272–302.

Castaneda, D. I., Manrique, L. F., & Cuellar, S. 2018. Is Organizational Learning Being Absorbed by Knowledge Management? A Systematic Review. *Journal of Knowledge Management*, 22, 299–325.

Chiva, R., Ghauri, P., & Alegre, J. 2014. Organizational Learning, Innovation and Internationalization: A Complex System Model. *British Journal of Management*, 25, 687–705.

Choi, B., Poon, S., & Davis, J. 2008. Effects of Knowledge Management Strategy on Organizational Performance: A Complementarity Theory-Based Approach. *Omega*, 36, 235–251.

Cohen, W. M. & Levinthal, D. A. 1990. Absorptive Capacity: A New Perspective on Learning and Innovation. *Administrative Science Quarterly*, 35, 128–152.

Cutcher, L., Dale, K., & Tyler, M. 2019. 'Remembering as Forgetting': Organizational Commemoration as a Politics of Recognition. *Organization Studies*, 40, 267–290.

Cyert, R. & March, J. 1963. *A Behavioral Theory of the Firm*. Englewood Cliffs, NJ, Prentice Hall.

De Holan, P. M., Phillips, N., & Lawrence, T. B. 2004. Managing Organizational Forgetting. *MIT Sloan Management Review*, 45, 45–51.

Dhanaraj, C., Lyles, M. A., Steensma, H. K., & Tihanyi, L. 2004. Managing Tacit and Explicit Knowledge Transfer in IJVs: The Role of Relational Embeddedness and the Impact on Performance. *Journal of International Business Studies*, 35, 428–442.

Dosi, G., Faillo, M., & Marengo, L. 2008. Organizational Capabilities, Patterns of Knowledge Accumulation and Governance Structures in Business Firms: An Introduction. *Organization Studies*, 29, 1165–1185.

Easterby-Smith, M. & Lyles, M. A. 2011. The Evolving Field of Organizational Learning and Knowledge Management. *In*: Easterby-Smith, M. & Lyles, M. A. (eds) *Handbook of Organizational Learning and Knowledge Management*. Chichester, John Wiley, 1–22.

Easterby-Smith, M., Lyles, M. A., & Tsang, E. W. K. 2008. Inter-Organizational Knowledge Transfer: Current Themes and Future Prospects. *Journal of Management Studies*, 45, 677–690.

Engeström, Y. 2008. *From Teams to Knots: Studies of Collaboration and Learning at Work*. Cambridge, UK, Cambridge University Press.

Eriksson, T. 2014. Processes, Antecedents and Outcomes of Dynamic Capabilities. *Scandinavian Journal of Management*, 30, 65–82.

Faraj, S., Von Krogh, G., Monteiro, E., & Lakhani, K. R. 2016. Special Section Introduction—Online Community as Space for Knowledge Flows. *Information Systems Research*, 27, 668–684.

Fiol, M. C. & Lyles, M. A. 1985. Organizational Learning. *Academy of Management Review*, 10, 803–813.

Gherardi, S. 2008. Situated Knowledge and Situated Action: What Do Practice-Based Studies Promise. *In*: Barry, D. & Hansen, H. (eds) *The Sage Handbook of New Approaches in Management and Organization*. London, Sage, 516–527.

Gherardi, S. 2009. Knowing and Learning in Practice-Based Studies: An Introduction. *The Learning Organization*, 16, 352–359.

Gherardi, S. 2016. To Start Practice Theorizing Anew: The Contribution of the Concepts of Agencement and Formativeness. *Organization*, 23, 680–698.

Gherardi, S. & Perrotta, M. 2014. Between the Hand and the Head. *Qualitative Research in Organizations and Management: An International Journal*, 9, 134–150.

Giddens, A. 1984. *The Constitution of Society*. Cambridge, UK, Polity.

Giuliani, E. 2007. The Selective Nature of Knowledge Networks in Clusters: Evidence from the Wine Industry. *Journal of Economic Geography*, 7, 139–168.

Glynn, M. A., Lant, T. K., & Milliken, F. J. 1994. Mapping Learning Processes in Organizations: A Multi-Level Framework Linking Learning and Organizing. *Advances in Managerial Cognition and Organizational Information Processing*, 5, 43–83.

Gourlay, S. 2006. Conceptualizing Knowledge Creation: A Critique of Nonaka's Theory. *Journal of Management Studies*, 43, 1415–1436.

Gupta, A. K., Tesluk, P. E., & Taylor, M. S. 2007. Innovation at and across Multiple Levels of Analysis. *Organization Science*, 18, 885–897.

Hayek, F. A. 1945. The Use of Knowledge in Society. *The American Economic Review*, 35, 519–530.

Helfat, C. E. & Peteraf, M. A. 2003. The Dynamic Resource-Based View: Capability Lifecyles. *Strategic Management Journal*, 24, 997–1010.

Khun, T. R. 2014. Knowledge and Knowing in Organizational Communication. *In*: Putman, L. L. & Mumby, D. K. (eds) *The Sage Handbook of Organizational Communication: Advances in Theory, Research, and Methods*. London, Sage, 481–502.

Kimble, C., De Vasconcelos, J. B., & Rocha, Á. 2016. Competence Management in Knowledge Intensive Organizations Using Consensual Knowledge and Ontologies. *Information Systems Frontiers*, 18, 1119–1130.

Kuhn, T. & Jackson, M. H. 2008. Accomplishing Knowledge. *Management Communication Quarterly*, 21, 454–485.

Lave, J. & Wenger, E. 1991. *Situated Learning: Legitimate Peripheral Participation*. Cambridge, UK, Cambridge University Press.

Lavie, D. & Rosenkopf, L. 2007. Balancing Exploration and Exploitation in Alliance Formation. *Academy of Management Journal*, 49, 797–818.

March, J. G. 1991. Exploration and Exploitation in Organizational Learning. *Organization Science*, 2, 71–87.

Mariano, S. & Awazu, Y. 2017. The Role of Collaborative Knowledge Building in the Co-creation of Artifacts: Influencing Factors and Propositions. *Journal of Knowledge Management*, 21, 779–795.

Mariano, S., Casey, A., & Olivera, F. 2018. Managers and Organizational Forgetting: A Synthesis. *The Learning Organization*, 25, 169–179.

McIver, D., Lengnick-Hall, C. A., Lengnick-Hall, M. L., & Ramachandran, I. 2012. Integrating Knowledge and Knowing: A Framework For Understanding Knowledge-In-Practice. *Human Resource Management Review*, 22, 86–99.

Mention, A.-L., Barlatier, P.-J., & Josserand, E. 2019. Using Social Media to Leverage and Develop Dynamic Capabilities For Innovation. *Technological Forecasting and Social Change*, 144, 242–250.

Miller, K. D. & Martignoni, D. 2016. Organizational Learning with Forgetting: Reconsidering the Exploration–Exploitation Tradeoff. *Strategic Organization*, 14, 53–72.

Nonaka, I. & Takeuchi, H. 1995. *The Knowledge-Creating Company: How Japanese Companies Create the Dynamics of Innovation*. Oxford, UK, Oxford University Press.

Nonaka, I. & Von Krogh, G. 2009. Perspective—Tacit Knowledge and Knowledge Conversion: Controversy and Advancement in Organizational Knowledge Creation Theory. *Organization Science*, 20, 635–652.

O'Reilly, C. A. & Tushman, M. L. 2013. Organizational Ambidexterity: Past, Present, and Future. *Academy of Management Perspectives*, 27, 324–338.

Orr, J.-E. 1996. *Talking About Machines: An Ethnography of a Modern Job*. Ithaca, NY, ILR Press.

Polanyi, M. 1966. *The Tacit Dimension*. Garden City, NJ, Doubleday.

Powell, T. H. & Ambrosini, V. 2017. Espoused versus Realized Knowledge Management Tool Usage in Knowledge Intensive Organizations. *The International Journal of Human Resource Management*, 28, 356–378.

Pyrko, I., Dorfler, V., & Eden, C. 2017. Thinking Together: What Makes Communities of Practice Work? *Human Relations*, 70, 389–409.

Ratten, V., Braga, V., & Marques, C. S. 2018. *Knowledge, Learning and Innovation. Research Insights on Cross-Sector Collaborations*. Cham, Switzerland, Springer International Publishing.

Rennstam, J., & Ashcraft, K. L. (2014). Knowing work: Cultivating a practice-based epistemology of knowledge in organization studies. *Human Relations*, 67, 1, 3-25.

Riviere, M. & Bass, A. E. 2019. How Dimensions of Internationalization Shape the MNE's Renewal Capability: Multidimensional and Multilevel Considerations. *Long Range Planning*, 52, 4 (52, 4), 101862.

Roper, S. & Love, J. H. 2018. Knowledge Context, Learning and Innovation: An Integrating Framework. *Industry and Innovation*, 25, 339–364.

Salunke, S., Weerawardena, J., & McColl-Kennedy, J. R. 2019. The Central Role of Knowledge Integration Capability in Service Innovation-Based Competitive Strategy. *Industrial Marketing Management*, 76, 144–156.

Sandberg, J., Rouleau, L., Langley, A., & Tsoukas, H. 2017. *Skillful Performance, Enacting Capabilities, Knowledge, Competence, and Expertise in Organizations.* Oxford, UK, Oxford University Press.

Schatzki, T. 2002. *The Site of the Social: A Philosophical Account of the Constitution of Social Life and Change.* University Park, PA, Pennsylvania State University Press.

Sewell, G. 2005. Nice Work? Rethinking Managerial Control in an Era of Knowledge Work. *Organization*, 12, 685–704.

Simpson, B., Tracey, R., & Weston, A. 2018. Traveling Concepts: Performative Movements in Learning/Playing. *Management Learning*, 49, 295–310.

Spry, T. 2006. A 'Performative-I' Copresence: Embodying the Ethnographic Turn in Performance and the Performative Turn in Ethnography. *Text and Performance Quarterly*, 26, 339–346.

Taylor, F.W. (1911). The Principles of Scientific Management, New York, USA, Harper & Brothers.

Teece, D. J. 2007. Explicating Dynamic Capabilities: The Nature and Microfoundations of (Sustainable) Enterprise Performance. *Strategic Management Journal*, 28, 1319–1350.

Teece, D. J., Pisano, G., & Shuen, A. 1997. Dynamic Capabilities and Strategic Management. *Strategic Management Journal*, 18, 509–533.

Tsoukas, H. 2005. *Complex Knowledge.* Oxford, UK, Oxford University Press.

Wang, C. L. & Ahmed, P. K. 2003. Organisational Learning: A Critical Review. *The Learning Organization*, 10, 8–17.

Wenger, E. 2010. Communities of Practice and Social Learning Systems: The Career of a Concept. *In*: Blackmore, C. (ed.) *Social Learning Systems and Communities of Practice*. London, Springer, 179–198.

Winter, S. G. 1982. An Essay on the Theory of Production. *In*: Hymans, S. H. (ed.) *Economics and the World Around It.* Ann Arbor, MI, University of Michigan Press, 55–91.

6
Discourse Studies

According to Lookwood, Giorgi, and Glynn (2018), discourse studies are relevant to the field of organizational theories (OTs) if only because 'we can do things with words'. Some decades ago, however, such a claim would have not been taken seriously. Of course, since the 1970s, it has been an acknowledged fact that communication is one of managers' main tasks (Mintzberg, 1973). Since then, the importance of communication and discursive activities in understanding organizations has gradually become paramount in OTs. This is quite understandable: today, managers and others spend countless hours talking with colleagues, customers, superiors, and subordinates, writing reports or emails, producing PowerPoints, taking notes, reading text messages, and so on. The ability of managers to openly engage a multitude of stakeholders around a common discourse is crucial, especially in a context where high-performance communication tools and social media are expanding at lightning speed. As organizations remain meaningful places that bring together individuals and teams, discourse studies offer sophisticated insights to sharpen our understanding of the complexities of organizational dynamics.

The increased interest in discourse studies in OTs was made possible by the diffusion of social constructionist and post-modernist epistemologies in the 1990s, which led organization theorists to take the 'linguistic turn' (Alvesson and Kärreman, 2000). The constructionist line of thought places actors at the centre of the social construction of reality (Berger and Luckmann, 1966). Thus, its tenets bring the complexity of language to the forefront of organizational analysis. According to this view, organizations are formed through multiple 'discursive constructions' (Fairhurst and Putnam, 2004). Post-modernist thinking has also had a major influence on the development of discourse studies in OTs. For post-modern researchers, language is at the centre of what constitutes the world (Gergen, Gergen, and Barret, 2004). By proposing to view organizations through the metaphor of 'texts', post-modern researchers seek to highlight the multiple effects of power inherent in organizational discourses.

Organization Theories in the Making. Linda Rouleau, Oxford University Press.
© Linda Rouleau (2022). DOI: 10.1093/oso/9780198792024.003.0007

The linguistic turn paved new paths in OTs, far removed from its initial and ubiquitous rationalization project. The linguistic turn's scope is wide, as organizational discourses are polyphonic and pervade all activities related to organizing. Therefore, discourse studies have been used to investigate a wide array of phenomena, including mergers and acquisitions (Vaara, Kleymann, and Seristô, 2004), change (Heracleous and Barrett, 2001; McClellan, 2014), innovation (Bartel and Garud, 2009), field-configuring events (Hardy and Maguire, 2010), strategic planning (Spee and Jarzabkowski, 2011), leadership (Fairhurst and Uhl-Bien, 2012), authority (Benoit-Barné and Cooren, 2009), sustainability (Ferns and Amaeshi, 2021), and work–family dynamics (Kangas, Lämsä, and Jyrkinen, 2019), to name a few. If we take for granted that words are the cornerstone of civilization, does this mean that discourse studies can provide a lens to study any organizational phenomena? For this to be possible, we must first accept the idea that organizations are nothing more than discourses. . . and such a view is laden with implications. This chapter will flesh out these implications.

This far-reaching interest for studying discourse initially appeared and was developed in Europe, and over the past 25 years has extended all around the world. In 1994, the first International Conference on Organizational Discourse took place in Cardiff, UK, on the theme of metaphors[1] (this conference is now held every two years, in July). In addition, the International Centre for Research in Organisational Discourse, Strategy and Change (ICRODSC—https://fbe.unimelb.edu.au/icrodsc) was launched in 2001. This centre's leading team[2] wanted to build a strong collaborative network of world-class scholars in organizational discourse. Since then, the field has been largely institutionalized, as evidenced by the many special issues in academic journals and handbooks discussing the topic (see recent literature reviews, e.g. Phillips and Oswick, 2012; Cederström and Spicer, 2014; Vaara, Sonenshein, and Boje, 2016; Lookwood et al., 2018).

Over the years, discourse studies have become a thriving subfield in OTs; however, discourse studies have also become fraught with confusion, and may be difficult to navigate (Alvesson and Kärreman, 2011). Indeed, each and every specific research stream entails a diversity of paradigmatic variations. Exploring all of these variations in a fine-tuned way would be almost impossible in an OTs book covering multiple perspectives in the field. Nevertheless, this chapter attempts to provide a streamlined roadmap of discourse studies,

[1] David Grant (formerly University of Sydney), Tom Keenoy (Cardiff University), and Cliff Oswick (Cass Business School) spearheaded the conference series.
[2] Cynthia Hardy (Melbourne University), Nelson Phillips, Thomas Lawrence, and Steve McGuire (formerly McGill University).

which will hopefully be helpful for newcomers in OTs. First, the chapter puts forth a brief overview of language and organizational discourse in order to provide an understanding of the importance of discourse studies in OTs. It will then map the main research streams in discourse studies; namely, narrative analysis (NA), communicative constitution of organizations (CCO), discourse analysis (DA), and critical discourse analysis (CDA). After exploring the pros and cons of the linguistic turn in OTs, the chapter will finally discuss the coalescence of discourse and materiality studies and look towards their future.

6.1 From language to organizational discourse

Before mapping the territory of discourse studies, let me briefly reflect on the nature of language. In linguistics, language is essentially the result of a complex system of sounds, written symbols, and gestures. This system allows us to verbalize or to communicate our thoughts to others. The only way we can communicate the ideas that take shape in our minds is to speak, write, or move parts of our body through gestures. Therefore, the basic function of language consists of communicating our thoughts to others. As such, language is a medium that carries meaning. However, language is much more than that. In order for this system of sounds, symbols, and gestures to make sense, language requires us to understand the underlying social rules and norms that are intrinsic to social groups. Language and its specificities are intimately interwoven in a community's life, and differences in language use reflect differences in culture. Therefore, what organizational researchers are interested in is not so much language itself, but rather language as a medium that can help us broaden our understanding of the system of meanings underlying the richness of organizational life.

It is crucial to understand that language is not a transparent and reliable reproduction of reality. It is generative and context dependent. First, the generative propriety of language refers to native speakers' ability to use diverse combinations of words in creative ways while abiding by the grammatical system of rules governing the relations between these words. For example, each informant account is based on a specific way of putting words in action in order to deliver a set of meanings around a lived situation. The human capacity to formulate phrases and figurative expressions in an infinite number of ways is to some extent arbitrary. Each time someone expresses themselves, they produce a very particular if not unique version of what this set of words in use are supposed to represent.

Second, language is context dependent. One specific sentence may have different meanings in different situations. If I say, 'Well, that was a terrible crash!' it might refer to a car accident, a drop in the stock market, ocean waves hitting the shore, or a surprising sound. To understand what such a statement means, we need to know the context in which it is said. Analysing organizational discourse implies that we are exploring both 'what is said' and 'the context in which something is said'. In other words, to use the post-modern metaphor, we are exploring the 'text in context'. The text says almost nothing if it is not re-embedded in the social and organizational context in which it is produced. As these two characteristics of language (generativity and dependence on context) remain a matter of interpretation, opting for a discursive lens opens the door to multiple debates and questions about reality, truth, and its potential generalization (Alvesson and Kärreman, 2000, 2011; Cederström and Spicer, 2014).

Encompassing a broad range of approaches and disciplines, discourse studies seek to highlight the role of texts in the structuration of organizational life. Though highly contested and ambiguous, the term 'discourse' generally refers to a system of meanings that reproduces social and organizational order (Fairhurst and Putnam, 2004). These large-scale systems of meanings are carried on through conversations, stories, talks, narratives, speeches, and documents. In fact, discourses or texts generally include all forms of formal and informal verbal interactions and written texts (Grant, Keenoy, and Oswick, 2001). They can take the form of documents, but also of a wide variety of forms of talk (e.g. verbal reports, speeches, and informal documents). Hardy, Palmer, and Phillips (2000, p. 1231) define discourse as the 'sets of texts—statements, practices, etc. which bring an object into being'. Some authors even include the study of artefacts such as music, art, and architecture in this definition, such that everything related to signs can be considered part of organizational discourse.

Organizational discourse researchers examine the production, distribution and consumption of texts. For example, the production of a strategic plan concerns all the discursive activities around a strategy that shape strategy workshops or strategic planning exercises (Spee and Jarzabkowski, 2011). It is important to mention that the articulation of a strategy within a text (i.e. the strategic plan in itself) constitutes a specific 'communicational genre' that has recognizable characteristics and recurrent patterns (Cornut, Giroux, and Langley, 2012). The distribution of texts concerns the activities by which texts are made available to various stakeholders. The consumption of texts refers to how strategic texts are mobilized and appropriated by stakeholders in a multiplicity of discursive spaces such as board meetings, conversations in hallways, open strategy platforms, seminars, and so on.

A structuring conversation has been going on in the field over the years differentiating discourse with a small 'd' and Discourse with a capital 'D' (Alvesson and Kärreman, 2000). The former is related to talk and text productions at a micro level and involves retrospective accounts and real-time interactions and conversations. The latter is concerned with larger bodies of texts and utterances that are constructed over time and disseminated through different media. Intertextual analysis and deconstruction are thus the preferred methods of analysis of these macro-level discourses. Of course, we contend that it is difficult, if not impossible, to separate any form of discourse into discrete levels of analysis. Researchers make use of such distinction only for the purposes of clarity. The discursive accomplishment of organizing is a multi-level one (Phillips and Oswick, 2012).

In the following sections, four predominant streams of research structuring the field of discourse studies will be introduced: (i) NA; (ii) CCO; (iii) DA; and (iv) CDA. Table 6.1 provides a synoptic view of these streams of research according to a set of common aspects regarding knowledge production in OTs. It is worth noting that each of these streams of research is composed of diverse epistemological and methodological positions. However, only the most prominent one for each respective stream will be discussed in the text that follows.

6.2 Narrative analysis

The notion of narrative is complex and elusive, and has been used in a variety of ways since OTs took the 'narrative turn' at the end of the 1990s (Boje, 1995; Czarniawska, 1996). Sometimes, narrative refers to researchers' writings on the experience of others in papers, books, and so on. A case study or an ethnographic tale constitutes what is often called a 'narrative' in organizational research. Narratives are also often associated with the data gathered during research-based interviews. The word narrative is thus used to simply qualify the type of data on which a research design is based. In this chapter, however, narrative connotes a different meaning—one that is specific to this stream of discourse studies, where organizations are seen as storytelling arenas.

Table 6.1 Synoptic overview of discourse studies

	Narrative analysis	Communicative constitution of organizations	Discourse analysis	Critical discourse analysis
Definition (view of discourse)	Discursive constructions about the world having a beginning and an end (discourse as construction of stories, accounts, and rhetoric)	Text–conversation dynamics constitute the organization (discourse as constitutive of reality)	Systems of meaning re/producing organizational order (discourse as support of order and change)	Systems of meanings producing power effects and inequalities (discourse as constitutive emergence within constraints)
Research question	How do managers and others interpret organizational phenomena?	How does organization happen in communication?	How are organizational discourses aligned (or not) with one another?	How do organizational discourses struggle with one another?
Organization	Storytelling arenas	Plenum of human and material agencies	Discursive constructions	Discursive formations (regimes of truth and control)
Socio-linguistic influences	Bakhtin (1981); Ricoeur (1983); Greimas (1987); McAdams (1993)	Garfinkel (1967); Latour (1986)	Giddens (1984)	Foucault (1972); Fairclough (1995)
Organizational domains	Sensemaking and identity	Organizational communication	Organizational change	Strategic change

Continued

Table 6.1 *Continued*

	Narrative analysis	Communicative constitution of organizations	Discourse analysis	Critical discourse analysis
Conceptual resources	Narrative sensemaking, narrative identity, narrative struggle, and antenarratives	Metaconversation, presentification, ventriloquism, and organizationality	Discursive strategies and resources, discursive constellation, and discursive space	Discursive struggles, truth effects, discursive practices, and discursive legitimation
Level of analysis	Micro (individuals, i.e. *homo narrans*)	Micro (individual and textual agency)	Macro (organizational)	Macro (organizational and societal)
Epistemological model	Constructivism	Critical constructivism	Realism	Critical realism
Methods	Narratological tools (retrospective accounts)	Conversation analysis (real-time conversations and interactions)	Textual analysis (content analysis of stakeholders' interviews and texts)	Intertextual analysis (deconstruction of organizational and inter-organizational texts)
Exemplars	Barry and Elmes (1997); Boudes and Laroche (2009); Musca et al. (2018); Wolf (2019)	Taylor and Van Every (2000); Cooren (2004a, 2004b, 2012, 2015); Dobusch and Schoeneborn (2015); Vásquez et al. (2017)	McClellan (2014); Hardy and Maguire (2010); Zohar (2019); Hardy and Maguire (2020)	Vaara et al. (2006); Laine and Vaara (2007); Vaara and Monin (2010); Hardy and Maguire (2016); McCabe (2016); Ravazzani and Maier (2017)

In their literature review on narrative research in organization studies, Vaara et al. (2016, p. 496) define narratives as 'discursive constructions that provide a means for individual, social and organizational sensemaking and sensegiving'. There are two important dimensions in this definition and they are central to capturing the essence of the narrative approach. NA is based on a 'discourse constructs' view and considers that stories are powerful carriers of meanings. First, discursive construction involves the idea that a narration is a creative act of interpretation or authoring. Individuals, whether they are managers or not, are *homo narrans*. They order and interpret the events they experience in an organizational context by creating stories that are told and retold. A similar event might thus be assembled and reassembled in various stories. Second, narratives or stories are pivotal in sensemaking/sensegiving. According to Brown and Thompson (2013, p. 1145), 'narratives are a fundamental form of "meaning making" most often preoccupied with "human actions and events that affect human beings"'. They convey shared values and multiple meanings while reducing the equivocality of organizational life.

Similar to stories, narratives have distinctive features: temporality; emplotment; ordering; and agency. Temporality is central to NA, as a narrative comprises a beginning, a middle, and an end. Moreover, a good story contains traces of the past and of the future. During the narration process, past insights are evoked in the present, and future possible actions are pinpointed. Since they ascribe meaning to past events, narratives imply an appealing and preferred course of action (Barry and Elmes, 1997). Also, narratives transform a sequence of events into a meaningful plot that involves characters whose actions drive the plot forward. Hence the storyline, or plot, is a key feature of narratives. As a meaning-making device, narratives also order and distil ambiguous and triggering events, and in so doing ensure that the unfamiliar becomes understandable and *a fortiori* coherent. Finally, the descriptions of events made in narrative accounts contribute to shape the organizational reality and, in turn, organizational reality influences the narrative's form over time.

As organization encompasses both narration and narrating, we can find two ways of conducting NA in the field of OTs: a structural approach and a processual approach. In the former, researchers seek to interpret the 'underlying structure of meanings' behind the narration (i.e. a text or a spoken discourse). A structural NA aims to better understand a narrative's plot line. In the latter, narrating is viewed as a 'process' where researchers look at how narratives or stories are produced, disseminated, appropriated, supported, and even resisted. Of course, such a distinction between structural (narration) and processual (narrating) approaches is not always clear-cut, as NA sometimes combine elements of both. Let me introduce some illustrative examples extracted from organizational sensemaking and identity research—the main domains where NA has flourished over the past decades.

To perform a structural NA, researchers draw on a wide variety of narratological tools inspired from literary work and semiology (e.g. Barthes, 1966; Bakhtin, 1981; Greimas, 1987). For example, those narratological tools include, but are not limited to, voice and perspective, readership, actantial dynamics, syntactic structure, and so on (Vaara et al., 2016). It might also be relevant to look at structuring contradictions (e.g. credibility and novelty of a text (Barry and Elmes, 1997)) and repetitions (Dailey and Browning, 2014) that might pervade the narration. For instance, Boudes and Laroche (2009) studied the official post-crisis reports regarding the 2003 French heatwave and explained how these reports served to restore meanings and order after the crisis. To depict the central plot of those successive reports, they borrowed Greimas (1987)'s 'semiotic square', which led them to identify and demonstrate the underlying tension between 'knowing and acting in time' (Boudes and Laroche, 2009). These authors also used Greimas (1987)'s 'actantial model' to analyse how the reports were casting the roles of actors (e.g. heroes, opponents, adjutants) in order to uncover who was deemed responsible. In this paper, the Greimassian semiotic tools are used to demonstrate how meanings that would otherwise have gone unnoticed were crystallized in official post-crisis reports. Musca et al. (2018) analysed the logbook of the Darwin mountaineering expedition relying on the notion of chronotopes (chronos = time, topos = space) borrowed from Bakhtin (1981). A chronotope is a unique configuration of time and space used to organize a specific literary genre (e.g. physical roads in an adventure novel). They examined the syntactic structure of the logbook and found two central figures of speech— 'dropping the boat' and 'let's pack our bags'—that articulated the expedition's meanings during days 9 and 10, a moment that proved to be crucial. The authors show that the transition between these figures of speech was central in the process of reframing the expedition's meanings around different goals resulting from unexpected events.

Narrative processual analysis invites scholars to find ways of analysing individual or organizational narratives by using both semiotic and ethnographic techniques. On the individual side, narrative scholars seek to better understand how managers and others 'tell' their organizational lives. For example, drawing on a narrative identity perspective (McAdams, 1993), Wolf (2019) conducted 'life stories' of 29 managers and professionals dealing with significant shifts in their careers owing to new requirements of modern organizations. Doing so led her to reconstitute the common themes and patterns that characterize the life trajectories of non-linear careers. Similar approaches were used to understand other facets of managerial and professional identity work. Bardon, Brown, and Pezé (2017) examined the narrative struggle over what it meant to be a competent middle manager and to make decisions that are both effective and moral. Heikkinen and Lämsä (2017) analysed the narratives of male managers to see how they perceived their wives' support in relation to their careers. The men's interviews were framed around three different storylines: romance, 'happily-ever-after', and tragedy of spousal support. The romance narrative emphasizes the interrelated nature of family and career. In this kind of storyline, the spousal support is regularly negotiated between the partners. In the 'happily-ever-after' storyline, the gender role division is clearly articulated and the spousal support is thus narratively constructed as enriching the men's careers. When the storyline takes the form of a tragedy, the spousal support declines over the course of male managers' careers.

On the organizational side, the purpose of narrative research is to answer the following questions: How do stakeholders (e.g. managers, professionals, and employees) produce and reproduce organizational stories? How do organizational stories emerge, become dominant, become displaced, or even resisted? Here, organizational narratives refer to shared stories and meanings around a set of common values and actions. For example, Chreim (2005) looked at continuity and change in a bank's identity narratives on both individual and organizational levels. Her analysis of annual reports and press releases allowed her to describe a set of discursive strategies used by senior managers and management teams to position continuity and change in complementarity to one another (e.g. selective reporting of past, present, and future events). Rhodes, Pullen, and Clegg (2010) analysed stories of organizational change reported by employees and managers in an organization that had undergone persistent downsizing. They show how a central narrative of inevitable decline became dominant throughout the organization. By portraying the organization as a victim of the new capitalism area, this narrative had the ethical consequence of downplaying the organizational responsibility for its economic downturn.

NA is actually a substream of discourse studies in which researchers interpret stories that are told and retold within the context of organizational life. It is worth mentioning that NA is mostly based on the assumption that some organizational narratives or stories are more prevalent or 'dominant' than others (Vaara et al., 2016). Though less widespread, there is also research that uses NA to grasp the political dynamics at play in organizational texts through rhetoric and antenarratives (i.e. narratives that are not widely shared but can potentially merge into one; see Boje, 2008). Such rhetorical devices function to increase (or undermine) the credibility and dominance of some organizational narratives. Hence, rhetorical dynamics is sometimes used to 'authorize' change while masking counter or antenarratives.

6.3 Communicative constitution of organizations

The CCO substream of discourse studies was first developed in the field of organizational communication (Taylor and Van Every, 2000; Cooren, 2004a, 2004b, 2006, 2012; Robichaud, Giroux and Taylor, 2004; Ashcraft, Kuhn, and Cooren, 2009; Kuhn, 2012; Cooren, 2015). The CCO approach assumes that communicative phenomena are what constitute social realities and organizations. As Schoeneborn, Kuhn, and Kärreman (2019, p. 476) put it, 'organization [and organizing] happens in communication'. Organizational members not only communicate with others but also ultimately constitute others, as they are in turn constituted through ongoing communication acts and multiple communicative social practices such as verbal and non-verbal expressions. As it is concerned with the role of discourse in 'constituting' organization, CCO thus takes a 'discourse as constitutive of reality' view.

At first glance, the differences between NA and CCO might not be so obvious given that both share the understanding that organization is performed at a micro level. Yet, while NA focuses on the meanings of texts, the CCO stream of research emphasizes their effects and performative consequences. Also, unlike NA, CCO assumes that communication is grounded in action. Hence, organizations are 'talked, written and acted into existence' (Vásquez et al., 2017, p. 418) through conversations where organizing takes place. The basic premise is that an organization is not the sum of its members or of its professional roles, but rather of an incessant flood of conversations and texts evoking it and making it identifiable as a distinct entity (Taylor and Van Every, 2000; Cooren, 2010; Taylor and Van Every, 2010).

The CCO perspective also considers that organization and organizing is performed through the complex entanglement between humans and non-humans. Action is understood as the ability of a form of existence to make a difference in the course of events (Latour, 2005). This ability is not only the prerogative of living beings; it also applies to inanimate objects that can be mobilized or act automatically. Within the framework of CCO analysis, the goal is not to establish perfect symmetry between human and non-human entities, but to consider all agents of various ontologies that are an integral part of making an organization what it is (Ashcraft, Kuhn, and Cooren, 2009). According to CCO scholars, materiality is a *sine qua non* condition of existence. As a matter of fact, even ideas must be supported by a certain degree of materiality, given that certain molecules are required for them to be formulated in a person's brain (Cooren, 2004b). It follows that even though we are aware of its physical components, materiality cannot necessarily be seen by the naked eye (*Ibid.*). In this way, organization is a plenum of human and material agencies (Cooren, 2004b).

Aside from these baseline assumptions, CCO is a heterogeneous subset of discourse studies as it comprises different 'schools of CCO thinking' (Brummans, 2014). First developed in North America, this stream of discourse studies rapidly expanded in European countries over the past decade (e.g. there has been a subtheme dedicated to CCO at the European Group for Organisational Studies (EGOS) colloquium since 2015). Boivin, Brummans, and Barker (2017) propose an extensive literature review covering a span of 15 years (2000–2015) to demonstrate how CCO has been institutionalized over time. Located at the intersection of communication and organizational studies, CCO encompasses a diversity of theoretical and methodological influences such as structuration theory, actor–network theory, social system theory, ethnomethodology, speech acts, and conversation analysis, to name a few. This variety of influences allowed CCO to gain legitimacy within the greater fields of discourse and organization studies. Being able to unpack communicative phenomena from multiple angles is certainly a great advantage in disseminating a new set of ideas about organizing.

Under the leadership of 'The Montreal School' (TMS) of organizational communication, CCO research was able to consolidate its 'place at the interdisciplinary table' (Boivin, Brummans, and Barker, 2017, p. 348). It is no secret that TMS is considered the leading group of CCO (Schoeneborn, Kuhn, and Kärreman, 2019). Researchers associated with this school study the socio-linguistics dynamics necessary for cooperating in and constructing a common project. TMS focuses on unpacking how an organization emerges (or comes into existence) through networks of conversations, texts, and patterns of material and time–space coordination.

As of 2021, TMS counts three generations of CCO scholars. The first generation of researchers, led by James Taylor, developed the theoretical grounds of the CCO approach (Taylor and Van Every, 2000). Robichaud et al. (2004) define the notion of 'constitution' as both a process by which an organization is established through the interaction of its members and a product resulting from these interactions (e.g. the set of underlying understandings about the rights and responsibilities structuring organizational members' interactions). According to these authors, organizing occurs through 'meta-conversation'; that is, 'from the recursive processes of the conversations of the members, where each conversation narratively frames, implicitly or explicitly, the previous one' (Robichaud et al., 2004, p. 624). More specifically, Robichaud et al. (2004) illustrate the notion of metaconversation by examining the exchanges between a mayor and citizens during a public meeting about the services provided by the city's administration. Similarly, Cooren (2004a) examined excerpts from board meetings and illustrates how a 'collective mind' (a Weickian notion) emerges in a mundane conversation between managers. In so doing, he shows how one can engage in 'scaling up' from conversations to organization, thus proposing a way to resolve the so-called micro–macro gap in communication and organization studies. At the beginning of the 2000s, TMS was largely influenced by Giddens' structuration theory and the Four-Flows Model (an American school of CCO thinking, see Fairhurst and Putman, 2004).

The second generation of TMS scholars expand these ideas by considering all agents of various ontologies in organizing. The works of Cooren (2006, 2012, 2015) are central to the development of this second generation. Conducting fieldwork in mundane and emergency organizational settings, the author developed a vocabulary to explain how organizing and coordination take place when acting at a distance and across time through a chain of co-presence effects. What does this mean? To achieve coordination, control or even authority, managers and employees act at a distance—or 'teleact', to use Cooren's term—by appropriating for themselves the actions and words of pre-existing figures among others. Acting and speaking on behalf of others (e.g. organization, managers, co-workers, rules) or making others present in a conversation ('presentification', as he calls it) is a key feature of agency and organizing. In a paper on Médecins Sans Frontières (MSF, also known as Doctors Without Borders), Benoit-Barné and Cooren (2009) claim that authority is the result of an effect of presence and is not simply wielded by titles and status. Based on a video excerpt where Cooren is introduced by the hospital coordinator to its main units, the paper illustrates how diverse sources of authority (e.g. notes on the security rules on the wall, coordinator's status, government, MSF) were invoked during the conversation between the coordinator and the technicians on site. Therefore, entities with various ontologies were able to influence the flow of the interactions through these punctual and distributed effects of presence. Cooren (2012) sees communication as *ventriloquial*. When people speak, they also lend their voices to the principles, norms, viewpoints, and other 'figures' that materialize through their speech (Benoit-Barné and Cooren, 2009; Cooren, 2012, 2015). The metaphor of ventriloquism stresses that the relationship is reciprocal, as the figures people invoke in their speech also make them say and do things.

A third generation of scholars belonging to TMS but also including other CCO approaches is currently advancing CCO research in the field of OTs. For example, Dobusch and Schoeneborn (2015) examined the identity claims of an activist hacker's community and came up with the notion of 'organization-ality' to refer to new organizational forms characterized by fluid, networked, and boundaryless collective arrangements. Vásquez et al. (2017) looked at communicative practices, namely presentifying, substantiating, attributing, and crystallizing, by which some ideas gradually gain a strategic character in a community-based organization. Wilhoit-Larson (2020) explored alterna-tive workspaces (spaces where work is done outside the formal organization, such as aeroplanes, home offices, coffee shops, and so on). She aimed to understand how such temporary spaces become appropriated and made 'organizational' by workers. It is worth noting that this new generation of CCO scholars goes beyond reinterpreting organizational phenomena under the CCO lens. As a matter of fact, they also generate cumulative knowledge about other organizational phenomena.

The main contribution of CCO to OTs has been to foster the re-examination of organizational phenomena by proposing to see them as fluid and precarious communicative accomplishments. These scholars gen-erally conduct fine-grained empirical studies in their organizational settings (Vásquez et al., 2012). With regard to the linguistic turn in OTs, CCO has left its mark on OTs over the years by adopting a different approach to studying how organization, organizing, or organizationality is talked into existence.

6.4 Discourse analysis

DA, also called organizational discourse analysis ODA; see Alvesson and Kär-reman, 2000), promotes an understanding of discourse at a more formal and broader level than the previous two research streams described. Instead of zooming in on the micro level of narratives and conversations, DA looks at the macro level of 'grand narratives' or 'metanarratives'. One must note that it is not unusual to see the notion of discourse used interchangeably with that of narrative, especially when such discourse designates a large-scale system of meanings. Organizational discourse refers to master discourses 'circulat-ing' in society and organizations. For instance, the ecological discourse, the feminist discourse, the risk discourse, and the SuperNurse discourse dur-ing the COVID-19 crisis are all discourses, or grand narratives, circulating within and across society. Certain types of discourses are more specific to organizations. This is the case of organizational change, corporate responsibility, customer satisfaction, and stakeholder inclusion discourses, to name a few.

Hardy and Maguire (2010, p. 1367) define organizational discourse as collections of 'interrelated bodies of texts that determines "who and what is 'normal', standard and acceptable"' in social and organizational spheres. Its purpose is to legitimize and control organizational visions of the world as well as to produce unified identities and representations. For many researchers, organizational discourse embodies cultural meanings that enable social interaction and communication. Aligned with the core values of the organization, organizational discourse provides managers and others with discursive resources and textual strategies for creating or appropriating meaningful interpretations of organizational events. Nevertheless, organizational discourses are linked to broader societal discourses that reproduce dominant values and ideologies. For instance, as mentioned earlier, the COVID-19 pandemic has given rise to new discourses (e.g. the SuperNurse discourse and the virtual work discourse) within popular media that reflect and reinforce, in multiple ways, the gendered nature of the impacts of COVID-19 in service organizations.

DA provides a perspective on the nature of organization as discursive constructions. It seeks to explain how organizational texts are made meaningful through discursive activities, practices, and events. By revealing the discursive strategies and resources embedded within texts, DA thus takes a 'discourse as support' view of organizational order and change. DA research seeks to better understand how different organizational discourses are or can become aligned with one another in order to support the organizations' maintenance and/or change. As in NA, organizational discourse refers to the dominant discourse clusters, while its periphery is made up of counter-discourses. For example, the analysis of open government reform in Austria by Kornberger et al. (2017) reveals the existence of two discourses around this change: open government as the logical consequence of new public management policies (dominant discourse); and open government as a break from the new public management policies (counter-discourse). In spite of these differences, the authors observe that both discourses nevertheless led to a promotion of convergent actions (e.g. opening government-owned databases through diverse technological applications) that the city managers could live with, despite divergent goals.

DA carries two main orientations regarding the representation of what Fairhurst and Putnam (2004) call the 'discourse–organization relationship'. Organizational discourse can be seen either as organizational features and outcomes or as a process of organizational formation or becoming. These representations of the organization do not oppose one another nor are they mutually exclusive. Indeed, in the same article or book chapter, we can sometimes see both views coexisting. Let us take a closer look at what these representations consist of.

In cases where discourse is viewed as organizational features and outcomes, it is said to result from the intersection of mediations stemming from the use of pre-existing discursive materials produced by influential discursive agents (e.g. CEO, top managers, professionals, engineers). Here, the organization 'exists prior to discourse, remains stable over time, and has specified features or components that shape language use' (Fairhurst and Putnam, 2004, p. 2009). The two following examples show that organizational discourse, considered as organizational features and outcomes, is seen as something we can influence and possibly control. McClellan (2014) studied how organizational discourse within an international data solutions company providing data transfer services in diverse markets evolved after the announcement of a separation between its bureaucratic headquarters and one of its subsidiaries that was to become public. Following the announcement of this change, three different discourses prevailed in the subsidiary: a discourse of organization (an organization that is profitable but constrained by a bureaucratic centre); a discourse of change (surprise and uncertainty regarding the separation from the bureaucratic headquarters); and a discourse about the future (if freed from its bureaucratic headquarters, the subsidiary's financial success was expected to increase). McClellan (2014) shows how the three organizational discourses aligned with one another in a discursive constellation that reaffirmed the maintenance of organizational meanings. In a recent paper, Zohar (2019) studied how a discourse, or grand narrative, of inclusion emerged and was diffused and crystallized as a central feature of the global agenda of the Organisation for Economic Co-operation and Development (OECD) since 2006. The paper shows that this organizational discourse became entangled in every segment of the OECD's activities over the years. In this case, the author assumed that the discourse of inclusion was produced by, and simultaneously produced, the organization.

In the case where organizational discourse is seen as a process of organizational formation or becoming, it is considered as being constructed, maintained, reproduced, and even imposed on organizational members through global narratives that are recognizable in various domains, professions, and organization fields. Therefore, according to this orientation, discourse shapes the organization; meanwhile, the organization is in a constant state of change that is produced and reproduced through discourses in circulation. The work of Hardy and Maguire (2010) illustrates this processual orientation in DA. The authors studied the discourse around DDT—dichlorodiphenyltrichloroethane, an insecticide used in agriculture—that took shape during the Stockholm Convention on Persistent Organic Pollutants, which brought together multiple actors from different organizational fields. They drew on the notion of discursive space to examine the dynamics by which the Convention had been produced, distributed, and consumed between governmental, corporate, and civil organizations. A discursive space is a space in which actors discuss and debate important issues for the future of their group. Such a space can be physical (e.g. conversations in hallways, plenary talks, external communications) or virtual (e.g. platform meetings, online community) and it is governed by specific rules and understandings. Hardy and Maguire (2010) observed the existence of three main narratives or systems of meanings around the DDT controversy that have evolved over time: DDT as an evil threat (which was the dominant narrative from the beginning until 1998); DDT as a hero (the counter-narrative that emerged in 1999); and, finally, DDT as a necessary evil (which emerged as the concluding narrative). This transformation was possible owing to the existence of a multiplicity of discursive spaces providing peripheral actors with opportunities to influence the positions and understandings of others through their counter-discourse. In so doing, peripheral actors got to shape the reality in which they were embedded.

DA is often described as the systematic study of spoken and recorded forms of organizational discourse. Surprisingly, there is no definite or prescriptive way of analysing data from a DA perspective. Most of the time, organizational researchers must develop a customized approach to analyse their textual data. Some researchers look at modal markers and evidential devices in the text. For example, to examine the legitimizing strategies in online newspaper articles around the Scottish referendum, Alonso-Almeida and Carrió-Pastor (2019) used WordSmith corpus tools (a lexical analysis software) and identified diverse grammatical modal markers such as indirect inferential evidence (e.g. seem, appear, look, clearly); indirect reportative evidence (e.g. according to x, said, told, apparently, supposedly); epistemic modality (e.g. must, may, might, could, certainly, surely, probably, possibly, perhaps); and cognitive verbs (e.g. I/we know, I/we think, I/we believe, I/we suppose, it seems to me/us). Using modal markers to analyse a corpus of texts, researchers can find support for their interpretations with statistics or verify their qualitative findings. Yet, most of the time, researchers apply content analysis not on one single text but rather on a corpus of texts (Hardy, 2022).

While this type of analysis is supposed to be systematic, content analysis itself is a crafty method where the linguistic function and rules underlying the texts are analysed in great detail, which entails an enormous amount of work that is often underestimated. For instance, when one looks closely at how Hardy and Maguire (2020) analysed their data about novel risks based on prior work on chemical bisphenol A (BPA), it becomes patently clear that they went through a series of iterative steps to develop deep knowledge about how to interpret the plural texts' meanings. Also note that researchers can use both ways (modal markers and content analysis) to analyse one single corpus of texts.

The notion of organizational discourse in DA is applied broadly to the collection of texts actors draw on as they carry out their activities. Discourse is considered as global systems of meanings that either produce or are produced by the organization. However, most of the time, DA ignores how organizational discourse is constrained by underlying social structures. This, rather, is the aim of CDA.

6.5 Critical discourse analysis

Discourses can be vehicles of change and adaptation but also of resistance, contestation, oppression, and manipulation. Discourses produce and reproduce not only social and organizational orders but also inequalities. CDA (also called organizational critical discourse analysis (OCDA); Alvesson and Kärreman, 2000) differs from DA in that it recasts organizational discourses in their institutional constraints or social contexts, as well as in its main objective, which centres on power issues. CDA development in OTs stems from the development of applied linguistics approaches and the spreading of critical studies in different social science domains. CDA was originally founded by Fairclough (1992, 2005) and his colleagues (Gunther Kress, Teun van Dijk, Theo van Leeuwen, and Ruth Wodak). In OTs, as well as in strategic management, Eero Vaara and his colleagues have been central to the diffusion of CDA. Although there are several approaches in CDA, the Foucauldian influence remains preponderant in OTs.

CDA highlights the discursive 'power effects' at play in stabilizing organizational meanings and making them appear as taken for granted or 'normal'. As per the three dimensional framework developed by Fairclough (1995), in order to understand discourses and their normalizing and performative effects, we must also take into account the continuous and recursive relationships between texts, organizational discourse, and the institutional constraints in which they are embedded. CDA posits that we cannot understand specific texts and discourses without resituating them in their organizational and institutional contexts. Indeed, constraints may be reproduced through discursive processes and practices across multiple organizational texts. As such, Moodley and Schvaughn (2020) studied the discourses around the Ebola virus/disease in South African news reports (March 2014 to June 2015). Four types of discourses were found: threat to humanity; predation; invasion; and conspiracy. The authors show that these discourses reproduced the colonialist imagery. For instance, the conspiracy discourse was leveraged as a means of defence against colonial oppression and increased local and international political tensions during the Ebola outbreak.

CDA assumes that discourse emerges and develops according to the discursive rules of a 'hegemonic order', which is a set of unifying and regulating mechanisms that ensure its normalization. In their paper on what they call 'riskification' discourse, Hardy and Maguire (2016, p. 82) define discourse as 'a collection of interrelated texts and practices "that systematically form the object of which they speak" [Foucault, 1979: 49]'. As organizational discourses define or give meanings to concepts and events, CDA adopts a 'discourse as constitutive emergence' view. Over time, organizational discourses contribute to legitimating some ideas and meanings over others by naturalizing them. Hardy and Maguire (2016) further explain that the technical language of risk (e.g. high risk, acceptable risk) has become commonplace in both expert circles and popular groups to address a diversity of medically, environmentally, financially, or technically risky situations. The dissemination of this terminology gradually established a coherent way of defining what is acceptable or not in uncertain contexts. Indeed, the expression that we are living in a 'risky society' effectively translates the fact that the language of risk permeates contemporaneous life; Hardy and Maguire (2016, p. 95) call this phenomenon 'riskification', which refers to discourses 'whereby risk becomes further entrenched as "the natural way to talk about a variety of concerns"'.

While DA seeks to align discourses, the purpose of CDA is rather to highlight the dynamics of 'discursive struggles' between hegemonic discourses and counter-discourses. Organizations are not just sites where meanings are produced and negotiated; they also result from the struggle where different groups compete to shape their social reality. As regimes of truth and control, organizations are maintained and resisted through discursive struggles. The notion of discursive struggle can also be associated with the idea of 'distorted communication', which facilitates the suppression of counter-discourses in organizational settings. Looking at the strategy development process of an engineering group, Laine and Vaara (2007) show the struggle between three central discursive patterns: the formulation and launch of an official strategic discourse by the top management team; the creation by middle managers of their own strategic discourse as a means of resisting the official one; and the project engineers' development of a discourse emphasizing their experience and professionalism in order to distance themselves from the strategic discourses of top and middle managers. By demonstrating how discursive struggles are manifested in organizational settings, the authors highlight the dynamics between control and resistance as well as the disempowering/empowering effects intrinsic to strategic discourses.

CDA is often used in OTs to depict the discursive strategies or the discursive 'truth effect' whereby organizations legitimize their actions or delegitimize opposing views. For example, Vaara, Tianari, and Laurila (2006) studied how a controversial merger between a Finnish (Enso) and a Swedish (Stora) pulp and paper mill was portrayed as legitimate in respective local newspapers. They identify five discursive strategies by which the merger was legitimized: normalization; authorization; rationalization; moralization; and narrativization. Vaara and Monin (2010) examined the merger between French pharmaceutical companies BioMérieux and Pierre Fab. They highlight the fundamental role of naturalization as discursive legitimization and delegitimization strategies by demonstrating how the merger was publicly shaped by the companies as inevitable and necessary. The authors conclude by stressing that such discursive strategies revolve around rationality, authority, and morality. Ravazzani and Maier (2017) studied how an astronomical observatory dealt with protests against the construction of a telescope on Mauna Kea, a Hawaiian mountain considered sacred by the local culture. By analysing the corporation's posts on Facebook, they show that such posts were legitimizing the new telescope by invoking impersonal authority and echoing supporters' voices and actions.

Some researchers also adopt CDA to understand how discourse defines status and allows individuals to be seen as disciplined 'subjects'. Discourses such as the 'ideal customer', 'students' excellence', or 'employee of the month' all contribute to mould the subjectivities of individuals targeted by these discourses. The prevalence of such discourses results in customers, students, and employees behaving in ways that conform to those idealized managerial expectations. McCabe (2016) shows how frontline workers are transformed into numerical value following manager-defined ratios, scenario planning, workflows, and so on. When combined, these micro processes of 'numericalizing the other' exercise considerable power. By distancing themselves from what workers are living, managers contribute to reproducing ongoing workplace struggles central to capitalist enterprises.

By silencing some actors and giving voice to others, organizational discourses define the positions of subjects and shape their identities. Not only do managers shape the subjectivities of others through their discursive activities; their own selves are also impacted. Writing an organizational policy, pronouncing an organizational discourse, or explaining to subordinates how a job needs to be done are all highly political acts that contribute to managerial identity construction. For instance, Laine et al. (2016) highlight the subtle performative dynamic of identity construction in strategy talk. According to these authors, there is a close link between the socio-historical discourse of strategy and the strategists' subjectivity. They identify three dynamics of submission/mastery performed by managers in their strategy talk: illusion of control (the analytical strategist); omnipotence (the strategic leader); and personal glory (the state-of-the-art strategist). According to Mantere and Whittington (2021), the identity of strategist is ambiguous; therefore, becoming a strategist is often experienced as an existential challenge. Following the analysis of their data, the authors distinguish three identity work tactics (self-measurement, self-construction, and self-actualization), whereby strategic discourse has both disciplinary and emancipatory effects in shaping the role of strategist.

Methodologically, CDA aims to deconstruct the dominant organizational discourse and the corresponding counter-discourses. The goal is to identify latent or underlying manifestations of power–knowledge relations in texts and discursive practices. Moreover, CDA cannot be conducted without considering the context in which the discourses analysed are produced. This makes the task of choosing which specific texts to analyse even more difficult. Also, CDA is based on various types of textual data, including documents, interviews, and media texts. Largely influenced by media studies (e.g. see Vaara et al., 2006); Vaara and Monin (2010); Ravazzani and Maier, 2017), CDA relies on the researcher's craftsmanship, and the method is essentially based on multiple steps of theme or content analysis (Hardy, 2022).

CDA's ultimate goal is to highlight the critical link between the production of texts or large systems of meanings and the social context in which they emerge and evolve. Focusing on 'truth effects', it emphasizes the connection between the macro and micro levels of discursive activities. While it is duly recognized, it is probably the least developed substream of discursive studies in the field of OTs.

6.6 Towards a post-linguistic turn

The distinct but interrelated substreams of research in discourse studies explore how organizations, industries, and their environments are created, maintained, and changed through narratives, conversations, and large systems of meanings. In so doing, discourse studies make strong contributions towards advancing our understanding of organizations. However, discourse studies are not without their limitations. We began this chapter by referring to Lookwood et al. (2018), who suggest that 'we can do things with words'. Does this imply that organizations are nothing more than words or discourses? Before debating this question, I will review the main promises made by discourse studies as well as the challenges they face.

Though broad and heterogeneous, discourse studies have delivered on some of their promises by providing multiple opportunities for developing meaningful contributions in OTs. Discourse studies encompass a wide range of epistemological, theoretical, and methodological grounds. They represent a transdisciplinary field involving OTs, as well as communication, sociology, linguistics, cultural anthropology, and social psychology, to name a few. By emphasizing the plurivocal or polyphonic aspects of individual and organizational narratives and discursive practices, discourse studies offer opportunities to better understand how heterogeneous and multiple voices engage in organizing. They can be conducted at both levels of reality: micro reality (i.e. the analysis of how individuals express themselves and use language) and macro reality (i.e. the analysis of discourses provided by organizations, institutions, and society). This field of study calls on various methodological devices (e.g. conversation analysis, rhetorical analysis, narrative, metaphorical deconstruction, and media studies).

Characterized by multiple perspectives and paradigmatic positions, discourse studies lack integration and remain an ambiguous field of study. All trends are present and welcome. On the one hand, this is positive, as it opens the door to experimentation and renewal. On the other hand, it impinges on its credibility. For some researchers, language is simply an epiphenomenon of what is going on in organizations. It is not possible to grasp its meaning with certainty—much less measure it. We are in a world of interpretation and representation. In everyday life, the meanings of words are in constant flux. When an organizational member says something, how can we be sure that what they are saying corresponds to what they are thinking? As discursive studies remain based on subjective understandings, the resulting interpretations are not always easy to sell to the scientific community.

Moreover, difficulties arise, especially in the course of empirical research and data collection. While highly stimulating, finding one's own way of conducting research under this lens can rapidly turn into nightmare. Organizations produce a large number of texts in a variety of forms. Hence, deciding which ones should be analysed is a major recurring issue. In addition, there is no straightforward tool or procedure to conduct a narrative or discourse study. The justification around the few quotes analysed in depth is often rather rudimentary. In other words, the lack of rigour in sampling and analysing discourse is flagrant, and it often increases the suspicion of editors and reviewers, who are still relatively unfamiliar with the fundamentals of discourse studies. Numerous researchers are sceptical about the concrete implications of such studies; though very stimulating in terms of ideas, their practical implications remain underdeveloped.

Over time, the interest in depicting the complexity of organizational discourse seems to have vanished. Organizational discourse is increasingly used interchangeably with other notions like narrative, frame, competing rationality, logic, vocabulary, category, and so on. All of them refer to a more or less broad system of meanings, prompting OTs researchers to use narrative or discourse analysis in a metaphorical way. Rather than enriching our comprehension of organizational discourse by bringing to the forefront its socio-linguistics roots, the notion of organizational discourse is becoming multifarious and therefore in danger of 'standing for nothing and everything!'

In order to cope with these challenges, discourse studies are regenerating themselves by following the turn to materiality in OTs, thus taking a post-linguistic turn. Currently, 'materiality' and even 'multimodality' are the new topics in discourse studies. Not only do 'we do things with words' (Lookwood et al., 2018), but words also 'matter'. Critics of discourse studies claim that scholars have devoted too little concern to the material features and other modalities by which organizational discourse is performed. They question what they claim to be the tendency to reduce organizations to one form, in this case a discursive one, at the expense of materiality and other elements (e.g. bodies, objects, spaces, and even practices, according to Hardy and Thomas, 2015). Language serves to represent the world, but it also constitutes it; discourse is action, not only representation. As Cooren (2006) tells us, organizations are composed of a 'plenum of agencies'.

In discourse studies, organizational discourse is now increasingly seen as inseparable from and intertwined with the material world. There is a materiality to or within discourse; materiality acts as a constitutive element of organizational discourse, and vice versa. The inextricable link by which both are interwoven can be conceptualized in different ways (see the point and counterpoint 'New directions in studying discourse and materiality', in *Journal of Management Studies*, 2015). There are different routes to conceptualizing the relationships between materiality and discourses (see Section 7.4 in the Chapter 7), which makes the whole enterprise tricky indeed!

Overall, discourse studies are of great importance for OTs scholars. Inasmuch as questions of 'stories', 'textual agency', and 'discourses' are raised, it remains that this particular field of OTs needs enhanced reflexivity. We should never forget that we, as academics, produce stories, texts, and discourses. We use language to report on the nature of the organizational world and are therefore entangled in discursive webs. Words are carriers of 'truth' or 'knowledge', whether they be in the form articles, books, or teaching and business consultations. We should be more reflective about the capacity of language to represent reality. After all, academic discourses also produce power or performative effects!

References

Alonso-Almeida, F. & Carrió-Pastor, M. L. 2019. Constructing Legitimation in Scottish Newspapers: The Case of the Independence Referendum. *Discourse Studies*, 21, 621–635.

Alvesson, M. & Kärreman, D. 2000. Taking the Linguistic Turn in Organizational Research. *Journal of Applied Behavioral Science*, 36, 136–158.

Alvesson, M. & Kärreman, D. 2011. Decolonializing Discourse: Critical Reflections on Organizational Discourse Analysis. *Human Relations*, 64, 1121–1146.

Ashcraft, K. L., Kuhn, T. R., & Cooren, F. 2009. Constitutional Amendments: 'Materializing' Organizational Communication. *The Academy of Management Annals*. London, Routledge.

Bakhtin, M. M. 1981. *The Dialogic Imagination: Four Essays*. Austin, TX, University of Texas Press.

Bardon, T., Brown, A. D., & Pezé, S. 2017. Identity Regulation, Identity Work and Phronesis. *Human Relations*, 70, 940–965.

Barry, D. & Elmes, M. 1997. Strategy Retold: Toward a Narrative View of Strategic Discourse. *Academy of Management Review*, 22, 429–452.

Bartel, C. A. & Garud, R. 2009. The Role of Narratives in Sustaining Organizational Innovation. *Organization Science*, 20, 107–117.

Barthes, R. 1966. Introduction à l'analyse structurale des récits. *Communications*, 8, 1–27.

Benoit-Barné, C. & Cooren, F. 2009. The Accomplishment of Authority through Presentification. How Authority Is Distributed among and Negotiated by Organizational Members. *Management Communication Quarterly*, 23, 5–31.

Berger, P. L. & Luckmann, T. 1966. *The Social Construction of Reality*. New York, Anchor Books.

Boivin, G., Brummans, B. H. J. M., & Barker, J. R. 2017. The Institutionalization of CCO Scholarship: Trends from 2000 to 2015. *Management Communication Quarterly*, 31, 331–355.

Boje, D. 1995. Stories of the Storytelling Organization: A Postmodern Analysis of Disney as 'Tamara-Land'. *The Academy of Management Journal*, 38, 997–1035.

Boje, D. 2008. *Storytelling Organizations*. London, Sage.

Boudes, T. & Laroche, H. 2009. Taking Off the Heat: Narrative Sensemaking in Post-Crisis Inquiry Reports. *Organization Studies*, 30, 377–396.

Brown, A. D. & Thompson, E. R. 2013. A Narrative Approach to Strategy-as-Practice. *Business History*, 55, 1143–1167.

Brummans, B. H. J. M. 2014. Pathways to Mindful Qualitative Organizational Communication Research. *Management Communication Quarterly*, 28, 440–447.

Cederström, C. & Spicer, A. 2014. Discourse of the Real Kind: A Post-Foundational Approach to Organizational Discourse Analysis. *Organization*, 21, 178–205.

Chreim, S. 2005. The Continuity–Change Duality in Narrative Texts of Organizational Identity. *Journal of Management Studies*, 42, 567–593.

Cooren, F. 2004a. The Communicative Achievement of Collective Minding. *Management Communication Quarterly*, 17, 517–551.

Cooren, F. 2004b. Textual Agency: How Texts Do Things in Organizational Settings. *Organization*, 11, 373–393.

Cooren, F. 2006. The Organizational World as a Plenum of Agencies. *In*: Cooren, F., Taylor, J. R., & Van Every, E. J. (eds) *Communication as Organizing: Practical Approaches to Research into the Dynamic of Text and Conversation*. Mahwah, NJ, Lawrence-Erlbaum, 81–100.

Cooren, F. 2010. *Action and Agency in Dialogue: Passion, Incarnation and Ventriloquism*. Amsterdam, John Benjamins Publishing Company.

Cooren, F. 2012. Communication Theory at the Center: Ventriloquism and the Communicative Constitution of Reality. *Journal of Communication*, 62, 1–20.

Cooren, F. 2015. Studying Agency from a Ventriloqual Perspective. *Management Communication Quarterly*, 29, 475–480.

Cornut, F., Giroux, H., & Langley, A. 2012. The Strategic Plan as a Genre. *Discourse & Communication*, 6, 21–54.

Czarniawska, B. 1996. *A Narrative Approach to Organization Studies*, Thousand Oaks, CA, Sage.

Dailey, S. L. & Browning, L. 2014. Retelling Stories in Organizations: Understanding the Functions of Narrative Repetition. *Academy of Management Review*, 39, 22–43.

Dobusch, L. & Schoeneborn, D. 2015. Fluidity, Identity, and Organizationality: The Communicative Constitution of Anonymous. *Journal of Management Studies*, 52, 1005–1035.

Fairclough, N. 1992. Discourse and Text: Linguistic and Intertextual Analysis within Discourse Analysis. *Discourse & Society*, 3, 193–217.

Fairclough, N. 1995. *Critical Discourse Analysis*. Harlow, Longman.

Fairclough, N. 2005. Peripheral Vision. Discourse Analysis in Organization Studies: The Case for Critical Realism. *Organization Studies*, 26, 915–939.

Fairhurst, G. T. & Putnam, L. 2004. Organizations as Discursive Construction. *Communication Theory*, 14, 5–26.

Fairhurst, G. T. & Uhl-Bien, M. 2012. Organizational Discourse Analysis (ODA): Examining Leadership as a Relational Process. *Leadership Quarterly*, 23, 1043–1062.

Ferns, G. & Amaeshi, A. 2021. Fueling Climate (In)Action: How Organizations Engage in Hegemonization to Avoid Transformational Action on Climate Change. *Organization Studies*, 42, 1005–1029.

Foucault, M. 1972. *The Archaeology of Knowledge*. New York, Harper and Row.

Garfinkel, H. 1967. *Studies in Ethnomethodology*. Englewood Cliffs, NJ, Prentice-Hall.

Gergen, M., Gergen, K., & Barret, F. 2004. Appreciative Inquiry as Dialogue: Generative and Transformative. *Advances in Appreciative Inquiry*, 1, 3–27.

Giddens, A. 1984. *The Constitution of Society*. Cambridge, UK, Polity.

Grant, D., Keenoy, T., & Oswick, C. 2001. Organizational Discourse Key Contributions and Challenges. *International Studies of Management and Organization*, 31, 5–24.

Greimas, A. 1987. *On Meaning: Selected Writings in Semiotic Theory*. London, Frances Pinter.

Hardy, C. & Maguire, S. 2010. Discourse, Field-Configuring Events, and Change in Organizations and Institutional Fields: Narratives of DDT and the Stockholm Convention. *Academy of Management Journal*, 53, 1365–1392.

Hardy, C. & Maguire, S. 2016. Organizing Risk: Discourse, Power, and 'Riskification'. *Academy of Management Review*, 41, 80–108.

Hardy, C. & Maguire, S. 2020. Organizations, Risk Translation, and the Ecology of Risks: The Discursive Construction of a Novel Risk. *Academy of Management Journal*, 63, 685–716.

Hardy, C., Palmer, I., & Phillips, N. 2000. Discourse as a Strategic Resource. *Human Relations*, 53, 1227–1248.

Hardy, C. & Thomas, R. 2015. Discourse in a Material World. *Journal of Management Studies*, 52, 680–696.

Hardy, C. (2022). *How to Use a Discursive Approach to Study Organizations*, Cheltenham, UK, Edward Elgar Publishing.

Heikkinen, S. & Lämsä, A. M. 2017. Narratives of Spousal Support for the Careers of Men in Managerial Posts. *Gender, Work & Organization*, 24, 171–193.

Heracleous, L. & Barrett, M. 2001. Organizational Change as Discourse: Communicative Actions and Deep Structures in the Context of Information Technology Implementation. *The Academy of Management Journal*, 44, 755–778.

Kangas, E., Lämsä, A. M., & Jyrkinen, M. 2019. Is Fatherhood Allowed? Media Discourses of Fatherhood in Organizational Life. *Gender, Work & Organization*, 26, 1433–1450.

Kornberger, M., Meyer, R. E., Brandtner, C., & Höllerer, M. A. 2017. When Bureaucracy Meets the Crowd: Studying 'Open Government' in the Vienna City Administration. *Organization Studies*, 38, 179–200.

Kuhn, T. 2012. Negotiating the Micro-Macro Divide. *Management Communication Quarterly*, 26, 543–584.

Laine, P.-M. & Vaara, E. 2007. Struggling Over Subjectivity: A Discursive Analysis of Strategic Development in an Engineering Group. *Human Relations*, 60, 29–58.

Laine, P.-M., Meriläinen, S., Tienari, J., & Vaara, E. 2016. Mastery, Submission, and Subversion: On the Performative Construction of Strategist Identity. *Organization*, 23, 505–524.

Latour, B. 1986. The Power of Association. *In*: Law, J. & Kegan, P. (eds) *Power, Action and Belief*. London, Routledge, 264–280.

Latour, B. 2005. *Reassembling the Social: An Introduction to Actor–Network Theory*, Oxford, Oxford University Press.

Lookwood, C., Giorgi, S., & Glynn, M. A. 2018. 'How to Do Things with Words': Mechanisms Bridging Language and Action in Management Research. *Journal of Management*, 45, 7–34.

Mantere, S. & Whittington, R. 2021. Becoming a Strategist: The Roles of Strategy Discourse and Ontological Security in Managerial Identity Work. *Strategic Organization*, 1–26.

McAdams, D. P. 1993. *The Stories We Live By: Personal Myths and the Making of the Self*. New York, Guilford Press.

McCabe, D. 2016. Numericalizing the Other: A Critical Analysis of a Strategy Discourse in a UK Bank. *Organization*, 23, 525–549.

McClellan, J. G. 2014. Announcing Change: Discourse, Uncertainty, and Organizational Control. *Journal of Change Management*, 14, 192–209.

Mintzberg, H. 1973. *The Nature of Managerial Work*. New York, Harper and Row.

Moodley, P. & Schvaughn, S. 2020. A Discourse Analysis of Ebola in South African Newspapers (2014–2015). *South African Journal of Psychology*, 50, 158–169.

Musca, G., Rouleau, L., Mellet, C., Sitri, F. D. R., & de Vogüé, S. 2018. From Boat to Bags: The Role of Material Chronotopes in Adaptive Sensemaking. *M@n@gement*, 21, 705–737.

Phillips, N. & Oswick, C. 2012. Organizational Discourse: Domains, Debates, and Directions. *The Academy of Management Annals*, 6, 435–481.

Ravazzani, S. & Maier, C. D. 2017. Strategic Organizational Discourse and Framing in Hypermodal Spaces. *Corporate Communications: An International Journal*, 22, 507–522.

Ricoeur, P. 1983. *Temps et récit. La configuration dans le récit de fiction*. Paris, Le Seuil.

Robichaud, D., Giroux, H., & Taylor, J. R. 2004. The Metaconversation: The Recursive Property of Language as a Key to Organizing. *Academy of Management Review*, 29, 617–634.

Rhodes, C., Pullen, A., & Clegg, S. R. (2010). 'If I should fall from grace. . .': Stories of change and organizational ethics, *Journal of Business Ethics*, 91, 4, 535–551.

Schoeneborn, D., Kuhn, T. R., & Kärreman, D. 2019. The Communicative Constitution of Organization, Organizing, and Organizationality. *Organization Studies*, 40, 475–496.

Spee, A. P. & Jarzabkowski, P. 2011. Strategic Planning as Communicative Process. *Organization Studies*, 32, 1217–1245.

Taylor, J. R. & Van Every, E. J. 2000. *The Emergent Organization: Communication as its Site and Service*. Mahwah, NJ, Lawrence Erlbaum.

Taylor, J. R. & Van Every, E. J. 2010. *The Situated Organization: Case Studies in the Pragmatics of Communication Research*. London, Taylor & Francis.

Vaara, E. & Monin, P. 2010. A Recursive Perspective on Discursive Legitimation and Organizational Action in Mergers and Acquisitions. *Organization Science*, 21, 3–22.

Vaara, E., Kleymann, B., & Seristô, H. 2004. Strategies as Discursive Constructions: The Case of Airline Alliances. *Journal of Management Studies*, 41, 1–35.

Vaara, E., Tienari, J., & Laurila, J. 2006. Pulp and Paper Fiction: On the Discursive Legitimation of Global Industrial Restructuring. *Organization Studies*, 27, 789–813.

Vaara, E., Sonenshein, S., & Boje, D. 2016. Narratives as Sources of Stability and Change in Organizations: Approaches and Directions for Future Research. *The Academy of Management Annals*, 10, 495–560.

Vásquez, C., Brummans, B. H. J. M., & Groleau, C. 2012. Notes From the Field on Organizational Shadowing as Framing. *Qualitative Research in Organizations and Management: An International Journal*, 7, 144–165.

Vásquez, C., Bencherki, N., Cooren, F., & Sergi, V. 2017. From 'Matters of Concern' to 'Matters of Authority': Studying the Performativity of Strategy from a Communicative Constitution of Organization (CCO) Approach. *Long Range Planning*, 51, 417–435.

Wilhoit-Larson, E. 2020. Where Is an Organization? How Workspaces Are Appropriated to Become (Partial and Temporary) Organizational Spaces. *Management Communication Quarterly*, 34, 299–327.

Wolf, C. 2019. Not Lost in Translation: Managerial Career Narratives and the Construction of Protean Identities. *Human Relations*, 72, 505–533.

Zohar, G. 2019. Institutionalization of the OECD Grand-Narrative of Inclusivity (1983–2012). *Qualitative Research in Organizations and Management: An International Journal*, 14, 94–118.

7
Practice Studies

Since the dawn of the twenty-first century, organizations have been facing new challenges. To ensure rapid and innovative responses to competition, they are becoming more open and decentralized. This has flattened hierarchies and transformed the span of managerial control. In this global context, managers also have to deal with geographically distant and dispersed units and teams. Moreover, success in today's customer-oriented organizations is less and less attributed to senior managers alone. The strategic importance of managers on the periphery or at the boundaries between units and organizational networks as well as managers close to customers and to other external stakeholders is being taken increasingly seriously. These challenges have accelerated the movement towards embracing the 'practice turn' in the field of organization theories (OTs).

In line with the so-called practice turn in social sciences (Schatzki, 2001), the notion of practice has shown a burst of popularity in management and OTs over the past two decades. Indeed, we now find a wide range of expressions in OTs that reflect the practice perspective. For example, the French talk about the 'fabric' of organizing while the English often use the 'activity-based view' label. Topics or issues said to be 'situated' within a context (e.g. situated cognition or learning) also fall under the heading of practice studies. This is also true of scholars referring to 'work studies' (Lawrence and Phillips, 2019). Practice studies have also fuelled the development of many new conversations in a variety of management disciplines, including accounting-as-practice (Ahrens and Chapman, 2007), project-as-practice (Blomquist et al., 2010), entrepreneurship-as-practice (De Clercq and Voronov, 2009), strategy-as-practice (Golsorkhi et al., 2015), leadership-as-practice (Carroll, Levy, and Richmond, 2008; Raelin, 2016), diversity-as-practice (Janssens and Steyaert, 2020), and so on. Even medicine has taken the turn towards practice (Peddie, 2016).

However, there remains a lot of confusion in OTs about the scope and meaning of practice studies. Under the practice label, OTs aim to better understand how practitioners act through an interlocked nexus of practices and activities, which can be organizational (micro, meso, or macro) as well as

Organization Theories in the Making. Linda Rouleau, Oxford University Press.
© Linda Rouleau (2022). DOI: 10.1093/oso/9780198792024.003.0008

institutional in nature. After nearly a century of studying organizations and their management, we still know little about the detailed activities and skills through which managers and other organizational groups are enacting and re-enacting the day-to-day of organizational life. And yet, should we really be surprised? After all, over the years, multiple masterful contributions have attempted to answer the question, 'What do managers do?' However, most of them have followed the scientific management tradition. According to Tengblad (2012, p. 5), 'Many researchers have divided managerial work into small, separate tasks and have created models using sequential charts and decision trees'. We all have in mind the famous 'POLC' (Planning, Organizing, Leading, and Controlling) framework as one of the first management tools that was developed, which is still taught in business schools today!

In parallel, generations of OTs researchers have mainly conceptualized organizations as structures, institutions, cultures, political arenas, sets of networks, and so on. Over the decades, OTs have thus overlooked the 'concrete' or specific workplace activities through which managers, professionals, employees, and even external stakeholders accomplish their tasks, despite the fact that the very first organizational theorists were practitioners (e.g. Taylor, Fayol, Parker-Follet, and Gulick). Hence, at first glance, by taking the practice turn, it appears that the OTs field has had to make a singularly long detour before finding its way back to where it first started. Does adopting a practice lens to study organizational phenomena entail throwing off the yoke of past organizational theories? Or is the practice turn in OTs a way to overcome its pitfalls by allowing researchers to engage in a direct and reflexive dialogue with practitioners? Are we back to square one, rubbing elbows with the Taylors, Fayols, Parker-Follets, and other practitioners who tried to define the contours of managerial work? This chapter intends to answer these questions.

Nevertheless, it would be unfair not to mention pioneering works that have put the real work of managers at the centre of their research. Among them, Mintzberg (1973), one of the first researchers to observe managers in action, suggests that the essence of managerial work is inherent to the fragmentation of both their activities and their communication skills. A decade later, Schön (1983) introduced the idea of 'reflexive practitioners' who follow their intuition and are sensitive to context. Watson (1994) describes managerial work in terms of 'crafting' and recognizes that it is characterized by conflicting expectations, cynicism, and disillusion about management tools and discourse. However, while these seminal works have been around for a while, OTs only embraced the practice turn at the turn of the new century.

This chapter begins by introducing the similarities and differences between process and practice studies. It then offers a selective immersion in the world of practice studies in OTs by targeting four streams based on different views of practice: practice as managerial work, practice as social accomplishment, practice as (socio)materiality, and practice as embodiment. While each of these views can be considered a distinct way of approaching the notion of practice, many scholars believe that 'in practice' they are entangled with one another. The chapter ends by discussing whether taking the practice turn has led OTs to move forward or backward.

7.1 From process to practice studies

In the past few decades, there has been a lasting conversation about similarities and differences between process and practice perspectives. Both of these perspectives have virtually the same onto-epistemological foundations, as they are generally—but not necessarily—embedded in a social constructionist view of reality. Process and practice perspectives have been used as ways to open the black box of phenomena studied by OTs scholars. Put differently, they constitute an original and distinctive critique of mainstream or rationalistic perspectives in the field of OTs. For instance, in the field of strategy, the mainstream approach is concerned with the patterns of strategies adopted by firms to position themselves competitively in their economic environments. Rather than looking at strategies at the industry level, a process perspective explores their formation at the organizational level, while a practice perspective looks inside organizational processes to examine the strategic episodes through which a strategy is formulated and implemented by managers and others. It is also worth noting that a practice perspective criticizes the fact that content and sometimes even process perspectives grant too much importance to managerial elites.

The process perspective emerged at the beginning of the new century and subsequently gained momentum in the OTs through special issues (e.g. *American Management Journal*, 2013; *Strategic Management Journal*, 2018) and conferences (e.g. the annual Academy of Management process Professional Development Workshop and the *International Symposium Process*). Adopting a process perspective entails considering any organizational phenomenon as being in motion. As Langley et al. (2013, p. 1) tell us, 'process studies focus attention on how and why things emerge, develop, grow, and terminate over time'. Change, time, and motion are central to process studies. Process researchers seek to understand and explain the complex dynamics underpinning organizational stability and change. The process perspective gained momentum in OTs through special issues. Everything

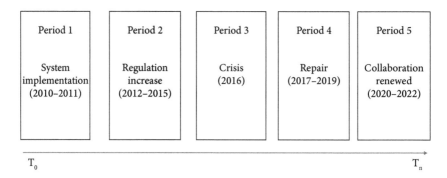

Figure 7.1 Typical form of process study

you want to know but never dared to ask about the process approach is in the *Sage Handbook of Process Organization Studies*, edited in 2017 by Langley and Tsoukas, two central scholars dedicated to the dissemination of process-based research in OTs.

There is a plurality of onto-epistemological positions in organizational process research. In other words, OTs might be more or less process oriented, depending on the underlying assumptions about the nature of reality and of the knowledge that pervades them. The diversity of process orientations can be positioned on a continuum along which two poles are typically referred to as 'weak' (or synoptic) and 'strong' (or performative) process perspectives. In the former type of process research, scholars are interested in understanding how and why organizational entities and events change or evolve in chronological order from one point to another over time (Langley and Tsoukas, 2017). Typical examples of process research concern studies of change over several months or even decades (see Figure 7.1). This temporal bracketing of the change allows the researcher to identify specific patterns of organizational initiatives for each period, stage, or cycle. In the latter type of process research, scholars are looking at how organizational life is reconstituted in the flow of experience (Langley et al., 2013). In a strong process perspective, organizational or strategic change is explored 'in the moment' of its production and from within. Therefore, researchers are interested in the complexity whereby processes are accomplished in the recurrent and situated nature of everyday life.

Coming back to the debate around the similarities and differences between process and practice perspectives, they do meet or intersect when scholars adopt a 'strong' view of process research. For a long time, practice studies were seen as an extension of process research under the umbrella of a 'post-processual view' (Chia and MacKay, 2007; Gherardi, 2016). Recently, Burgelman et al. (2017) proposed a joint view of strategy process and practice

(SAPP), where both are seen 'as closely intertwined aspects of the same phenomena'. But as Whittington (2006) put it some years ago, 'practice will be better as cousin than sibling' of process studies. But why is this so? It occurs that one of the main distinctions between both perspectives concerns their units of analysis. While process scholars are more interested in investigating a change process at the macro level of the organization, practice scholars are generally more concerned with the micro level of the detailed activities of managerial work. For instance, a process study of strategy investigates the unfolding process of strategic change over time, while a practice approach will seek to better understand the unexpected significance of the day-to-day strategy-making activities and episodes during the change.

The debate around the micro–macro distinction is central to practice studies. It emerges from the rejection of dualisms between subject and object, action and structure, and mind and body. Based on a sensitivity to connections and relationships, practice studies focus on the co-constitutive aspect of these dualisms and presuppose that action and structure are both part of a same phenomenon. In fact, practices are inherently contextual, performed by skilful actors involved in networks of activities regulated through diverse patterns of more or less integrated action. This radical reformulation of the intractable problem of action and structure in OTs involves a major shift in the research agenda when adopting a practice perspective. Scholars are thus invited to start not from organization as a whole—firm, business unit, and so on—but from the activities of people upon which key practices depend. Instead of assuming that the 'whole (organization) is more than the sum of its parts (practices)', as is currently the case with the mainstream approach in OTs, the practice perspective rather considers that the 'whole (organization) is contained within the parts (practices)'. To understand this, consider the microscope metaphor. For a close-up on practices, it is as though we put them under a microscope for a better idea of what is happening at the organizational level. Much like the relationship between cells and plants and animals, practices are the basic building blocks for organizations and society as a whole.

Practice studies emphasize the complexity of everyday life and foreground the importance of relations and situatedness in organizational and social contexts. For better or for worse, they form a collection of studies on organizing inspired by distinct scholarly traditions within the broader field of OTs. These scholarly traditions refer to a variety of vocabularies, units of analysis, and methodologies. As a result, there is no single unified theory of practice. While the task of articulating the respective differences between the different views found under the practice umbrella is no simple matter, similarities can be observed across the different scholarly communities that promote their own specific views of practice studies.

As previously mentioned, this chapter introduces four different streams of practice studies: practice as managerial work; practice as social accomplishment; practice as (socio)materiality; and practice as embodiment (see Table 7.1). Each stream respectively corresponds to the contributions of specific subfields of study (and communities) in OTs: managerial studies (Strategy-as-Practice, or SAP); knowledge and innovation studies (Innovation, Knowledge & Organization Networks, or IKON); technology studies (Workshop on Organizations, Artefacts and Practices, or OAP, and Research Group on Collaborative Spaces, or RGCS); and emotion and sensorial studies (Centre for Sensorial Studies, or CSS).

7.2 Practice as managerial work

This stream of practice studies places human actors front and centre. It aims to analyse the purposeful activities of practitioners (e.g. managers, consultants, employees, and external stakeholders). As the property of individuals who enact various locally negotiated regimes of actions, practices are located within the activities and the relationships between the individuals, groups, and networks of people upon which key managerial and organizing practices depend. According to Corradi, Gherardi, and Verzelloni (2010), this stream of research maintains a strong focus on concrete activities and the purposeful agency of actors. Scholars interested in practice as managerial work recognize that practitioners—who have their own backgrounds, interests, and goals—struggle to accomplish their tasks and make a difference in the organizations they work for. Nevertheless, they pay great attention to the organizational environment within which this managerial work is conceived, coordinated, transformed, and implemented.

This focus on the awareness of practitioners calls for an investigation of what is being done and by whom, as evidenced by the main research question of scholars from this stream of research: how is the work of organizing actually done? More specifically: what do people do when they are managing, strategizing, enterprising, leading, and so on (in accordance with the managerial domain targeted)? The answers involve using a gerund (the 'ing' form, e.g. organizing instead of organization) to describe organizational order and change in terms of routines, becoming, and enactment. By focusing on people's everyday activities as units of analysis, a managerial work as practice view considers that practices emerge at the 'nexus of doings and sayings'

Table 7.1 Synoptic overview of practice studies

	Practice as managerial work	Practice as social accomplishment	Practice as (socio)materiality	Practice as embodiment
Definition	Purposeful activities and efforts of managers (to have a managerial practice)	Patterns of actions emerging from everyday activities (to be constituted in practice)	Patterns of behaviours involving the use of materials (to be constitutive of practices)	Patterns of bodily practices sustaining sensible knowledge (to be constitutive of practices)
Key research question	What do managers do? What is done in praxis and by whom?	How and why is organizing done in one way or another?	How is materiality used in practice?	What can bodies do in practice?
Unit of analysis	Practitioners' activities (doings and sayings)	Everyday practices	(Socio)material practices	Bodily (emotional and sensorial) practices
Organization	The flow of managerial activities enabling/constraining organizational outcomes	Nexus of practices through which the flow of relations is ordered and reordered	A combination of social and material practices	A shifting assemblage of bodily (emotional/sensorial) practices

Continued

Table 7.1 Continued

	Practice as managerial work	Practice as social accomplishment	Practice as (socio)materiality	Practice as embodiment
Influences	Mintzberg (1973); Johnson et al. (2003); Whittington (2006); Golsorkhi et al. (2015); Jarzabkowski et al. (2007)	Schön (1983); Schatzki (2001); Schatzki et al. (2001); Gherardi (2016, 2019); Nicolini (2013)	Latour (2005); Barad (2003); Orlikowski (2007); Orlikowski and Scott (2008); Leonardi (2013); Bruni (2005)	Mauss (1936); Merleau-Ponty (1945); Simmel (1907); Dale (2001); Howes and Classen (2013); Pink (2015)
Research areas	Managerial and strategy studies (SAP)	Workplace and knowing studies (IKON)	Science and technological studies (CSI, OAP)	Emotions and sensory studies (Emonet, inVisio, CSS)
Conceptual resources	Praxis, practices and practitioners, episodes, meeting practices, and strategy work	Mutual intelligibility, practical understanding, and sites of knowing/diversalizing	(Socio)materiality as consequence, assemblage, affordance, and performativity	Embodied spatial practices, embodied knowing, sensory ordering, and organizational scent
Methods	Organizational ethnography (case studies/interviews)	Video-ethnography (instruction of the double)	Ethnography of non-humans (shadowing objects/software)	Auto and sensory ethnography (traces of emotion/senses)
Exemplars	Bednarek et al. (2017); Jarzabkowski and Bednarek (2018); Seidl and Werle (2017);	Nicolini (2011); Le Baron et al. (2016); Best and Hindmarsh (2019); Janssens and Steyaert (2020)	Stigliani and Ravasi (2012); Barley (2015); Bilodeau et al. (2019); Wallenburg et al. (2016); Leonardi et al. (2019)	Bell and King (2010); Gümüsay et al. (2018); Stigliani and Ravasi (2018); Gardiner (2019); Grosjean et al. (2021)

(Chia and MacKay, 2007, p. 227). Researchers are thus interested in all forms of managerial work, such as writing and diffusing corporate discourses, holding formal management meetings and workshops, crafting press releases, and even engaging in informal conversations around the coffee machine, spreading rumours, and gossiping about stakeholders. The aim of this substream of practice studies consists of bringing to light hidden or unnoticed practices and the significance of their pervasive effects in shaping the organizational world.

The scholarship community of SAP is the most prolific example of a management discipline that has adopted a practice view as managerial work. Incubated in Europe at the beginning of the 2000s, this research community has rapidly spread to North America and elsewhere. A dynamic international network (see www.sap-in.org) has facilitated the institutionalization of the SAP perspective and the development of this research community within the broader field of strategic management. SAP scholars consider strategy not as something that a firm possesses but rather as something that people do (Johnson, Melin, and Whittington, 2003; Johnson et al., 2007). Thus, SAP focuses on the concrete activities carried out by strategy practitioners, the tools they mobilize while strategizing, and the skills and roles they have while engaging in strategic activity. In what follows, I will use SAP research as an example of what I call 'practice as managerial work'.

Leading SAP researchers have put forth an overreaching '3P framework' (Figure 7.2) defining the broad parameters of a practice perspective: Praxis, Practices, and Practitioners (Whittington, 2006; Jarzabkowski, Balogun, and Seidl, 2007). Strategizing is located at the intersection of these three elements, which pervade all practice theories. In other words, this framework provides a means for understanding strategy work as embedded in praxis, practices, and practitioners. Recently, Whittington (2019) suggested that strategizing practices also inform us of what constitutes the profession of strategists. Therefore, he suggested adding another 'P' to take into account the cross-organizational dimension of Profession in the framework of Praxis, Practices, and Practitioners. This framework has served to classify SAP studies according to their empirical focus (Vaara and Whittington, 2012).

Praxis refers to the flow of activities that people engage in while enacting strategy in a particular setting. According to Jarzabkowski et al. (2007, p. 8), an activity 'is considered strategic to the extent that it is consequential for the strategic outcomes, directions, survival and competitive advantage of the firm (Johnson et al., 2003), even where these consequences are not part of an intended and formally articulated strategy'. The primary empirical focus of SAP papers associated with a praxis dimension consists of highlighting

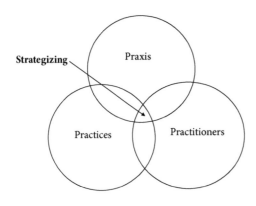

Figure 7.2 SAP framework*
*Adapted from Jarzabkowski, Balogun, and Seidl, 2007

what goes on in each of the strategy-making phases. As you will see in the following two examples, such studies endorse a 'weak-process' orientation. Jarzabkowski and Balogun (2009) examine the implementation of a new strategic planning system that attempts to facilitate the integration between a multinational's business units across Europe. Drawing on a longitudinal case study, they show that over the three implementation phases of the new planning system, experienced and powerful business units react differently to business units with less experience and power. Seidl and Werle (2017) study the process of inter-organizational sensemaking around complex strategic problems that pervade entire sectors (e.g. water management, ecological threats, and new sectorial technological change). Based on two longitudinal case studies, they put forward a model explaining the two-phase dynamics of this process. First, potential partners negotiate the interpretation of the strategic problem in keeping with their respective interests. As some potential partners leave the collaboration, new ones join; this dynamic is repeated until a consensus is achieved. This then marks the transition towards the second phase, where actors are willing to cooperate and advance in the same direction to find solutions to the strategic problem addressed through the inter-organizational collaboration.

Practitioners are the actors who are engaged in strategizing; that is, who are seeking to participate at one level or another in strategy-making. SAP research has moved away from the 'omnipotent' strategist (generally top managers) to a more inclusive understanding of strategy work by acknowledging a broader range of actors involved in strategy-making. The empirical focus of SAP papers associated with practitioners consists of paying attention to the roles and identities of strategists with the aim of improving their skills to perform their strategy work. In addition to top managers, SAP researchers have closely examined middle managers' strategy work (Rouleau, Balogun, and Floyd, 2015) by enquiring about the sensemaking, discursive, political, and institutional aspects of their strategy work. Today, middle managers occupy diverse mediating positions that prompt us to explore their boundary practices inside and outside organizations. Recently, the SAP field has also shown a timid interest in the strategy work of frontline supervisors and even employees. Balogun, Best, and Lê (2015, p. 1285) demonstrate 'the subtle and intricate nature of the embodied work of frontline workers (e.g., tour guides) as they "bring into being" the strategic aims of an organization'. According to these authors, it is the skilful combination of discursive, material, and bodily expressions (i.e. their interactional competence) that allows these non-managerial workers to help realize the deliberate strategy of their organization.

Practices correspond to the patterns of cognitive, symbolic, political, and material activities accomplished by practitioners. More specifically, Whittington (2006, p. 619) refers to practices as the 'shared routines of behaviour, including traditions, norms and procedures for thinking, acting and using "things"'. In this vein, SAP researchers aim to identify the strategic practices underlying the surface of events or the formal aspects of strategy work. The empirical focus of SAP papers associated with practices consists of highlighting their unintended but significant enabling or constraining effects on strategic outcomes. For example, Jarzabkowski and Seidl (2008) examine the role of meeting practices and their consequences for strategic orientations. By comparing 51 meetings from 3 universities, they highlight specific meeting practices instantiated during the initiation, conduct, and termination of meetings (see Table 7.2). They also show that 'it is the combination of different practices across several meetings that shape whether a proposed variation stabilizes or destabilizes strategic orientations' (Jarzabkowski and Seidl, 2008, p. 1417). Bednarek, Paroutis, and Sillince (2017) examine three science-producing organizations that are meeting contradictory but interrelated objectives (commercial versus social objectives and science excellence versus science impact) that are strategic for their survival. They found that their response to these contradictory objectives (by dealing with the two objective poles and their complex interdependences) is constituted of four rhetorical practices, namely, ordering, aspiring, signifying, and embodying. Drawing on these rhetorical practices, they put forward a view of transcendence as an oscillating process between content/context, stability/change, and distance maintaining/distance reducing.

Methodologically speaking, and similarly to many management disciplines, capturing practices has remained a major issue in SAP research over the years. The use of interviews, self-report methods, and focus groups

Table 7.2 Meeting practices

Initiation	Conduct	Termination
Bracketing participants in a central location	Emerging and developing free discussion	Building bridges to other meetings
Setting the agenda	Constraining emergence of variations	Rescheduling
Chairing meeting	Deselecting variations in discussion	Voting
	Administrative discussion	Stage-managing

* Excerpt from Jarzabkowski and Seidl (2008)

complemented by periodic presences in the field and archival data have remained prominent methods used over the years (for a review of the SAP research designs from 2000 to 2015, see Abdallah, Basque, and Rouleau, 2018). It is worth noting that recent years have seen a growing interest in using video-ethnographic and visual methods (e.g. photographs, drawings). Regardless of the methodology used in designing SAP research, it is critical to approach strategy work in accordance with the definition of the practice carried out throughout the research.

Despite its concern with practice and its strong claim that strategy is a social phenomenon which takes form in what people do, SAP research has nonetheless been subject to criticism. First, most studies are still based on a mainstream definition of strategy, which reflects a managerial agenda. Indeed, SAP research conceives strategy as 'the activities around what is labelled "strategy" in the organization (strategy meetings, plans, retreats, episodes, etc.)', though it does admit that 'strategy in action or strategy as practice is broader in that it encompasses everything people understand as strategic in the organization' (Abdallah, Basque, and Rouleau, 2018, p. 340). Second, in SAP research, the figure of the strategist remains largely anchored in the managerial hierarchy, as though everything was resulting from the purposeful actions of top and middle managers. As such, despite all their efforts at being more inclusive, most SAP studies still act on a strong desire to improve managerial practices. Third, the issues surrounding situatedness have remained questionable over the years. By targeting the strategic context in which practitioners' activities lead to strategic outcomes, SAP researchers fail to strongly address the contingent and the social or collective embeddedness of agency in strategy work. As a result, the majority of SAP research as well as practice research in other managerial domains belong to a so-called 'weak-practice' perspective.

Still, SAP research has considerably evolved since its early days. More studies assume that practice is located at the interplay between the social, material, and discursive activities of strategy work. Balogun et al. (2014) argue for 'connecting' the study of strategy discourse to socio-material, sensemaking, and power dimensions in order to understand complex social processes. Jarzabkowski and Bednarek (2018) studied the everyday competitive practices in the reinsurance industry based on what they called a relational perspective. According to these authors, reinsurers compete with one another through 'the nested relationships among their common practices' instead of strictly between themselves (Jarzabkowski and Bednarek, 2018, p. 799). It is the practical knowledge of trading deals within their industry that allows reinsurers to coordinate their action around a deal without talking to each other. As will be demonstrated in the next section, the study by Jarzabkowski and Bednarek (2018) has close affinities to a view of practice as social accomplishment.

7.3 Practice as social accomplishment

The practice as social accomplishment substream of practice studies places the emphasis on 'how' and 'why' things are done in a particular way and given a specific context, rather than on 'what' is done and by 'whom'. A view of practice as social accomplishment investigates the local practices that make up organizational phenomena such as strategy, leadership, coordination, and so on. Instead of focusing on the practitioners' activities as a unit of analysis, a view of practice as social accomplishment gives ontological primacy to the practices themselves. Given the centrality of practices, the focus is placed on the patterns of everyday actions emerging from relationships between practitioners, as opposed to the managerial activities purposefully carried out by managers (as assumed by SAP researchers). Therefore, 'practices are not so much the visible doings of actors per se, but culturally and historically transmitted *regularities* detectable through the patterns of activities actually carried out' (Chia and MacKay, 2007, p. 227). Put differently, it is not so much the intentionality of individuals but rather their socio-cultural predispositions that generate the possibilities for strategy or any other organizational phenomenon. Rather than 'having' a practice, according to the practice as social accomplishment view, practitioners are themselves constituted through their ongoing everyday activities. Such a view fosters the adoption of an 'in-practice' label rather than the widespread 'as-practice' appellation.

A view of practice as social accomplishment calls for a 'post-humanist' epistemology of practices (Gherardi, 2016). Social practices are not inside the mind of individuals or the result of external structures; they are the product of both. A view of practice as social accomplishment conveys a 'strong-practice' approach, as it involves interpreting a phenomenon according to its historical, socio-cultural, and situated character. Consider, for example, the practice of presenting papers in international conferences. Each presenter has a regional speaking accent and specific habits and dispositions acquired through immersion in their national and local communities. All presenters are therefore constituted, defined, and identified by these specific socio-cultural traits. Intentionally or not, some speakers will use these characteristics to their advantage (e.g. by emphasizing one or several of these traits to create a favourable climate) throughout the presentation. Even when they don't, they cannot escape from their own socio-cultural embeddedness when practising their profession; those characteristics will eventually be revealed. Over the years, speakers will develop certain consistent patterns of actions when delivering papers, coupled with a practical sense of what works and what does not work when presenting them. They will therefore get better at adjusting themselves according to their audiences and to the specific context of their presentation.

As the building blocks of organizing, practices are tied up with 'what is going on here and now'. This claim involves two dimensions. First, 'what is going on' implies the fabrication of organizing or the process of its activation in the flux of more or less controllable events. It suggests that researchers favour the 'practice-complexes' or the 'field of practices' by which organizing is put into action. Any practice is achieved within socio-material conditions and power relations and involves embodied capacities such as tacit understanding, emotions, and senses. As Nicolini (2013, p. 174) states, 'the world [read: the organization] is a vast nexus of practices'; that is, an assemblage of heterogeneous elements that come together to create and recreate some organizational ordering. Second, 'here and now' refers to the 'situated' aspect of practices. As a matter of fact, the challenge of the practice as social accomplishment view is to capture the practical sense with which organizational life is lived in the moment. It therefore involves seriously taking into consideration the spatio-temporality of practices. Hence, instead of being part of a passive background, the 'situated' or the context-specificity of practising is part of the human performance emerging from an array of local practices.

Let me now return to the previous example. A conference presentation is not merely the result of discursive utterances. It also takes place within an ecology of connected elements: speakers use PowerPoint, computers, and microphones, and they exhibit, consciously or not, a panoply of emotions such as pride, pleasure, anxiety, and so on. Moreover, the fact of delivering a talk in the morning or at the end of the day makes a difference. It is not the same if the conference is in an amphitheatre or in a small room, in your own university or in a different country. All these spatio-temporal conditions matter in practice. The connection and reconnection between these elements in keeping with conference rules and norms constitute the practice of presenting papers at international conferences.

The emergence of the academic community around the view of practice as social accomplishment can be traced back to the special issue on 'Work and Knowledge' in *Sociologie du Travail* (1994), a publication that brings together North American, English, and French scholars (Gherardi, 2019). The name of this special issue is hardly anecdotal. This stream of research has developed at the intersection of workplace and knowing studies (see Chapter 5, Section 5.5). During the 2000s, the research group RUCOLA (Research Unit on Communication, Organizational Learning and Aesthetics), run by Silvia Gherardi, Chair of Sociology of Work and Organization at the University of Trento, was a pillar in the development of the view of practice as accomplishment. In the following decade, the multidisciplinary research unit IKON became a leader in the promotion of practice studies. Co-directed by Jacky Swan and Davide Nicolini, the group is largely known for organizing doctoral summer schools on practice and process studies.

Inspired by the tradition of symbolic interactionism and ethnomethodology, workplace studies have brought into the conversation the anthropological condition of 'action intelligibility' (Schatzki, 2002, p. 75) that distinguishes human beings from animals. In all circumstances, people act according to how they make sense of what is going on in their social and organizational life. Therefore, practice resonates with coping skills activated in everyday situations. Multiple notions have been brought up by OTs researchers to designate the practical ability of human agents to carry out their day-to-day activities: skilful performance (Sandberg et al., 2017), shared practical understanding (Schatzki, 2001), and logic of practice (Bourdieu, 1990), to name a few. All suggest that 'it is agents and processes that are subordinate to, and constituted from practices and practice-complexes' (Chia and MacKay, 2007). In the same vein, Le Baron et al. (2016) recently put forth the notion of 'mutual intelligibility' by examining how shared understanding is created and maintained during handoff routines in medical care.

Drawing on routine dynamics and ethnomethodology, Le Baron et al. (2016) studied the practice of transferring patient information and knowledge during the shift changes of physicians in a community hospital. They videorecorded the conduct of physicians doing handoffs and analysed their conversations. It appears that in each handoff routine, physicians behaved according to a specific conversational pattern based on the following moves: patient identification; past events; current issues; future plans; and family matters. During these conversations, physicians also engaged in mutual adjustment through a set of audible and visual behaviours indicating whether they confirmed or deviated from expected moves (e.g. stopped writing, looked up, asked a question, or turned a page). Even though these behaviours may initially appear anecdotal, they are essential for ensuring a flexible, collegial coordination with each other. While they have to tailor the handoff routine to each patient's needs, they must still cooperate smoothly with their colleagues over time. Hence, by highlighting the mutual intelligibility with which physicians accomplished their handoff routines, Le Baron et al. (2016) show the dynamics of how physicians share their task in order to deal with the situation at hand. You may also consider your own way of interacting with your teammates when meeting for writing a conference or journal paper—you will certainly be able to find similar ongoing tactics of mutual adjustment.

In their paper on the interactive experience of site tours, Best and Hindmarsh (2019) provide another example of a practice as social accomplishment view inspired by workplace studies. In the emerging stream of research on space as lived experience, these authors investigate how tour guides and audiences coordinate successful tours by co-producing a temporary workspace. As we have all taken museum tours facilitated by experienced guides, we can easily visualize guides as they constantly seek the best spot to position themselves in anticipation of the audience's movements. When walking down a path between series of small spaces and objects, guides and visitors subtly position themselves in such a way as to allow the visitors to see and appreciate the exhibit. For instance, when moving from one painting to another, the guide always waits for visitors to come to a stop before talking or pointing out a specific element of the exhibit. When the guide starts talking, most visitors stop talking. In their paper, Best and Hindmarsh (2019) show that space is not produced by one single individual—such as the tour guide—but is rather the co-production of all participants (guide + audience) and objects (e.g. paintings) involved in the interaction (i.e. the tour). Ultimately, the view of practice as social accomplishment is about the situated and fine-grained articulation and coordination of work.

It was previously mentioned that the foundational nature of practice as social accomplishment lies in learning and knowing as situated activity. According to this view, doing and knowing (or action and interpretation) are not separate. Therefore, practice makes it possible to represent and make sense of the world. According to Nicolini (2011, p. 602), 'practice is where knowledgeability manifests itself and agency becomes possible'. This author suggests conceptualizing practice as the 'site of knowing'. Based on vignettes and illustrations of teleconsultation, Nicolini (2011) argues that knowing is 'located' in social, material, and practical conditions inscribed in the practice of medical calls. He uses as an example a difficult call that a nurse had to make to a cardiac patient. First, the author describes how the nurse prepares for the call:

> the nurse has her pieces of paper (the agenda, test, ECG, and therapy sheet) all strategically positioned on the desk in front of her. Leaning towards the ring binder, which is now at the end of the table near the wall, she reads the telephone number and calls the patient. (Nicolini, 2011, p. 608)

Then, Nicolini (2011) describes all the gestures the nurse makes when talking with the patient (e.g. looks at the tests results, takes notes, pulls up the therapy sheet). Finally, he illustrates the need for the nurse to report the call and what happened during the call to the cardiologist in charge. Nicolini reconstitutes the logic of this post-call interaction this way:

> Often doctors listen to you only briefly and support your decisions. However, it is vital you talk to the same doctor and it is he or she who makes decisions. You are a nurse. Your job is to 'stay in your place' (while ensuring that doctors do the same). (Nicolini, 2011, p. 608)

In these three sequences of a telemedicine vignette, Nicolini conceptualizes the relationship between practice and knowing.

In the same vein as Nicolini (2011), Janssens and Steyaert (2020) revisit the notion of inclusion by adopting a view of diversity as social accomplishment. They study the real-time practising of a dance production involving performers of different ages. From their two years of observation, they put forth the idea of 'site of diversalizing', defined as 'a nexus of practices and their associations in time and space that recursively produce multiplicity [read: inclusion] in a processual way' (Janssens and Steyaert, 2020, p. 1146). They advance the diversity literature by suggesting the need to conceptualize inclusion as the entanglement of three aspects of practice, namely, discourse, materiality, and body. According to these authors, diversity is a practical accomplishment where human inclusion skills manifest themselves in the process of practising dancing.

After reading this section, you should now understand that capturing practices as ongoing accomplishment requires a high awareness of the 'murmurings of the everyday' or a kind of anthropological sixth sense. Such awareness induces an openness to longitudinal case studies based on observational methods such as ethnography, participant observation, ethnomethodology, and shadowing. In order to avoid getting trapped into centring observations on individuals rather than on practices, video-ethnography is also used by organizational researchers that take on a practice as social accomplishment approach (Le Baron et al., 2016; Best and Hindmarsh, 2019; Janssens and Steyaert, 2020). A renewed interest for 'the instruction to the double' interview technique has been proposed by Nicolini (2009) and Gherardi (2019). When using this projective technique, the interviewer asks the interviewee what they need to know to accomplish their work. Put differently, the researcher wants to know all the 'tricks of the trade' to perform the job. In a recent methodological paper, Théron (2020) proposes a research design mixing this data collection technique with shadowing and conversation in order to access the practical underpinnings of situated action.

During the past decade, scholars subscribed to the view of practice as managerial work and the view of practice as social accomplishment began emphasizing practice dimensions such as materiality and body. Those dimensions are now receiving a great deal of attention in the broader field of OTs. Indeed, the views of practice as (socio)materiality and embodiment now constitute specific research streams in practice studies and are supported and carried on by lively research communities. In the next two sections, I explore practice as (socio)materiality and practice as embodiment views.

7.4 Practice as (socio)materiality

The primary concern of the view of practice as (socio)materiality is the use of artefacts and objects, including technology and physical spaces. When invoking materiality, OTs scholars broadly refer to 'images, logos, videos, building materials, graphic and product design, and a range of other material and visual tools and expressions [used] to compete, communicate, form identity and organize activities' (Boxenbaum et al., 2018, p. 598). With the new communication technologies (email, cell phones, Internet, social media), the material world around us is changing and is becoming omnipresent. This influences the course of interactions within and outside the organization. Most importantly, information technologies have transformed the borders between the human, digital, and physical spheres. In a practice approach, such divisions collapse into each other through practice. This is why practice studies are bringing materiality back into OTs.

When we examine a practice—for example, handoff routine, guided visit, cardiological teleconsultation, dance rehearsal (all practices described in Section 7.3)—we implicitly see the material world in which this practice is accomplished. Nevertheless, studying material practices entails more than simply examining the proprieties of tangible artefacts, objects, and technologies. In OTs, materiality happens to be a dimension of all organizational and social practices. According to Stigliani and Ravasi (2012, p. 1238), material practices refer to 'patterns of behaviours involving the collection, production, manipulation, or use of one or more types of material artifacts'. Therefore, studies of material practices examine how materiality is used via these patterns of behaviours. The organization is thus viewed as a combination of social and material practices (Leonardi, 2013).

The study of materiality has a long history in science and technology studies. In science studies (e.g. Barad, 2003; Latour, 2005), 'materiality' is generally associated with the ordinary use of artefacts and objects. In technology studies (Orlikowski, 2007; Leonardi, Nardi, and Kallinikos, 2012), 'materiality' is mainly technological but not exclusively so. Research communities in science and technology studies are made up of scholars from diverse disciplines studying how institutions, cultures, and politics impact, or are impacted by, social and technological innovation. For instance, the Centre for the Sociology of Innovation (CSI), based at Mines Paris Tech (where Callon and Latour developed actor–network theory; see Chapter 4) has been and still is a leading research group in the field. Set up in 2011 at Paris-Dauphine, the OAP workshop (Organization/Organizing, Artefacts and Practices), which is grounded in the materiality turn, is an annual meeting point for European and American organizational researchers studying materiality and its related processes and practices.

The main debate around materiality revolves around the way the relationships between the social and the material are ontologically conceptualized and applied when conducting research on organizing. This debate can be traced back to contingency theory in the 1970s, when Tavistock scholars came up with the idea that the organization should be conceived as a 'sociotechnical system'. According to the Tavistock scholars, there needs to be a fit between these two subsystems and equal attention must be paid to both in order to achieve worker satisfaction and organizational performance. Almost three decades later, Orlikowski (2007) was one of the first authors to challenge the separation of technology from organizational matters by suggesting that practices using technology shape the technology structure and vice versa.

This perspective was termed as 'technology-in-practice'. Along the same line of thought, Orlikowski and Scott (2008) posit that material things are 'entangled' or intrinsically conjoined with social practices. Indeed, this was how the 'sociomateriality' perspective emerged, in so doing adding a new facet to the materiality turn in OTs.

In OTs, the term sociomateriality is used to express the fact that within a practice, meaning and matter, discourse and material, or the social and the technological, are inextricably related. It is worth recalling Orlikowski's highly cited claim that 'there is no social that is not also material, and no material that is not also social' (Orlikowski, 2007, p. 1437). The presence or absence of the hyphen in sociomateriality is no mere question of grammar, and in fact refers to two different ontologies about the relation between the social and the material. When the term is written *with* a hyphen, it signals that the social and the material are understood as empirically entangled, yet ontologically distinct. In other words, the social and the material affect each other recursively, or are mutually shaped, yet not simultaneously. When the term is written *without* a hyphen, it means that the social and the material are ontologically equivalent and inseparable and are constituted in, and through, practices (see Figure 7.3). The former corresponds to a 'weak-sociomateriality' orientation. Such an orientation assumes that materiality mediates or surrounds human actions. It is a similar ontological position that underpins the notion of 'material practices'. The latter endorses a 'strong-sociomateriality' view where equal weight is given to humans and non-humans. In this case, materiality is constitutive of human action (Gherardi, 2017). As you have probably noticed in the heading of the present section, when 'socio' is placed within parentheses, it advocates for an inclusive 'and/or' orientation rather than one that targets either of the two views (i.e. 'weak-sociomateriality' or 'strong-sociomateriality').

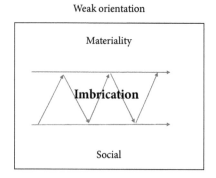
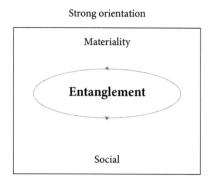

Figure 7.3 Orientations toward (socio)materiality*
*Adapted from Leonardi, 2013

Beyond these ontological nuances, there is an array of approaches aimed at studying the relationships between the social and the material. Indeed, these relationships can be approached in terms of consequence, assemblage, affordance, and performativity (Leonardi et al., 2012; Putnam, 2015). It is worth considering their underlying assumptions in greater depth.

First, the material aspect of organizing can be conceptualized in terms of the consequences of its social use. Researchers are thus interested in the process of becoming material (materializing) or influencing a specific course of events. For instance, ultimately, rumours and jokes might be seen as material if they have real consequences for others. A false rumour or a bad joke spread by word of mouth or social media might incite individuals, groups, and even organizations to move from one community to another or to change their behaviours. Such a perspective highlights the materiality of discourse and communications as they occur in live and web interactions. The focus is therefore on the interactional setting in which the material and the social are at play. For example, Stigliani and Ravasi (2012) show that material practices related to sketches and designs allow middle managers to move from an individual comprehension of a problem they face to a collective understanding across multiple hierarchical levels. For his part, Barley (2015) examines how the Internet has altered the work of salespersons by conducting a dramaturgical analysis of car sales encounters. In some ways, a consequential approach corresponds to a pragmatic view of materiality in which material practices and artefacts support cognitive and interactive work.

Second, the assemblage approach explores the imbrication of multiple social and material agencies. It looks at how objects, discursive practices, spaces, and bodies are bound up together in organizing. For example, patients, electronic health records, pills, beds, caring practices, medical discourses, and knowledges are assembled to form a network or an infrastructure of imbricated heterogeneous agencies (Bruni, 2005). In this vein, Bilodeau et al. (2019) studied three local neighbourhood communities in the Montreal (Canada) area to tackle the complexity of health interventions within the population. They show how the effects of interventions are the results of linkages between social forces (e.g. heterogeneous agencies such as committees, town councils, public, and private healthcare organizations) and materials forces (e.g. knowledge, reports, policies, technologies, and funding). These assemblages between human and non-human actors form a network of governance allowing them to enable cooperative work to improve a population's health. When controversies arise, actors' roles are negotiated and reconfigured. An assemblage perspective allowed the researchers to explain how population health interventions are the results of networks of social and material agencies, the actions undertaken by these networks, the context in which they act, and the effect they produce on communities.

Third, materiality as affordances is based on the assumption that perceptions tend to alter and modify how objects and artefacts are used and acted upon. Intuitively, a chair is for people to sit on. However, in a theatrical presentation, a chair might be used by actors to afford other symbolic functions. The meanings surrounding an object are malleable rather than fixed, as meanings emerge in the practice of using. In technology and organizing studies, the technical vocabulary of experts defines a technology and its formal and conceptual properties (e.g. interactive platforms designed for working). But the real actions afforded by this technology depend on the intuitive and, sometimes, the creative or unexpected ways users will appropriate for themselves (or be constrained by) the technology, according to their own goals (e.g. interactive platforms used for partying). According to Leonardi, Bailey and Pierce (2019, p. 669), 'affordances are the perceptual mechanism that relates materiality and goals through practice'. These authors examine how objects (digital and physical) facilitate communication across a diversity of organizational boundaries (e.g. geographic (USA, Mexico and India) vs cognitive (knowledge of aerospace software used in automotive engineering)) separating organizational members from an international automobile corporation. They insist on the role of materiality and affordances in the context of maintenance and changing boundaries. For instance, American and Mexican engineers had to provide PowerPoint slide decks (physical or discursive object) to Indian engineers in order for them to take advantage of the possibilities afforded by a simulation model (digital object) according to their own goals. Afterwards, while the cognitive boundaries between engineers dissolved, others appeared as they performed their collaborative work.

Fourth, the performativity approach shifts the focus of attention to the mutual entanglement between sociality and materiality. Ranking devices comparing universities, researchers, professors, and so on are performative discourses anchored in the materiality of the numbers, ratios, and visuals comprising them. Far from being passive recordings, ranking devices shape the reality that they are describing by leading university managers, researchers, and others to act according to these ratios. Wallenburg, Quartz, and Bal (2016) show precisely this in their study comparing the effects of rankings in three hospitals. While rankings appear to be highly criticized, they are nevertheless taken into account by quality staff, hospital managers, physicians, and nurses engaged in the governance of clinical practices.

According to these authors, this opens new spaces for rendering care delivery processes manageable. They have observed that each hospital generates data according to specific performance indicators composing the rankings that lead to changes in work routines, roles, and responsibilities. Even though they produce and quantify their clinical practices differently, the whole constitutive effect of these rankings essentially leads to the same outcome: the professionalization of hospital governance.

Conducting research on materiality remains a challenge. As Barley (2015, p. 26) argues, 'It is one thing to propose that the material and the social are ontologically mutually constitutive; it is another to develop methods to systematically investigate that entanglement'. Bruni (2005) put forth a new ethnographic genre called ethnographic materialism by following non-humans—or in this case, electronic and clinical patient records. Shadowing objects or software allows 'the ethnographer to be able to orient his/her observations to the material practices that perform relations' (Bruni, 2005, p. 374).

While Hindmarsh and Llewellyn (2018) opted for video-ethnographic data to study the influence of materiality on organizations and organizing, Royer (2020) suggests three types of observation techniques: observing materiality in actions; observing beyond seeing; and making participants observe. Organizational researchers who want to explore practice as (socio)materiality should find ways to gain access to rich, 'thick', and real-time data.

7.5 Practice as embodiment

A view of practice as social accomplishment is also concerned with the embodied dimension of practice. From the moment we draw our first breath, our bodies are essential to all of our activities. Let's consider a PhD student revamping a version of an academic paper. At first glance, this activity seems to be disembodied. However, her fingers are tapping away on the keyboard as she tries to find an inspiring idea that will help her meet her reviewers' demands. This process triggers some anxiety, which is slightly visible through the myriad movements her body makes: typing nervously, taking a sip of coffee, combing her fingers through her hair, and so on. Eventually, her concentration sharpens, and her movements become more deliberate. As she begins reformulating the findings according to the new angle of the literature review, the nervous tics disappear, her typing accelerates, her lips curl slightly in the start of a smile, and satisfaction starts to creep in. Though largely solitary, research practice is embodied in the sensuous and sometimes aesthetic experience of mastering words, ideas, and figures that will hopefully lead to a new way of building theory on an old research question.

Nevertheless, OTs have historically paid little attention to the bodies of managers and workers. Both have generally been conceptualized as disembodied subjects (Dale, 2001). In the past few decades, practice studies have paved new roads in the field of OTs by addressing a view of practice 'from within' or as embodiment (knowing the world through the body's emotions/affects and perceptions). This obviously applies even more to an organizational setting, where body movements form an assemblage with the object of the practice (e.g. a manufactured product in an industrial farm, a patient in a hospital, a paper in science, a digital app in an engineering firm, or an animal on a farm) and the technology used. A working practice results from the relationships between human bodies and the object of their practice and the technology used. For the sake of illustration, think about a potter working with a piece of clay. It is by touching, grasping, and squeezing the clay that the potter's hands shape a beautiful and unique ceramic piece. This generates some satisfaction for the potter. Central to this crafting practice is the potter's bodily engagement with the wheel needed to skilfully master the subtle movement of the clay according to their creative goals. The wheel enhances the embodied skills of the potter for shaping the clay. In this crafting activity, as in any practice, mind, body, and materiality engage in a complex synthesis.

A practice approach as embodiment rejects the dualism between mind and body and insists on the co-constitutive relationships between mind, body, and materiality. Instead of targeting the body as an object of movement and gesture, a practice approach as embodiment emphasizes the patterns of bodily practices (e.g. touching the clay and increasing pleasure) that sustain some embodied knowing. Another example of this idea of 'embodied knowing' can be found in the Best and Hindmarsh (2019) paper examining the work of tour guides in a museum. They put forth the notion of 'embodied spatial practices' to describe the shifting assemblage of bodily practices accomplished by tour guides and their audiences in specific spaces to coordinate successful tours. A practice approach as embodiment examines how organizing and workplace practices are performed through skilful bodies mastering the object of their practices. The organization is thus viewed as a constant shifting assemblage of bodily practices in a material and spatial context. The shared but always provisional and partial embodied know-how with which individuals, collectively or not, perform their work is central to organizing practices—and this holds true whether these practices are performed by academics, potters, physicians, tour guides, and so on.

A practice approach as embodiment looks at the 'lived body' as a locus of practical knowledge, expressed through feelings and senses, which is used to skilfully act upon the world (Dall'Alba, Sandberg, and Sidhu, 2017). We should never forget, however, that the body's actions are always the result of how the outside world interacts with the body through the latter's feelings and senses. In fact, the relationships between the 'body-in-the-world' and the 'world-in-the-body' are reciprocal (Dall'Alba et al., 2017). As we have seen with the previous examples of the academic writer and the potter, when practising their work activity, their bodies 'move' and 'feel'. Bodily practices are put into action through emotional and sensorial modalities in a world in flux. Both contribute to a better understanding of embodied knowing.

The study of practice as embodiment has a long history in social sciences. While emotion and sensoriality were of major concern to British and French social sciences at the start of the past century (Simmel, 1907; Mauss, 1936; Merleau-Ponty, 1945), they have been the target of a renewed interest in the twenty-first century. Moreover, the study of bodily practices through emotions and sensoriality resonates strongly both with both disciplines (e.g. sociology and anthropology) and applied fields (e.g. education and healthcare). In OTs, two pioneering books on the body in organization were published at the beginning of the 2000s (Hassard, Holliday, and Willmott, 2000; Dale, 2001). This was followed by a rapid growth of the approach of bodily practices through emotion and sensoriality in OTs over the past two decades. Emotions studies emerged at the end of the 1990s, as a group of European and American organizational scholars working on emotions (Barsade, Rafaeli, Pratt, and Ashkanasy) started a discussion list called Emonet (www.emotionsnet.org), which became the webpage listing the recent news on emotions research and events. Every two years, the network organizes an International Conference on Emotions and Worklife. Emotions studies are advancing our understanding of emotions in organizations by bridging the emotional realm with complementary metaphors or qualities such as emotional skills, emotional dynamics, emotional contagion, toxic emotions, and so on. Emotions researchers are primarily concerned with the display of basic emotions (happiness, sadness, fear, anger, disgust, and surprise) in different contexts.

In OTs, sensory studies emerged in the shadow of the RUCOLA group (Nicolini, 2007; Strati, 2007). They then spread in Europe through the leadership of the International Network of Visual Studies in Organization (Invisio).

Researchers in this network aim to advance our understanding of emotional needs by analysing sensory experiences in the workplace (Strati, 2007; Riach and Warren, 2015; Clancy and Vince, 2019). Based in North America, the Centre for Sensory Studies (www.sensorystudies.org) is dedicated to the study of sense and perception in various organizational settings across different cultures (Howes and Classen, 2013). Recently, some OTs scholars called for a closer examination of the ways in which power operates on and through bodies, and of the various forms of corporeal differentiation—for instance, between men and women, abled and disabled persons, migrants and immigrants, and so on (Fotaki and Pullen, 2019).

Emotions grew in importance in OTs concurrently with the finding that cognition cannot be separated from emotion. As the neuroscientist Damasio (1994) showed in his book *Descartes' Error: Emotion, Reason and the Human Brain*, emotions belong to vital body processes and play their part in decision-making. Since then, revisiting the potential rationality of emotions has become a timely issue in OTs as a way to broaden our understanding of decision-making, sensemaking, workplace relationships, managerial work, and so on. A large part of emotion research, however, is dedicated to the management of emotions as a central feature of organizing. The seminal book of Hochschild (1983) on the work of flight attendants kicked off research on emotion management. In her book, Hochschild put forth the notion of 'emotional labour' to explain the regulation of our own emotions and of those of others in accordance with the organizational context. More specifically, emotional labour consists of 'the management of feelings to create a publicly observable facial and bodily display' (Hochschild, 1983: 7). Emotional labour is particularly important in service and professional sector jobs (e.g., salespeople, nurses, teachers, actors, police, and even managers) where the workers have to suppress their emotions in order to display the expected emotions within the context of their activities. In their literature review on emotion management, Bianchi et al. (2016) called on scholars to further advance our knowledge about moral emotions and to pursue research on the embodied understanding of ethical engagement more seriously.

Broadly put, emotions (and/or affects) are physical responses of the body to an external event. It is what puts your body in 'motion' in a 'circuit of feelings and sensations' (Fotaki, Kenny, and Vachhani, 2017). Related to what occurs between interacting bodies in a specific space or situation, emotions and affects permeate all organizations. As emotions are hardly private, intangible, or even unknowable, it is their social character that is relevant for practice scholars. For each and every organizational setting, there are corresponding social norms on specific ways to feel, embody, and display emotions. For example, Bell and King (2010) look at academic conferences (inter-corporeal spaces), where the 'gendered' body is at play (participants walk from one room to another, stand near or move away from each other, present papers, drink coffee, talk, eat, leave the site, and so on). The authors show how the bodies of conference participants are the locus by which junior faculty members and PhD students acquire skills (e.g. stage-craft and concealment of emotions) and dispositions (e.g. physical endurance) that will eventually make them recognized as members of a research community while also shaping their own identities as academics. Practice and emotions researchers who share a common interest in the body consider that social interactions encompass human bodies and a form of knowledgeability through emotions. Hence, in the context of a practice approach, emotions are therefore seen as embodied knowing.

Sensoriality refers to the active engagement of our body in senses via touch, hearing, smell, sight, and taste. By producing sensory knowledge, our senses inform us of the outside world and provide us with multiple cues about how to act. In all jobs, people use their bodies and activate their senses to learn and share how to do things. Stigliani and Ravasi (2018) illustrate the relationship between designers' aesthetic knowledge and visual cues. They show how 'combining visual, verbal and material forms of communication (or shifting across them)' enables design team members to coordinate their work (Stigliani and Ravasi, 2018, p. 777). Grosjean, Matte, and Nahon-Serfaty (2021) on their part suggest the notion of 'sensory ordering' to describe the multisensorial resources nurses sequentially and interactionally use to make clinical decisions. To build evidence about a patient, nurses rely on the use of both embodied data (direct sensing such as seeing the colour of the skin, touching swollen legs, or hearing a pulse) and disembodied data (produced via technology such as a stethoscope or a saturometer, and so on). Interestingly, in both papers, the notion of intuition (sixth sense) is seen as part of sensory work.

Though unnoticed until recently, studies on smell (Riach and Warren, 2015; Islam, Endrissat, and Noppeney, 2016) and taste (Hennion, 2015; Gardiner, 2019) are now burgeoning in OTs. Gümüsay, Höllerer, and Meyer (2018) invite OTs researchers to take scent seriously and regard it as a semiotic mode or a cultural resource for meaning construction. According to these authors, scent can be studied at the institutional, organizational, and individual levels. Taste also provides sensory knowledge about organizations. As Gherardi (2009) puts it: 'Practice? It's a matter of taste!' According to her, 'taste is a sense of what is aesthetically fitting within a community of practitioners' (Gherardi, 2009, p. 535). Taste is a collective and situated activity resulting from an assemblage of bodies, things, and practices illustrating how preferences are collectively shaped on different occasions (e.g. when organizational members share food and drink).

Studying emotion and sensoriality as embodied practices constitutes a major challenge in qualitative research because it is all about capturing what is generally 'felt' rather than verbalized. Nevertheless, according to Gherardi et al. (2019), it is always possible to see the traces of emotions and sensory manifestations in a transcript, in a logbook, or in audio/video support. By developing insider accounts based on lived experience, auto-ethnography can also be a fruitful way of gathering data on body practices. Pink (2015) uses the term 'sensory ethnography' to stress the importance of consciously using our senses in ethnographic research and developing innovative methods that draw on the senses to represent our findings (e.g. using films, dances, artistic compositions).

7.6 Back to square one?

The origin of OTs can be traced back to practitioners who wrote essays based on their own experience of organizing and managing (e.g. Taylor, Fayol, Parker-Follet, and Gulick). Since then, academics have taken over and developed multiple research perspectives inspired by various human and social sciences. Practice studies bring us back to where it all began; that is, managerial work and activities. Does the focus of practice researchers on the 'concrete' or specific workplace activities of managers, professionals, employees, and even external stakeholders mean that OTs are back to square one, a full century later? Did the OTs field simply take a roundabout way to come back home? Or is the practice turn in OTs a way to overcome its pitfalls as it allows researchers to engage in a direct and reflexive dialogue with practitioners?

The answer to these questions lies in the very notion of practice. 'Practice' is a polysemic notion that carries at least four interrelated meanings. In the singular form, practice infers any kind of human performance. For example, I can say, 'It is common practice to build theory from empirical data when writing academic papers' or 'It is common practice to make a plan before implementing an organizational change'. When pluralized, practices refer to routinized patterns of behaviours based on specific skills (e.g. writing or organizing abilities) acquired through socialization and experience. One can also use practice in the sense of 'best practice' to describe a way of acting (e.g. building theory or planning) that has been recognized as superior to any alternatives by a group of experts. Finally, practice can also be associated with the idea of a 'professional' practice; that is, a practice that is regulated according to a set of standards and codes of conduct with the aim of protecting the public. A positive consequence of the polysemic character of the term practice relates to its capacity to be attractive to different audiences (e.g. practitioners, business school managers, PhD students, professors, and consultants), but for different motives.

However, the polysemy associated with the notion of practice compromises the possibility of cumulating knowledge in practice studies. For many OTs scholars, looking at nitty-gritty practices is of little importance as they might be incidental in the life of an organization. On an epistemological level, Floyd et al. (2011, p. 935) suggest that practice is in fact what they call an 'umbrella construct', meaning that it 'encompasses multiple constructs and phenomena'. This has allowed practice studies to offer mainly comprehensive or conceptual knowledge with the aim of rethinking mainstream issues around various OTs subfields. This is certainly a big step for advancing our knowledge of organizing. However, is it enough? The notion of practice can hardly be 'bridged' with other constructs in a way that could expand practice studies in developing new research streams. By contrast, the notion of institution is somewhat of an umbrella construct in the same way as practice is, given that there is no clear answer to the question of what an institution is or is not. However, institutional theorists were able to develop a series of new substreams by bridging the notion of institution with other constructs, such as logic (institutional logic), entrepreneur (institutional entrepreneur), and work (institutional work) (see Chapter 2). Hence, the organizational institutionalism field is constantly expanding by developing new areas of knowledge. Practice studies cannot grow this way. They are almost condemned to extend their influence by merely proposing a fresh look at old stories of organizing.

When adopting a practice lens to study an organizational phenomenon, do we need to throw all of the existing theories out of the window? The answer to this question partly depends on researchers' onto-epistemological positioning. I believe it is imperative to have a view as clear as possible of the nature of 'practice' when researching an organizational phenomenon under the practice lens. Remember that, ideally, the aim of practice studies is to identify the meanings underlying a set or a nexus of practices. Even though the term practice does connote a strong capacity for acting on the world, social practices are hidden and interwoven in organizational intricacies. From a social practice viewpoint, everyday practices are discernible patterns of actions arising from habituated tendencies and internalized dispositions rather than from deliberate, purposeful goal-setting initiatives. As there are multiple social theories of practice, the challenge resides in finding which one is the most relevant to study a specific organizational phenomenon or situation.

To identify which social theories of practice can fit with a specific research interest, one can begin with Nicolini's book (2013) entitled *Practice Theory, Work and Organization*. This book, itself an invitation to embrace a 'strong-practice' research programme, introduces diverse scholarly traditions of social practice theory based on classical authors (e.g. Giddens and Bourdieu; Lave and Wenger; Engeström; Garfinkel; Schatzki; and Foucault). As Gherardi (2016) noticed, the components of a social practice theory—actions, predispositions, contexts, materiality, norms, meanings, texts, and discourses—somewhat overlap, but their arrangement and salience are quite different. This is part of what Turner (1994) calls the problem of the opacity of the practice concept.

Management and organization theories such as sensemaking, routines, capabilities, institutionalism, and so on can also be used to support a definition of practice. Numerous scholars attempted to highlight the complementarity between those diverse streams of research that have evolved separately. For instance, Régner (2015) examines the intersection between the strategy-as-practice and resource-based views. Consciously or not, management theories and OTs are likely to come up with a definition of practice in which humans occupy a preponderant position. In that sense, they are likely to introduce some 'normative' bias. Hence, adopting a managerial or OTs lens increases the possibility of being trapped in a 'weak-practice' approach. It can no longer be denied that the definition of practice has been and also remains the object of a never-ending debate within the communities of practice studies.

According to social practice theories, practices are not directly accessible or measurable. This raises the following question: is it possible to capture the social practices shaping organizational life? In each view of practice presented in this chapter, I gave some tips about the qualitative and exploratory methods generally used under such a view. All of them assume that studying practices requires a deep engagement with practitioners in the field *in situ* in order to understand them as they engage with their working activities. The rich descriptions historically and contextually emanating from such research produce knowledge of conceptual value offering insights that can then be extended to other situations. Of course, collecting and analysing such data is time consuming and challenging in many aspects.

Are practice studies the solution for closing the theory—practice gap that has been pervading management and OTs over the years? At first glance, the answer is yes. Ideally, findings from practice research should serve to develop practitioners' skills in order to make our organizations more efficient as well as more human—a goal shared by researchers and practitioners alike. In the past 25 years, business schools have been criticized for disseminating a view of management as applied science, notably by teaching normative management models. Today, however, managers and managers in training are expected to develop practical skills and competencies that correspond to the new challenges they are facing. Surprisingly, research produced under the practice lens is far from being practically oriented as it rather emphasizes its theoretical and methodological implications at the expense of its managerial implications. While the publication system certainly plays a role in this outcome, there are other factors at play.

To shed further light on this dilemma, we must return to the central question posed throughout this chapter: Does the practice turn bring OTs back to square one? And if so, does this represent progress, or is it a step back? Practice research has advanced OTs on the theoretical level in two ways: First, practice studies require that OTs researchers embrace a higher level of theorization in order to be able to depict what is tacit and embedded in social life. Second, our interest in social practices helps us to overcome the bias of being constrained by the managerial and organizational categories in order to explain how organizing is accomplished. The renewed interest in practice, especially when practice is seen as a social accomplishment, allows researchers to reinforce the importance of social sciences in OTs. In this sense, practice studies, by constituting a 'science-socialization' of OTs, represent a strong step forward in the field.

However, we should not allow ourselves to be duped. Paradoxically, the practice turn could also be interpreted as a step back in OTs if we consider the enduring rationalization project at the root of this field. Remember that from day one, the scientific management project was devoted to capturing workers' knowledge in order to better control them. Can the same be said of practice studies, especially with regard to the view of practice as managerial work? Examining the practices of managers (and, to a lesser extent, the practices of others in organizations) is also a way to capture their knowledge. After a century of OTs, we still struggle to answer the question, 'What do managers do?' In this light, by attempting to study managerial in detail, practice studies appear to be reinvigorating the founders' original vision and simply applying it to a more powerful category of organizational member. And in this sense, the rise of practice studies certainly harkens back to the past.

References

Abdallah, C., Basque, J., & Rouleau, L. 2018. Designing Strategy as Practice Research. *In*: Cassell, C. G. (ed.) *The Sage Handbook of Qualitative Business and Management Research Methods*. London, Sage, p. 328–344.

Ahrens, T. & Chapman, C. S. 2007. Management Accounting as Practice. *Organizations and Society*, 32, 1–27.

Balogun, J., Jacobs, C., Jarzabkowski, P., Mantere, S., & Vaara, E. 2014. Placing Strategy Discourse in Context: Sociomateriality, Sensemaking, and Power. *Journal of Management Studies*, 51, 175–201.

Balogun, J., Best, K., & Lê, J. 2015. Selling the Object of Strategy: How Frontline Workers Realize Strategy Through Their Daily Work. *Organization Studies*, 36, 1285–1313.

Barad, K. 2003. Posthumanist Performativity: Toward an Understanding of How Matter Comes to Matter. *Gender and Science: New Issues*, 28, 801–831.

Barley, S. R. 2015. Why the Internet Makes Buying a Car Less Loathsome: How Technologies Change Role Relations. *Academy of Management Discoveries*, 1, 5–35.

Bednarek, R., Paroutis, S., & Sillince, J. 2017. Transcendence through Rhetorical Practices: Responding to Paradox in the Science Sector. *Organization Studies*, 38, 77–101.

Bell, E. & King, D. 2010. The Elephant in the Room: Critical Management Studies Conferences as a Site of Body Pedagogics. *Management Learning*, 41, 429–442.

Bell, E., Schroeder, J., & Warren, S. 2014. *The Routledge Companion to Visual Organization*. London, Routledge.

Best, K. & Hindmarsh, J. 2019. Embodied Spatial Practices and Everyday Organization: The Work of Tour Guides and Their Audiences. *Human Relations*, 72, 248–271.

Bianchi, A., Ruch, A. M., Ritter, M. J., & Kim, J. H. 2016. Emotion Management: Unexpected Research Opportunities. *Sociology Compass*, 10, 172–183.

Bilodeau, A., Galarneau, M., Lefebvre, C., & Potvin, L. 2019. Linking Process and Effects of Intersectoral Action on Local Neighbourhoods: Systemic Modelling Based on Actor-Network Theory. *Sociological Health International*, 41, 165–179.

Blomquist, T., Hällgren, M., Nilsson, A., & Söderholm, A. 2010. Project-as-Practice: In Search of Project Management Research that Matters. *Project Management Journal*, 41, 5–16.

Bourdieu, P. 1990. Structures, Habitus, Practices. *In*: *The Logic of Practice*. Cambridge, UK, Polity.

Boxenbaum, E., Jones, C., Meyer, R., & Svejenova, S. 2018. Towards an Articulation of the Material and Visual Turn in Organization Studies. *Organization Studies*, 39, 597–616.

Bruni, A. 2005. Shadowing Software and Clinical Records: On the Ethnography of Non-Humans and Heterogeneous Contexts. *Organization*, 12, 357–378.

Burgelman, R. A., Floyd, S. W., Laamanen, T., Mantere, S., Vaara, E., & Whittington, R. 2017. Strategy Processes and Practices: Dialogues and Intersections. *Strategic Management Journal*, 39, 531–558.

Carroll, B., Levy, L., & Richmond, D. 2008. Leadership as Practice: Challenging the Competency Paradigm. *Leadership*, 4, 363–379.

Chia, R. & Mackay, B. 2007. Post-Processual Challenges for the Emerging Strategy-as-Practice Perspective: Discovering Strategy in the Logic of Practice. *Human Relations*, 60, 217–242.

Clancy, A. & Vince, R. 2019. Theory as Fantasy: Emotional Dimensions to Grounded Theory. *British Journal of Management*, 30, 203–216.

Corradi, G., Gherardi, S., & Verzelloni, L. 2010. Through the Practice Lens: Where is the Bandwagon of Practice-Based Studies Heading? *Management Learning*, 41, 265–283.

Dale, K. 2001. *Anatomising Embodiment and Organisation Theory*. New York, Palgrave.

Dall'alba, G., Sandberg, J., & Sidhu, R. K. 2017. Embodying Skilful Performance: Co-Constituting Body and World in Biotechnology. *Educational Philosophy and Theory*, 50, 270–286.

Damasio, A. R. 1994. *Descartes' Error: Emotion, Reason, and the Human Brain*. New York, G.P. Putnam's Sons Publishing.

De Clercq, D. & Voronov, M. 2009. Toward a Practice Perspective of Entrepreneurship. *International Small Business Journal: Researching Entrepreneurship*, 27, 395–419.

Floyd, S. W., Cornelissen, J. P., Wright, M., & Delios, A. 2011. Processes and Practices of Strategizing and Organizing: Review, Development, and the Role of Bridging and Umbrella Constructs. *Journal of Management Studies*, 48, 933–952.

Fotaki, M., Kenny, K., & Vachhani, S. J. 2017. Thinking Critically About Affect in Organization Studies: Why It Matters. *Organization*, 24, 3–17.

Fotaki, M. & Pullen, A. 2019. *Diversity, Affect and Embodiment in Organizing*. Cham, Switzerland, Palgrave Macmillan.

Gardiner, R. A. 2019. Taste and Organization Studies. Organization Studies, 1543–1555.

Gherardi, S. 2009. Practice? It's a Matter of Taste! *Management Learning*, 40, 535–550.

Gherardi, S. 2016. To Start Practice Theorizing Anew: The Contribution of the Concepts of Agencement and Formativeness. *Organization*, 23, 680–698.

Gherardi, S. 2017. Sociomateriality in Posthuman Practice Theory. *In*: Hui, A., Shove, E., & Schatzki, T. (eds.) *The Nexus of Practices: Connections, Constellations, and Practitioners*. Abingdon, UK, Routledge, pp. 38–51.

Gherardi, S. 2019. *How to Conduct a Practice-Based Study. Problems and Methods.* Cheltenham, UK, Edward Elgar Publishing Limited.

Gherardi, S., Murgia, A., Bellè, E., Miele, F., & Carreri, A. 2019. Tracking the Sociomaterial Traces of Affect at the Crossroads of Affect and Practice Theories. *Qualitative Research in Organizations and Management: An International Journal*, 14, 295–316.

Golsorkhi, D., Rouleau, L., Seidl, D., Vaara, E., Golsorkhi, D., Rouleau, L., Langley, A., & Cloutier, C. 2015. *Cambridge Handbook of Strategy as Practice*, Cambridge, UK, Cambridge University Press.

Grosjean, S., Matte, F., & Nahon-Serfaty, I. 2021. "Sensory Ordering" in Nurses' Clinical Decision-Making: Making Visible Senses, Sensing, and "Sensory Work" in the Hospital. *Symbolic Interaction*, 44, 163–182.

Gümüsay, A. A., Höllerer, M. A., & Meyer, R. E. 2018. Organizational Scent. *M@n@gement*, 21, 1424–1428.

Hassard, J., Holliday, R., & Willmott, H. 2000. *Body and Organization*. London, Sage.

Hennion, A. 2015. Paying Attention: What Is Tasting Wine About? *In*: Berthoin, A., Hutter, M., & Stark, D. (eds.) *Moments of Valuation: Exploring Sites of Dissonance*. Oxford, UK Oxford University Press, pp. 37–56.

Hindmarsh, J. & Llewellyn, N. 2018. Video in Sociomaterial Investigations. *Organizational Research Methods*, 21, 412–437.

Hochschild, A. R. 1983. *The Managed Heart: Commercialization of Human Feeling*. Oakland, CA, University of California Press.

Howes, D. & Classen, C. 2013. *Ways of Sensing: Understanding the Senses in Society*. Abingdon, UK, Routledge.

Islam, G., Endrissat, N., & Noppeney, C. 2016. Beyond 'the Eye' of the Beholder: Scent Innovation Through Analogical Reconfiguration. *Organization Studies*, 37, 769–795.

Janssens, M. & Steyaert, C. 2020. The Site of Diversalizing: The Accomplishment of Inclusion in Intergenerational Dance. *Journal of Management Studies*, 57, 1143–1173.

Jarzabkowski, P. & Balogun, J. 2009. The Practice and Process of Delivering Integration through Strategic Planning. *Journal of Management Studies*, 46, 1255–1288.

Jarzabkowski, P., Balogun, J., & Seidl, D. 2007. Strategizing: The Challenges of a Practice Perspective. *Human Relations*, 60, 5–27.

Jarzabkowski, P. & Bednarek, R. 2018. Toward a Social Practice Theory of Relational Competing. *Strategic Management Journal*, 39, 794–829.

Jarzabkowski, P. & Seidl, D. 2008. The Role of Meetings in the Social Practice of Strategy. *Organization Studies*, 29, 1391–1426.

Johnson, G., Melin, L., & Whittington, R. 2003. Micro Strategy and Strategizing: Towards an Activity-Based View. *Journal of Management Studies*, 40, 3–22.

Johnson, G., Langley, A., Melin, L., & Whittington, R. 2007. *Strategy as Practice: Research Directions and Resources*. Cambridge, UK, Cambridge University Press.

Langley, A., Smallman, C., Tsoukas, H., & Van De Ven, A. H. 2013. Process Studies of Change in Organization and Management: Unveiling Temporality, Activity, and Flow. *Academy of Management Journal*, 56, 1–13.

Langley, A. & Tsoukas, H. 2017. *The SAGE Handbook of Process Organization Studies*. London, Sage Publications.

Latour, B. 2005. *Reassembling the Social: An Introduction to Actor-Network-Theory*. Oxford, UK, Oxford University Press.

Lawrence, T. B. & Phillips, N. 2019. *Constructing Organizational Life: How Social-Symbolic Work Shapes Selves, Organizations, and Institutions*. Oxford, UK, Oxford University Press.

Le Baron, C., Christianson, M. K., Garrett, L., & Ilan, R. 2016. Coordinating Flexible Performance During Everyday Work: An Ethnomethodological Study of Handoff Routines. *Organization Science*, 27, 514–534.

Leonardi, P. M. 2013. Theoretical Foundations for the Study of Sociomateriality. *Information and Organization*, 23, 59–76.

Leonardi, P. M., Nardi, B. A., & Kallinikos, J. (eds.) 2012. *Materiality and Organizing: Social Interaction in a Technological World*. Oxford, UK, Oxford University Press.

Leonardi, P. M., Bailey, D. E., & Pierce, C. S. 2019. The Coevolution of Objects and Boundaries over Time: Materiality, Affordances, and Boundary Salience. *Information Systems Research*, 30, 665–686.

Mauss, M. 1936. Les techniques du corps. *Journal de Psychologie*, 32, 5–23.

Merleau-Ponty, M. 1945. *Phenomenology of Perception*. London, Routledge & Kegan Paul.

Mintzberg, H. 1973. *The Nature of Managerial Work*. New York, Harper and Row.

Nicolini, D. 2007. Studying Visual Practices in Construction. *Building Research & Information*, 35, 576–580.

Nicolini, D. 2009. Articulating Practice Through the Interview to the Double. *Management Learning*, 40, 195–212.

Nicolini, D. 2011. Practice as the Site of Knowing: Insights from the Field of Telemedicine. *Organization Science*, 22, 602–620.

Nicolini, D. 2013. *Practice Theory, Work, and Organization*. Oxford, UK, Oxford University Press.

Orlikowski, W. J. 2007. Sociomaterial Practices: Exploring Technology at Work. *Organization Studies*, 28, 1435–1448.

Orlikowski, W. J. & Scott, S. V. 2008. Sociomateriality: Challenging the Separation of Technology, Work and Organization. *The Academy of Management Annals*, 2, 433–474.

Peddie, D. 2016. *The Turn to Practice in Medicine: Towards Situated Drug Safety* [Online]. Vancouver, Simon Fraser University.

Pink, S. 2015. *Doing Sensory Ethnography*. London, Sage.

Putnam, L. L. 2015. Unpacking the Dialectic: Alternative Views on the Discourse-Materiality Relationship. *Journal of Management Studies*, 52, 706–716.

Raelin, J. A. 2016. *Leadership-as-Practice: Theory and Application*. New York, Routledge.

Rasche, A. & Chia, R. 2009. Researching Strategy Practices: A Genealogical Social Theory Perspective. *Organization Studies*, 30, 713–734.

Régner, P. 2015. Relating Strategy as Practice to the Resource-Based View, Capabilities Perspectives and the Micro-Foundations Approach. *In*: Golsorkhi, D., Rouleau, L., Seidl, D., & Vaara, E. (eds.) *Cambridge Handbook of Strategy as Practice*. Cambridge, UK Cambridge University Press, pp. 301–316.

Riach, K. & Warren, S. 2015. Smell Organization: Bodies and Corporeal Porosity in Office Work. *Human Relations*, 68, 789–809.

Rouleau, L., Balogun, J., & Floyd, S. W. 2015. Strategy-as-Practice Research on Middle Managers Strategy Work. *In*: Golsorkhi, D., Rouleau, L., Seidl, D. & Vaara, E. (eds.) *Cambridge Handbook of Strategy as Practice*. Cambridge, UK, Cambridge University Press.

Royer, I. 2020. Observing Materiality in Organizations. *M@n@gement*, 23, 9–27.

Sandberg, J., Rouleau, L., Langley, A., & Tsoukas, H. 2017. *Skillful Performance, Enacting Capabilities, Knowledge, Competence, and Expertise in Organizations*. Oxford, UK, Oxford University Press.

Schatzki, T. R. 2001. Practice Theory: An Introduction. *In*: Schatzki, T. R., Knorr-Cetina, K., & Von Savigny, E. (eds.) *The Practice Turn in Contemporary Theory*. London, Routledge, pp. 10–23.

Schatzki, T. 2002. *The Site of the Social: A Philosophical Account of the Constitution of Social Life and Change*. University Park, PA, Pennsylvania State University Press.

Schatzki, T. R., Knorr-Cetina, K., & Von Savigny, E. 2001. *The Practice Turn in Contemporary Theory*. London, Routledge.

Schön, D. A. 1983. *The Reflective Practitioner: How Professionals Think in Action*. New York, Basic Books.

Seidl, D. & Werle, F. 2017. Inter-Organizational Sensemaking in the Face of Strategic Meta-Problems: Requisite Variety and Dynamics of Participation. *Strategic Management Journal*, 39, 830–858.

Simmel, G. 1907. Sociology of the Senses. *In*: Frisby, D. & Featherstone, M. (eds.) *Simmel on Culture*. London, Sage, pp. 109–120.

Stigliani, I. & Ravasi, D. 2012. Organizing Thoughts and Connecting Brains: Material Practices and the Transition from Individual to Group-Level Prospective Sensemaking. *Academy of Management Journal*, 55, 1232–1259.

Stigliani, I. & Ravasi, D. 2018. The Shaping of Form: Exploring Designers' Use of Aesthetic Knowledge. *Organization Studies*, 39, 747–784.

Strati, A. 2007. Sensible Knowledge and Practice-Based Learning. *Management Learning*, 38, 61–77.

Tengblad, S. (ed.) 2012. *The Work of Managers: Towards a Practice Theory of Management*. Oxford, Oxford University Press.

Théron, C. 2020. Enhancing In Situ Observation with the SCI Design (Shadowing–Conversations–Interview to the Double) to Capture the Cognitive Underpinnings of Action. *M@n@gement*, 23, 28–44.

Turner, A. 1994. *The Social Theory of Practices: Tradition, Tacit Knowledge, and Presuppositions*. Chicago, IL, University of Chicago Press.

Vaara, E. & Whittington, R. 2012. Strategy-as-Practice: Taking Social Practices Seriously. *The Academy of Management Annals*, 6, 285–336.

Wallenburg, I., Quartz, J., & Bal, R. 2016. Making Hospitals Governable: Performativity and Institutional Work in Ranking Practices. *Administration & Society*, 51, 637–663.

Watson, T. 1994. *In Search of Management. Culture, Chaos and Control in Managerial Work*. London, Routledge.

Whittington, R. 2006. Completing the Practice Turn in Strategy Research. *Organization Studies*, 27, 613–634.

Whittington, R. 2019. *Opening Strategy: Professionals Strategists and Practice Change. 1960 to Today*. Oxford, Oxford University Press.

8

The Next 25 Years of Theorizing Organizations

As mentioned in the Introduction, this book is meant for junior researchers and PhD students. My initial goal had been to reconstruct and make sense of the recent organization theories (OTs) perspectives in order to help readers acquire leading-edge knowledge of OTs in the making. However, along the way, my aim eventually broadened. My goal became less about outlining an objective picture of OTs or portraying the 'right' or 'best' image of a perspective and its various streams of research, and more about providing you with the knowledge you need to make your own way in this field. I hope this book has been successful in directing your attention to what you need to know in the fluid territory of OTs, rather than simply mirroring the fixed attributes of a diversity of perspectives. I have tried to do this as faithfully as possible.

Now that we've reached the end of this journey, I will not wrap up the main ideas circulating in OTs or provide a view of the interconnected themes around which the perspectives reviewed in this book have been developed. While this exercise would have certainly been relevant and stimulating, I have a more important goal in mind for this final chapter. As I suggested at the beginning of the book, perspectives are about seeing. They are positions from which we view the world. As we are in an era of extraordinary reflexivity in the field of OTs, I want to end this chapter by helping you to better foresee and imagine 'OTs in the making' for the next 25 years.

This chapter begins by addressing one crucial question that will most likely orient future developments in OTs: where are organizations in our theories? I will then position OTs as a survival toolkit that will help you develop your abilities to better 'see' the organizational world we live in. Finally, I will conclude with a brief overview of potential future trends that are currently emerging in the field.

Organization Theories in the Making. Linda Rouleau, Oxford University Press.
© Linda Rouleau (2022). DOI: 10.1093/oso/9780198792024.003.0009

8.1 Where are organizations in our theories?

In the previous pages, the discussions primarily focused on institutions, conventions, networks, knowledge, discourse, practices, and processes rather than on 'organizations' per se. However, OTs researchers are supposed to share a common preoccupation—organizations! Previously associated with bureaucracy and hierarchy, it looks as if organizations are becoming a phenomenon of the past. In our societies, firms and enterprises are increasingly forgoing the form of traditional bureaucratic organizations, and instead opting for the form of structured networks among a huge diversity of individual and collective actors. Accelerating changes in global politics and information technology have led to greater 'pluralism' and 'openness' within and between organizations. As a result, the coordination of multiple internal constituents has become a sensitive process putting pressure on formal procedures at a time when boundaries between organizations and their environments have become increasingly blurred.

In the past 25 years, OTs have developed new and broader ways of seeing and defining organizations. Indeed, the very term 'organization'—the mainstay of classical OTs—seems to have become obsolete. Rather, 'organizing' is now the new credo of OTs regardless of the paradigmatic position researchers take. For example, Faraj and Pachidi (2021) put forth the notion of 'regime of organizing' to emphasize how arrangements of practices, valuation schemes, authority, and technology are all intertwined. This new credo seems to have evicted the central theme of our field; that is, the organization. However, is this really the case? This strong interest in organizing does not mean that organizations are no longer in our theories. Even though new forms of organizing are supposedly challenging traditional ones, we cannot understand what is happening in these new forms without making compromises between tradition and novelty when we are producing theoretical explanations (Patriotta, 2017). In the same way, organizations and organizing cohabit throughout the perspectives described in this book. To better understand what I mean, let's have a look at what the OTs researchers who are examining new forms of organizing are telling us.

Within the past 25 years, a great deal of scholarly effort has been made to capture the essence of the new forms of organizing, resulting in concepts such as hybrid organizations, meta-organizations, self-managing organizations, virtual organizations, collaborative organizations, and alternative organizations, to name a few. Hybrid organizations such as social enterprises are organizations that combine diverse institutional logics from the public, private, and non-profit sectors (Battilana and Lee, 2014). Meta-organizations are associations of organizations engaged in collective action within their sector. Trade or sectorial associations are considered the ideal exemplar of meta-organizations (Berkowitz and Bor, 2018). Lee and Edmondson (2017, p. 50) define self-managing organizations (SMOs) as organizations 'that formally and radically decentralize authority throughout an organization, thereby eliminating the manager-subordinate authority relationship'. Organizations operating through technological platforms (e.g. online communities) and organizations dedicated to collaboration between autonomous workers and entrepreneurs (coworking spaces) are also new forms of organizing that are of interests to OTs scholars. These organizations are characterized by 'a culture of openness and collaboration concerning knowledge-sharing, skills and tools' (Boutillier et al., 2020, p. 2). Finally, alternative organizations are defined as different and in contrast with the dominant economic system (Parker et al., 2014). They can be either market-oriented (e.g. liberated organization) or, on the contrary, positioned as contesting the fundamental characteristics of capitalism; that is, property rights and capital accumulation (e.g. cooperative organizations).

Each new form of organization gives rise to unique organizing challenges. However, all of these new forms have one thing in common; that is, they present themselves as less bureaucratic, less hierarchical, and more human and democratic. They do so by revisiting the central tenets of organizing: Who are the members? How are goals pursued? How are rules defined? How are decisions made? How are rewards and sanctions applied? A recurring theme throughout all of these new forms of organizing concerns the transformation of control, power, and authority. In their own way, these new forms of organizing respond to increasing societal demands for accountability, transparency, and inclusion in organizational activities and processes.

But are they really new forms of organizing? It should not be forgotten that the idea of newness about organizing has been an increasingly common discourse in management for many decades. Each era has brought its share of 'new forms of organizing'. Whatever the label, they all describe the transformation of management and work organization modes. Some of them have transcended time, and others not. Most OTs researchers are fascinated by these new forms of organizing and suggest that far-reaching change is needed in the way we theorize about them. However, even as they study these new forms of organizing, researchers continue to highlight the fact that the traditional way of organizing is never very far away (Diefenbach and Sillince, 2011; Sturdy, Wright, and Wylie, 2016). I agree with them. I don't think we are witnessing the end of the rational and bureaucratic way of organizing. In fact, most of these new forms of organizing combine the old and the new, from the centralized and decentralized modes of control to the bureaucratic and distributed modes of coordination.

Many of these new forms of organizing have teams- or projects-based orientation. However, these collaborative work arrangements facilitate social and peer control given that team members are expected to keep an eye on each other's contributions and performance. These organizations are thus likely to be the locus of informal subjectivized forms of coercive control. Even in organizations governed by strong democratic values, there are always informal and even political organizing processes that return certain power issues to the picture. In these organizations, some individuals are more active and involved than others. Over time, they become informal leaders who exercise their influence through their networks and in so doing dominate decision-making processes. In tandem with these informal political processes, as such democratic organizations start becoming successful in some way, there is a natural tendency to implement professionalized rules and norms, thereby engendering some form of bureaucracy.

According to Sturdy, Wright, and Wylie (2016, p. 187), a key feature of these new forms of organizing consists of 'relatively few hierarchical levels (decentralization), combined with centralization of control' (e.g. through information technology). Often, attempts to reduce hierarchies contribute to their reinforcement. Diefenbach and Sillince (2011) put forth the notion of 'informal hierarchy' to describe the persistent hierarchal order that permeates these new forms of organizing. These authors propose the following hypothesis: 'whenever in common types of organizations formal hierarchy decreases, informal hierarchy increases' (Diefenbach and Sillince, 2011, p. 1516). OTs researchers who are studying these new forms of organizing emphasize the consequences of melding the virtues of both hierarchy and heterarchy. They are generally showing the difficulties, tensions, and paradoxes that emerge in these new modes of organizing. For example, the traditional hierarchical career becomes more lateral but simultaneously engenders more insecurity. While these new forms of organizing bring more flexibility, they inevitably produce other sorts of negative issues.

OTs have never been as relevant as now for understanding the nature of organizations in the twenty-first century. Despite the fluidity and complexity of the new forms of organizing, the perspectives presented in the book remain powerful lenses for understanding these phenomena. Of course, the theories mobilized by researchers (e.g. narrative theory and structuration theory) in these perspectives are not necessarily 'new' (Suddaby, Hardy, and Huy, 2011). But by developing perspectives around new objects (e.g. institutions, conventions, networks, knowledge, discourses, and practices), researchers reimagine our ways of seeing what is happening in organizations. OTs are not so much in crisis as they are in a state of effervescence as never seen before!

8.2 Organization theories as a way of seeing beneath the surface

If you have read this book, you are probably by now convinced of the usefulness of OTs in your academic life. Knowing the OTs field is essential for doing and publishing research on organizational phenomena. That said, there are many academics who disagree with this affirmation. Over the past 25 years, there has been a growing focus on methods, which has relegated OTs to a stimulating afterthought. Young scholars often start writing papers without having a clear idea of their theoretical proclivities or of their own work's distinctiveness. They are exceedingly anxious to get started on working the data. The pressure to 'publish or perish' has pushed all of us to invest considerably in our methodological competencies but to the detriment of our theoretical ones. Based on my experience, organizing a methodology workshop is very straightforward, as participants are easy to find. It's a different story when it comes to organizing theoretical workshops. It takes a lot of effort to recruit the necessary participants. As a result, the skills needed to generate theoretical explanations have atrophied over the years in our academic community, despite all the forums and editorial essays around publishing papers. This is rather surprising, as it is almost impossible to develop sufficient and novel contributions without putting forth theoretical explanations.

Even though it appears to be somewhat esoteric, theory is the distinctive character of scholarly work. Indeed, theory is one of the hardest and most difficult and demanding forms of cognitive endeavour. Much like organization and organizing, theory and theorizing go hand in hand. Theory takes the shape of what we already know as much as it is something we do! Whatever forms it may take (Cornelissen, Höllerer, and Seidl, 2021), theorizing is the active process of making sense of the organizational world. It is a process of 'disciplined imagination' (Weick, 1989, p. 518) where the researcher 'continuously should weave back and forth between intuition and data-based theorizing and between induction and deduction'. Theory is helping us to see and therefore to explain and depict patterns, dynamics, or processes and practices that live and breathe beneath the surface of the organizational life.

OTs offer us a huge diversity of perspectives that tell us 'what to see' and 'how to see' the organizational world (Allan, 2005). Theorizing organizations and organizing requires a highly developed set of skills, ample imagination, and a keen appreciation of the latest developments in OTs. To that end, I have created a toolkit filled with tips and advice to help you navigate this space, produce knowledge, and theorize in OTs, whether you are writing a thesis, a research report, or a paper. With serious and regular consideration of the points below, you can make this toolkit your own, and refer to it whenever you experience doubts about your current or future research.

8.2.1 What to see

Paraphrasing Mills (1970) on social sciences, OTs are the 'practice of craft' by which different communities elaborate specific language games. To develop your own identity as a scholar, you need to master these language games. What is good research at one moment in time is relative to the community you are working in. Each community or perspective provides us with a way of seeing what seems to be opaque in the organization (namely through its onto-epistemological position, e.g. realism, constructionism) that guides and structures our scholarly work as well as a set of conceptual resources and relationships that can be leveraged to explain an organizational phenomenon and develop contributions.

Our onto-epistemological position is at the very heart of organizational scholarship, as it influences how a research problem is framed. The expression 'what you see depends on where you stand' is particularly relevant here. Because organizations are the product of human life, our positioning about reality and science is a central and unavoidable part of our research work, even though we don't pay great heed to it most of the time. Whatever phenomena we choose to research, we encounter the world through our positioning and our perspectives. Our onto-epistemological position also serves as a key criterion for evaluating the coherence of our scholarly work. The quality of an academic production is judged by its overall coherence; that is, the coherence between the statement problem, the theoretical background, the methodological approach, and the contributions. For instance, in papers claiming a practice perspective and relying on interviews, it is not rare that in the peer review process, reviewers will question the coherence between the paper's positioning and its methods. In the same vein, claiming to be a process scholar and looking for the factors influencing organizational performance is not coherent. Being aware of how we see reality and science is crucial to building a coherent argument in a paper or thesis. However, such awareness must often be triggered and nurtured. In my PhD seminar, most students tend to position themselves as constructivist; however, the more they read, discuss with others, and analyse a diversity of papers, the more they realize they are less constructivist than they originally assumed—despite their rational or social sensibility about this paradigmatic positioning.

The conceptual resources provided by OTs perspectives also help us to be more aware of 'what to see' when trying to solve a research problem or frame a research design. Theorizing is driven by concerns, issues, or problems and the way we conceptualize them. Once your research question is formulated based on your knowledge of the existing literature on your empirical object, you need to decide and explain from which theoretical point of view you will answer it. In fact, a theoretical perspective is the lens you will use to look at the organizational world. It will help you to decide on which elements or dimensions of the organizational phenomena to focus your attention, and which ones to set aside (e.g. discourse, network, and knowledge). It also provides you with the conceptual resources to talk about the phenomenon observed (e.g. discursive struggle, skilful performance, and network centrality). The conceptual resources we used to theorize a topic or an empirical object make the organizational world comprehensible in a specific way. Also, it falls to the researcher to use some conceptual resources to answer their research question that provide the core building blocks to develop theoretical insights and contributions.

As you will recall, most chapters in this book have featured a synoptic table that summarized the main scholarly components within each stream of research (definition, research question, level of analysis, influences, disciplines, view of the organization, conceptual resources, methods, and current exemplars). These components tell you how to see the world in each of these streams of research. For instance, seeing the world from an institutional perspective will enable you to ask questions and use conceptual resources that are different from if you saw the world from a discursive perspective. The beauty of such a table is that it gives you a base from which you can improve your theorizing abilities. Theorizing begins with a conscious base on which we can build. Be sure to return to these tables again and again, as they can inspire you to frame 'what to see' in your research. These tables can help you to formulate your research question and to look at which conceptual resources can be used to problematize your research or to frame a theoretical explanation.

8.2.2 How to see

Once your theoretical argument is framed and makes sense, it will act as your own lens through which to look at your research data. Recursively, your findings will allow you to extend this argument and, all being well, to 'see' some theoretical contributions emerging from these findings. The relevant question now becomes: how can you see such theoretical contributions emerge? This step is one of the most difficult for junior researchers and PhD students. Theorizing organizations involves a back-and-forth movement between your research data and OTs readings. You cannot synthesize or formalize your findings at a higher level of abstraction without reading. Believe it or not, to improve your theorizing skills, you need to read, and read carefully; that is, 'to read in a way that will remake your mind' (Allan, 2005, p. 381). Reading makes us think differently, and sometimes brings us right outside of the box. When reading papers, keep in mind and practise the four following tips:

- *Read between the lines.* To assimilate what an author has to tell us, you must enter into a dialogue with papers and books. Ask yourself a systematic set of questions about how conceptual resources were previously used by researchers to ultimately extend theory. What is the main argument of their papers or books? What is the onto-epistemological position of the author(s)? What are the major concepts used by the author(s) to frame the problematization? How are they related? How have they been extended? Can their theoretical contributions be made more abstract? Theorizing is an activity where comparison is key to the generation of strong contributions. As Weick (2007, p. 14) said: 'It takes richness to grasp richness'. Therefore, compare and contrast your answers to the above-mentioned questions with your own work, using papers from both the same and different perspectives.
- *Read the classics.* This advice may sound strange in a world where we are highly encouraged to be aware of the most recent works in our field. As you have probably noticed, the OTs presented in this book often have roots in other disciplines and most of them draw on classical thinking in social theory. Classic theorists (e.g. Giddens, Foucault, Latour, and Greimas) can be of some inspiration to build strong theoretical contributions. Most of the classics in social sciences were written at a time of tremendous social change. Therefore, their books provide us with foundational theoretical explanations about questions that remain highly topical in OTs, such as change, order, human nature, action, domination, institution, and so on. You can also be inspired by rediscovering the OTs classics (e.g., Selznick, Gouldner, and Coase).
- *Read outside management and OTs.* Organizations do not exist per se, but people do. Organizations are made of human beings who come with their own background, values, beliefs, and so on. Therefore, they do not behave very differently when they are at work from when they are engaging in sports or even partying with family and friends. This is why it is always interesting to look at situations outside management

and organizations. For example, pick up a novel or a book of poetry, or visit a museum to enjoy the latest art exhibit. When immersed in theorizing, artistic productions can trigger new ideas or stimulate new ways of seeing things. You can also find inspiration in movies, plays, and concerts as well as in any kind of activities that you are passionate about. Such outside activities might provide useful metaphors and analogies to stimulate your thinking towards a finer comprehension of human behaviour.

- *Read creatively.* Theorizing is not only about rational thinking—it is also a deeply mindful and creative process. Theorists ask questions that makes sense to them; in a way, the answers they find say a lot about who they are and how they live. Their personal and professional backgrounds and the conditions in which they produce knowledge have an impact on their theorizing process. How could it be otherwise? This is what allows them to see things that no one else has seen or could see in the same way. Theorizing is intimately connected with our own selves and how we use our imagination to think outside the box.

8.3 What's next?

OTs are barrelling forward, keeping pace with the organizational world we inhabit. This brings us to the most common question I get asked by PhD students: what's next? What will be the new perspectives to emerge in OTs over the next 25 years? Absent a crystal ball, it is difficult to forecast the development of new knowledge communities and know for certain what the future of OTs has in store. It is however worth mentioning that some new perspectives—which emerged in the past decade—have not been covered in this book because they are still too novel. For instance, this is the case of the study of paradoxes, which has had a dazzling success in the past few years (Smith and Lewis, 2011; Smith et al., 2017). However, the new perspectives will materialize; let me propose a few trends that I believe will gain momentum in the near future. Indeed, they will help us better adjust with the contemporary spirit that values open theorizing, multimodal research, and new forms of organizational agency.

8.3.1 Towards open theorizing

The past 25 years in OTs have been marked by a tendency towards more flexible theorizing; that is, resorting to various conceptual resources from different perspectives in order to see multiple facets of the same phenomenon. OTs progressed following a heterodox pattern as perspectives were essentially developed through mutual enrichment. To wit, consider organizational institutionalism. Being familiar with different perspectives proves helpful when it comes to mastering multiple ways of theorizing about organizations. The more perspectives we are comfortable with, the more we can perceive the complexity and fluidity of the organizational world. Of course, this remains true as long as the conceptual resources we resort to are defined and integrated according to a coherent onto-epistemological positioning. This tendency towards flexibility in theorizing will continue and certainly accelerate over the next decades.

Theorizing is also becoming more 'open'. Over the past decade in science and education, an open mode of knowledge production, based on a variety of digital tools, has been developed and disseminated (e.g. 'open university', 'open access', 'open data', and 'open publishing'). The philosophy behind this alternative mode of knowledge production consists of sharing data, research material, and ideas around perspectives to foster collaboration and innovation. This philosophy of openness in knowledge production draws on the value of reproducibility of the research process and transparency across all scholars. According to Leone, Mantere, and Faraj (2021, p. 5), open theorizing 'occurs when loosely coordinated researchers realize they can draw on each other's empirical, methodological, or theoretical material to develop theoretical contributions'. In their paper, they examine how open theorizing processes can benefit or hinder the advancement of OTs.

Open theorizing can take multiple forms of collaborative arrangements between scholars. International research collaborations involving OTs scholars from different statuses and backgrounds have provided a fertile ground for open theorizing. These collaborations are now becoming the 'new normal' for producing the strong theoretical contributions needed to publish papers in high-quality journals. Such arrangements are generally strategic in so far as they are shaped according to what each partner can bring to the advancement of a paper project. PhD students and junior faculty often play a pivotal role in these collaborations by sharing their data sets and ideas. Advanced scholars, who are often engaged in multiple collaborations, can allow younger scholars to benefit from their conceptual knowledge and publishing experience. This process of open theorizing has greatly advanced the conceptual resources both within and between perspectives.

8.3.2 Multimodality research

OTs scholars are constantly searching for new 'turns'; that is, new directions in organizational research. As a case in point, a multimodal turn—still in its infancy—is now emerging (Höllerer, Daudigeos, and Jancsary, 2018). However, though very innovative, this turn is not actually completely new as its origins can be traced back to classic semiotic studies of the 1950s and 1960s (note that Barthes (1964) was pivotal in the development of this discipline). In brief, semiotics is interested in all types of signs and symbols (i.e. not just linguistics ones) that are intrinsic to communication and transmission of information. The semiotic discipline has extended to social sciences, and we can now find a vibrant community of researchers around what is now called multimodal studies (Höllerer et al., 2019). In OTs, these influences came up as a critique of the linguistic turn. To some extent, the multimodal turn constitutes a rearticulation of the linguistic, material, and even the practice turns that were the object of the previous chapters. Rather than focusing only on texts or objects, a multimodal approach looks at the multiple modes and media by which communication occurs. It looks at texts but also at spaces, objects, and materials. Organizing happens because managers and others 'rely on images, logos, videos, building materials, graphic and product design, and a range of other material and visual tools and expressions' (Boxenbaum et al., 2018).

We can expect that multimodal research will gain new impetus, and in so doing revitalize and extend the advancement of OTs in the coming years. A multimodal approach means that researchers aim to theorize multiple aspects or signs involved in the social construction of an organizational phenomenon. This 'multi' argument is a promising avenue for advancing research in OTs as we need broader explanations to capture the complexity of the organizational world. Moreover, multimodal research might be used to study micro-level interactions (e.g. strategizing, team behaviours, emotions) but also more macro phenomenon, such as organizational identity, institutions, and sensemaking. It might also be a relevant tool to better understand the multiple modes by which we are communicating through digital media. Though challenging, multimodal research will certainly help us reinvigorate the field.

8.3.3 New forms of organizational agency

Over the past 25 years, the philosophical notion of agency has broken into OTs. Agency has traditionally been associated with and limited to the human capacity to act intentionally in order to alter the course of events. Influenced by actor–network theory, OTs researchers took the concept a step further by arguing that agency should not be limited to individual sovereignty. They have recognized that objects (or 'non-humans') have the capacity to enter into relational dynamics, and in so doing play an active role in agency. This revisited view of agency as belonging in equal measure to both humans and non-humans and material domains has considerably impacted the OTs in the past 25 years. But what about 'live' non-humans such as animals and vegetal species? Do they have agency? In short: of course, they do! Though they cannot be considered 'agents with intent', they nonetheless act on the world in an unpredictable way. For example, actor–network theory came to life in part when Callon (1986) tried to explain why the 'scallops' did not develop as expected by the scientific community. O'Doherty (2016) explores how a lost cat found in an airport contributed to mediating its organizational politics. This author argued that we should extend our view of agency in OTs by seeing the organization as a multi-species ecology.

However, talking in terms of human and non-human agency still involves a dualistic distinction that gives a higher status to human over other living beings. More recently, efforts have been made to explore the relations between human and animals within organizations and in the natural world (Labatut, Munro, and Desmond, 2016; Lennerfors and Sköld, 2018 Sayers, Hamilton, and Sand, 2019). These efforts bring another more all-encompassing form of agency to the debate: the 'living being' agency. To wit, this perspective argues that any living being that has a capacity to act or change the world needs to be included in organizational research. We cannot rank living being agency as all are related to one another in a rather blurred way. This renewed conception of agency reconciles the false dichotomy between humans and other species. Additionally, it is particularly relevant to various areas that have thus far been neglected by the OTs, such as animal-centred organizations (e.g. farms, veterinary clinics, and pet shops), organizations fighting for endangered species and for animal welfare, and organizations focused on finding alternative ways of producing food that reconfigure the entire food production system (e.g. urban agriculture, beyond-meat production, and new agricultural products). OTs should start seriously taking into account the role of the natural environment in organizational life. There is a pressing need to explore the acting capacities of non-human species in diverse organizational contexts. This will certainly be one of the new trends in OTs in the next 25 years!

My primary motivation when writing this book was to draw a comprehensive portrait of the field of OTs as it currently stands for junior scholars and PhD students. I hope that I have given you a sufficient roadmap to continue navigating this field. This book sought to shine a light on how organizational researchers have 'seen' organizations over the past 25 years. OTs constitute a collective memory—one that I encourage you to continuously draw on for inspiration as you push your research further. It is now time for you to embark upon your own journey of theorizing and contribute to building the future of OTs. Remember that theorizing starts with a question. . . and asking questions is what researchers do best.

References

Allan, K. 2005. *Explorations in Classical Sociological Theory*. Thousand Oaks, CA, Pine Forge.

Barthes, R. 1964. *Elements of Semiology*. London, Jonathan Cape.

Battilana, J. & Lee, M. 2014. Advancing Research on Hybrid Organizing—Insights from the Study of Social Enterprises. *Academy of Management Annals*, 8, 397–441.

Berkowitz, H. & Bor, S. 2018. Why Meta-Organizations Matter: A Response to Lawton et al. and Spillman. *Journal of Management Inquiry*, 27, 204–211.

Boutillier, S., Capdevila, I., Dupont, L., & Morel, L. 2020. Collaborative Spaces Promoting Creativity and Innovation. *Journal of Innovation Economics & Management*, 31, 1–9.

Boxenbaum, E., Jones, C., Meyer, R., & Svejenova, S. 2018. Towards an Articulation of the Material and Visual Turn in Organization Studies. *Organization Studies*, 39, 597–616.

Callon, M. 1986. Some Elements of a Sociology of Translation: Domestication of the Scallops and the Fishermen of St Brieuc Bay. *In*: Law, J. (ed.) *Power, Action and Belief: A New Sociology of Knowledge?* London, Routledge & Kegan-Paul, pp. 193–233.

Cornelissen, J., Höllerer, M. A., & Seidl, D. 2021. What Theory Is and Can Be: Forms of Theorizing in Organizational Scholarship. *Organization Theory*, 2, 1–19.

Diefenbach, T. & Sillince, J. A. A. 2011. Formal and Informal Hierarchy in Different Types of Organization. *Organization Studies*, 32, 1515–1537.

Faraj, S. & Pachidi, S. 2021. Beyond Uberization: The Co-Constitution of Technology and Organizing. *Organization Theory*, 2, 1–14.

Höllerer, M. A., Daudigeos, T., & Jancsary, D. 2018. *Multimodality, Meaning, and Institutions*. Bingley, UK, Emerald Publishing Limited.

Höllerer, M. A., Van Leeuwen, T., Jancsary, D., Meyer, R. E., Andersen, T. H., & Vaara, E. 2019. *Visual and Multimodal Research in Organization and Management Studies*. London, Routledge.

Labatut, J., Munro, I., & Desmond, J. 2016. Animals and Organizations. *Organization*, 23, 315–329.

Lee, M. Y. & Edmondson, A. C. 2017. Self-Managing Organizations: Exploring the Limits of Less-Hierarchical Organizing. *Research in Organizational Behavior*, 37, 35–58.

Lennerfors, T. T. & Sköld, D. 2018. The Animal. *Culture and Organization*, 24, 263–267.

Leone, P. V., Mantere, S., & Faraj, S. 2021. Open Theorizing in Management and Organization Studies. *Academy of Management Review*, 46, 725–749.

Mills, W. C. 1970. *The Sociological Imagination*. Harmondsworth, UK, Penguin.

O'Doherty, D. P. 2016. Feline Politics in Organization: The Nine Lives of Holly the Cat. *Organization*, 23, 407–433.

Parker, M., Cheney, G., Fournier, V., & Land, C. 2014. *The Routledge Companion to Alternative Organization*. Abingdon, UK, Routledge.

Patriotta, G. 2017. Crafting Papers for Publication: Novelty and Convention in Academic Writing. *Journal of Management Studies*, 54, 747–759.

Sayers, J., Hamilton, L., & Sang, K. 2019. Organizing Animals: Species, Gender and Power at Work. *Gender, Work & Organization*, 36, 239–245.

Smith, W. K. & Lewis, M. W. 2011. Towards a Theory of Paradox: A Dynamic Equilibrium Model of Organizing. *Academy of Management Review*, 36, 381–403.

Smith, W. K., Lewis, M. W., Jarzabkowski, P., & Langley, A. 2017. *The Oxford Handbook of Organizational Paradox*. Oxford, UK, Oxford University Press.

Sturdy, A., Wright, C., & Wylie, N. 2016. Managers as Consultants: The Hybridity and Tensions of Neo-Bureaucratic Management. *Organization*, 23, 184–205.

Suddaby, R., Hardy, C., & Nguyen, H. 2011. Introduction to Special Topic Forum: Where are the New Theories of Organization? *The Academy of Management Review*, 36, 236–246.

Weick, K. E. 1989. Theory Construction as Disciplined Imagination. *Academy of Management Review*, 14, 516–531.

Weick, K. E. 2007. The Generative Properties of Richness. *Academy of Management Journal*, 50, 14–19.

Afterword
Theorizing Organizations in a Turbulent World

Can theory building change the organizational world? All of us would like to answer this relevant but puzzling question affirmatively. While theorizing can be subversive to the status quo, the fact remains that, most of the time, it is not. Additionally, the performativity of our theories partly depends on the socio-historical conditions in which academic communities are embedded. As such, tomorrow's organizations will most likely weather more than one storm! Simply think of the COVID-19 pandemic, the migrant crisis, natural catastrophes, terrorist attacks, societal inequalities, and new social movements (e.g. #MeToo, #BlackLivesMatter), to name a few. Such unpredictability is certain to have an impact on the way organizations will be theorized in the future.

Organization theories (OTs) scholars have already begun taking such critical and disruptive issues more seriously. Recently, vibrant OTs research communities tackling 'wicked problems' (Reinecke and Ansari, 2016) have emerged. For example, the OTs community concerned with tackling 'grand challenges' brings together researchers interested in studying the social and environmental issues currently faced by society, including social inequalities, climate change, migration, poverty, and sustainability (George et al., 2016; Howard-Grenville, 2016). Members of the 'extreme contexts' community are zooming in on settings where extreme events have strong consequences for people (e.g. aerospace, health care emergencies, firefighting, police, and natural catastrophes; Hannah et al., 2009; Hällgren, Rouleau, and De Rond, 2018). 'Social diversity and precarity' is also the topic of an emergent community in OTs. The goal of these scholars is to shed new light on the gendered and diversity-based challenges that the varied forms of precarious organizations create and maintain over time (Vincent, 2016; Samdanis and Özbilgin, 2019; Meliou, 2020).

OTs researchers in these communities share the desire to make their research impactful—and with good reason, as all these critical and disruptive issues are challenging our organizing processes and capacities. For instance, although COVID-19 has been largely looked at in epidemiological terms, the pandemic was also a crisis of our modes of organizing! Indeed, during the pandemic, the healthcare system had to reorganize itself, as did almost all other types of organizations! Surprisingly, even though they had the theoretical toolkits on hand, OTs scholars were not on the front lines to help facilitate these rapid changes. Hopefully, they will be better prepared to lend a hand when a future crisis inevitably pops up!

OTs researchers in these communities argue that research on such societal and organizational issues is likely to increase the relevance of our theorizing. I stand with these researchers! Theorizing is driven by concerns, tensions, and complex problems. The radical changes that have an impact on organizations and societies provide a unique opportunity to peek under the hood. Examining environmental and social issues or disrupted situations provides the intellectual puzzlement that can trigger us to develop new ways of 'seeing' organizational coordination and change. Moreover, focusing on such multilevel and complex phenomena may challenge us to emerge from our ivory tower and develop more democratic and responsible ways of theorizing. However, our ability to achieve this hinges on how we understand our role as OTs scholars. I strongly believe that we should be more socially reflexive and ask ourselves 'for whom' we are researching. Are we producing knowledge for managers and already powerful stakeholders? To empower those on the margins, including people affected by these challenges, or simply to position ourselves in our research community? The choice, dear reader, is yours.

References

George, G., Howard-Grenville, J., Joshi, A., & Tihanyi, L. 2016. Understanding and Tackling Societal Grand Challenges through Management Research. *Academy of Management Journal*, 59, 1880–1895.

Hällgren, M., Rouleau, L., & De Rond, M. 2018. A Matter of Life or Death: How Extreme Context Research Matters for Management and Organization Studies. *Academy of Management Annals*, 12, 111–153.

Hannah, S. T., Uhl-Bien, M., Avolio, B. J., & Cavarretta, F. L. 2009. A framework for examining leadership in extreme contexts. *The Leadership Quarterly*, 20, 897–919.

Howard-Grenville, J. 2016. Grand Challenges, Covid-19 and the Future of Organizational Scholarship. *Journal of Management Studies*, 58, 254–258.

Meliou, E. 2020. Family as a Eudaimonic Bubble: Women Entrepreneurs Mobilizing Resources of Care During Persistent Financial Crisis and Austerity. *Gender, Work & Organization*, 27, 218–235.

Reinecke, J. & Ansari, S. 2016. Taming Wicked Problems: The Role of Framing in the Construction of Corporate Social Responsibility. *Journal of Management Studies*, 53, 299–329.

Samdanis, M. & Özbilgin, M. 2019. The Duality of an Atypical Leader in Diversity Management: The Legitimization and Delegitimization of Diversity Beliefs in Organizations. *International Journal of Management Reviews*, 22, 101–119.

Vincent, S. 2016. Bourdieu and the Gendered Social Structure of Working Time: A Study of Selfemployed Human Resources Professionals. *Human Relations*, 69, 1163–1184.

Author Index

Subject Index